The Reference Shelf®

Representative American Speeches 2014–2015

The Reference Shelf
Volume 87 • Number 6
H.W. Wilson
A Division of EBSCO Information Services

Published by
GREY HOUSE PUBLISHING
Amenia, New York
2015

The Reference Shelf

The books in this series contain reprints of articles, excerpts from books, addresses on current issues, and studies of social trends in the United States and other countries. There are six separately bound numbers in each volume, all of which are usually published in the same calendar year. Numbers one through five are each devoted to a single subject, providing background information and discussion from various points of view and concluding with an index and comprehensive bibliography that lists books, pamphlets, and articles on the subject. The final number of each volume is a collection of recent speeches. Books in the series may be purchased individually or on subscription.

Publisher's Cataloging-In-Publication Data
(Prepared by The Donohue Group, Inc.)

Representative American speeches, 2014-2015 / [compiled by] H. W. Wilson, a division of EBSCO Information Services.

pages : illustrations ; cm. -- (The reference shelf ; volume 87, number 6)

Includes bibliographical references and index.
ISBN: 978-1-61925-695-8 (v.87, no.6)
ISBN: 978-1-61925-689-7 (volume set)

1. Speeches, addresses, etc., American--21st century. 2. United States--Politics and government--2009---Sources. 3. Civil rights--United States--Sources. 4. Criminal justice, Administration of--United States--Sources. 5. Electronic surveillance--United States--Sources. I. H.W. Wilson Company. II. Series: Reference shelf ; v. 87, no. 6.

PS661 .R46 2015
815/.008

Contents

3

Rethinking Criminal Justice

4

Surveillance and Privacy in the Digital Age

5

A Year in Review

6

A Global Perspective

Preface

Representative American Speeches 2014-2015 reflects current trends in American thought, from uplifting commencement speeches delivered on campuses of U.S. colleges and universities to biting political speeches from the halls of Congress.

The first section is devoted to commencement speeches from the past year. The speakers seek to inspire personal growth and insight, knowledge of our various histories, and individual and collective action toward a brighter future. First Lady Michelle Obama begins the collection with an address to the graduating class of Tuskegee University, simultaneously reminding the students of the legacy of racism and encouraging them to refuse to define themselves or their choices based on others' prejudice. Award-winning journalist Naomi Klein and feminist writer and activist Gloria Steinem both encourage their audience to bridge divides and work collaboratively to make the world a better place, in terms of environmental and social justice.

In a timely speech that takes on terrorism in the wake of the Islamist attack that killed twelve people on staff at the French satirical newspaper *Charlie Hebdo,* novelist Ian McEwan advocates for the uncompromising defense of free speech regardless of politics. Rounding out this section, founder and editor-in-chief of the *Huffington Post,* Arianna Huffington focuses on how graduating students can work toward developing their inner lives and passions amidst the noise of digital distractions, an increasingly relevant topic, as educators and sociologists continue to study and debate the effects of digital devices on individual development and our relationships with one another.

The theme of social justice connects many of the speeches in this volume. Just as Naomi Klein and Gloria Steinem encourage graduating students to engage in the betterment of their society and the world, the speakers included in the second section take up current issues and incidents that raise questions about civil rights and the need for public engagement in improving humanitarian causes. The section begins with a eulogy delivered by President Barack Obama for the Reverend Clementa Pinckney, one of nine people killed by white supremacist Dylann Roof who opened fire at Emanuel African Methodist Episcopal Church in Charleston, South Carolina on June 17, 2015. Obama situates this event in a long history of racially motivated violence in this country, which has often targeted black churches and their parishioners, and he imbues his speech with the themes of religion, forgiveness, and redemption of past sins. Following this speech is one by Massachusetts Senator Elizabeth Warren who takes up a broader examination of civil rights and state-sanctioned violence and inequity in the United States. These speeches complement one another in illuminating the issue of race in this country at a time when there is a growing movement to acknowledge and rectify persisting racial inequities.

In the following speech, President Obama talks about social renewal in New Orleans on the tenth anniversary of Hurricane Katrina, which destroyed much of the city and devastated the local economy and population. On a hopeful note, the president links the renewal of the local economy of New Orleans with the regrowth of the country's economy following the financial collapse just two years after Katrina.

Next, Pope Francis, an Argentinean by birth and the first pope to hail from the Americas, delivers a speech before the Joint Session of Congress, becoming the first pope to speak before this government body. Invoking the names of four great American thinkers and activists—Abraham Lincoln, Martin Luther King, Jr., Dorothy Day, and Thomas Merton—the pope implores his audience to keep in mind the greater good when tackling such important issues as global climate change, and he asks that they remember the spirit of kindness embodied by these American leaders when making policy decisions regarding those who are in need, such as refugees and other immigrants. The next speech by Secretary General of the United Nations Ban Ki-moon discusses some of the same global issues addressed by the pope, but from a political rather than religious standpoint, in his address to 70th session of the U.N. General Assembly.

Section three focuses on a stand-out social and political issue of the past year, reforming the criminal justice system in the United States. First, Director of the Federal Bureau of Investigation James Comey acknowledges a history of discrimination in policing and the law, but he warns against the simple assigning of blame to police officers and calls upon his country to examine greater, more complex societal problems at play. In the next two speeches, Hillary Clinton and Barack Obama develop various ideas about the causes for current problems in the criminal justice system, not only in regard to race and discrimination, but also with a critical eye toward the fact that the United States has a much larger percentage of its population imprisoned than any other country in the world. In addresses that complement one another, these speakers explore in detail the causes and possible solutions to problems in the U.S. criminal justice system.

Section four takes up surveillance and privacy in the digital age. In the past year the idea of online shaming and bullying has loomed large in the media and public eye, as have questions regarding government and corporate surveillance of private citizens in the name of homeland security. In the first speech of the section, former intern to President Bill Clinton, Monica Lewinsky discusses the public shaming she endured in the aftermath of the scandal surrounding her affair with the president—indeed, she claims, the first public shaming ever to occur on the Internet. Pointing out the malicious invasion of privacy posed by online shaming, Lewinsky pleads for more civility and decency in our public and online lives.

In the next speech, U.S. Senator from Kentucky Rand Paul voices opposition to the section of the PATRIOT Act that allows for mass surveillance and collection of private citizen's metadata, a section that was due to expire the following day. In opposition to his more hawkish colleagues in the Republican party like John McCain as well as Democrats, Paul contends that the replacement policy under the USA Freedom Act—which ultimately did pass within days of Paul's speech and despite his opposition—offers insufficient restrictions on government surveillance of private citizens. He argues that officials should have to obtain a warrant to gather information on potential suspects who have a constitutionally protected right to privacy.

In the next speech, David Medine, Chairman of the Privacy and Civil Liberties Oversight Board, describes how the PCLOB, an independent organization within the executive branch of government, came to the conclusion that Section 215 of the PATRIOT Act needed to be carefully reconsidered. Despite the expiration of this particular program, Paul and Medine's speeches still resonate as the public continues to debate what rights, if any, people can reasonably be expected to forego in the name of homeland security, alongside other aspects of privacy in the digital age.

The speeches in section five touch upon a host of topics that have dominated headlines, social media, and popular thinking in the past year, including health care, wealth inequality, the rights of the LGBT community, and women's rights. In a short speech featuring personal anecdotes, Dr. Steven J. Stack the recently elected president of the American Medical Association presents an insider's perspective on the challenges and triumphs of being a health care provider and an emergency room physician today.

President of the American Federation of Labor and Congress of Industrial Organizations (AFL-CIO), Richard L. Trumka delivers a speech arguing that the stark wealth inequality in this country requires the serious consideration and attention of those currently running for president, noting that neither Republicans nor Democrats have in recent history sufficiently answered this call. Vermont Senator, self-described Democratic Socialist, and presidential hopeful Bernie Sanders delivers the next speech in the section, in which he calls upon an audience at Liberty University, a college founded by religious conservative Jerry Falwell, to find common ground with him despite their differences. Surely, Sanders says, they can agree to condemn the incredible and growing discrepancy between the rich and poor in this country, a gap so large, he notes, as to violate religious ethics worldwide.

Principal Deputy Director of National Intelligence Stephanie O'Sullivan delivers the next speech on behalf of the Director of National Intelligence, James Clapper, at the LGBTA Summit, acknowledging the unjustness of past policies like "Don't Ask, Don't Tell," which, she notes, violated the rights of committed workers and soldiers. O'Sullivan applauds the increased awareness and acceptance of these marginalized communities, which she observes is partly due to newly visible people in the transgender community, like former Olympic gold medalist Caitlyn Jenner. Hillary Clinton's speech at the Women in the World Summit likewise points to great strides in recent years in the long march toward equal rights for women. She also acknowledges, however, that this work is far from over and that the United States, which one might expect to be leading the way on the issue, ranks surprisingly low in equal pay for women, a fact that, Clinton suggests, should spur people out of complacency and into feminist activism.

The sixth and final section of this book includes three representative speeches on global considerations. In the first speech we see an outside, critical view of American foreign policy delivered by the President of Cuba Raúl Castro in his first address to the United Nations General Assembly. In this speech, Castro makes the case to end the economic embargo of his country and aligns Cuba with other struggling nations in the world and particularly in Latin America. The second speech by President Obama defends his hotly debated nuclear ban treaty with Iran and promotes greater diplomacy in relations with the Middle East. The third and final speech in the collection, delivered by Secretary for the U.S. Department of Housing and Urban Development Julián Castro, advocates for an unbiased policy toward immigrants in response to those in the current political climate who make the case for deporting undocumented immigrants and closing the nation's borders. Arguing that the future of the United States is directly linked to that of its Latino population, the fastest growing ethnic group in the nation, Castro pleads for a more inclusionary domestic policy that looks beyond the borders of the nation, echoing the sentiment of several other speakers throughout the collection.

1
To the Graduating Class

Official White House Photo by Chuck Kennedy

First Lady Michelle Obama participates in the Tuskegee University class of 2015 commencement ceremony in Tuskegee, Alabama, May 9, 2015.

Remarks by the First Lady at Tuskegee University Commencement

By Michelle Obama

In a commencement speech at Tuskegee University, First Lady Michelle Obama reflects on the important history, both troubling and inspirational, of this historically black college. Obama remembers the prevailing racism at the time when the U.S. Army chose Tuskegee to be the training place for black pilots. The story of the first generation of Tuskegee pilots paved the way not only for all subsequent generations of students at the university, but also Obama says, for all African Americans as they fought for equal rights and triumphed over adversity. The flight of the pilots for Obama symbolizes "rising above" life's challenges and setbacks. As the first African American First Lady, Obama speaks to the pressures of being "the first" from a personal vantage point. Obama advises the graduating students to stay true to themselves and make choices based on their self-knowledge, not dictated by other people's expectations or prejudice. In this way, she says, they can move past life's "little indignities" and more pervasive structural obstacles in order to stay hopeful and shape the future of their own individual lives, as well as their communities and generations to come. Michelle Obama became First Lady of the United States in 2008. Before her husband was elected to the office, Obama worked for the University of Chicago Medical Center and was a member of the staff of Chicago mayor Richard M. Daley. As First Lady, Obama has focused on homelessness, education, LGBT rights, and childhood health.

Thank you all. (Applause.) Thank you so much. (Applause.) Let's let our graduates rest themselves. You've worked hard for those seats! (Applause.)

Let me start by thanking President Johnson for that very gracious introduction, and for awarding me with this honorary degree from an extraordinary institution. I am proud to have this degree—very proud. (Applause.) Thank you. Thank you so much. (Applause.)

I want to recognize Major General Williams; Congresswoman Sewell; Zachary; Kalauna; to all of the trustees, the faculty, the staff here at Tuskegee University. Thank you—thank you so much for this warm welcome, this tremendous hospitality. And I'm so glad to be here. (Applause.)

Before I begin, I just want to say that my heart goes out to everyone who knew and loved Eric Marks, Jr. I understand he was such a talented young man, a promising aerospace engineer who was well on his way to achieving his dream of following

Delivered May 9, 2015, at the Tuskegee University commencement, Tuskegee, Alabama, by Michelle Obama.

in the footsteps of the Tuskegee Airmen. And Eric was taken from us far too soon. And our thoughts and prayers will continue to be with his family, his friends, and this entire community. (Applause.)

I also have to recognize the Concert Choir. Wow, you guys are good! Well done! (Applause.) Beautiful song. (Applause.) And I have to join in recognizing all the folks up in the stands—the parents, siblings, friends—(applause)—so many others who have poured their love and support into these graduates every step of the way. Yeah, this is your day. (Applause.) Your day. (Applause.)

Now, on this day before Mother's Day, I've got to give a special shout-out to all the moms here. (Applause.) Yay, moms! And I want you to consider this as a public service announcement for anyone who hasn't bought the flowers or the cards or the gifts yet—all right? I'm trying to cover you. (Laughter.) But remember that one rule is "keep mom happy." (Laughter.) All right? (Applause.)

And finally, most of all, I want to congratulate the men and women of the Tuskegee University Class of 2015! (Applause.) T-U!

(AUDIENCE: You know!)

I love that. (Applause.) We can do that all day. (Laughter.) I'm so proud of you all. And you look good. (Applause.) Well done!

You all have come here from all across the country to study, to learn, maybe have a little fun along the way—from freshman year in Adams or Younge Hall—(applause)—to those late night food runs to The Coop. (Applause.) I did my research. (Applause.) To those mornings you woke up early to get a spot under The Shed to watch the Golden Tigers play. (Applause.) Yeah! I've been watching! (Laughter.) At the White House we have all kinds of ways. (Laughter.)

And whether you played sports yourself, or sang in the choir, or played in the band, or joined a fraternity or sorority—after today, all of you will take your spot in the long line of men and women who have come here and distinguished themselves and this university.

You will follow alums like many of your parents and grandparents, aunts and uncles—leaders like Robert Robinson Taylor, a groundbreaking architect and administrator here who was recently honored on a postage stamp. (Applause.) You will follow heroes like Dr. Boynton Robinson—(applause)—who survived the billy clubs and the tear gas of Bloody Sunday in Selma. The story of Tuskegee is full of stories like theirs—men and women who came to this city, seized their own futures, and wound up shaping the arc of history for African Americans and all Americans.

And I'd like to begin today by reflecting on that history—starting back at the time when the Army chose Tuskegee as the site of its airfield and flight school for black pilots. (Applause.)

Back then, black soldiers faced all kinds of obstacles. There were the so-called scientific studies that said that black men's brains were smaller than white men's. Official Army reports stated that black soldiers were "childlike," "shiftless," "unmoral and untruthful," and as one quote stated, "if fed, loyal and compliant."

So while the Airmen selected for this program were actually highly educated—many already had college degrees and pilots licenses—they were presumed to be inferior. During training, they were often assigned to menial tasks like housekeeping or landscaping. Many suffered verbal abuse at the hands of their instructors. When they ventured off base, the white sheriff here in town called them "boy" and ticketed them for the most minor offenses. And when they finally deployed overseas, white soldiers often wouldn't even return their salutes.

Just think about what that must have been like for those young men. Here they were, trained to operate some of the most complicated, high-tech machines of their day—flying at hundreds of miles an hour, with the tips of their wings just six inches apart. Yet when they hit the ground, folks treated them like they were nobody—as if their very existence meant nothing.

Now, those Airmen could easily have let that experience clip their wings. But as you all know, instead of being defined by the discrimination and the doubts of those around them, they became one of the most successful pursuit squadrons in our military. (Applause.) They went on to show the world that if black folks and white folks could fight together, and fly together, then surely—surely—they could eat at a lunch counter together. Surely their kids could go to school together. (Applause.)

You see, those Airmen always understood that they had a "double duty"—one to their country and another to all the black folks who were counting on them to pave the way forward. (Applause.) So for those Airmen, the act of flying itself was a symbol of liberation for themselves and for all African Americans.

One of those first pilots, a man named Charles DeBow, put it this way. He said that a takeoff was—in his words—"a never-failing miracle" where all "the bumps would smooth off. . . [you're] in the air. . . out of this world. . . free."

And when he was up in the sky, Charles sometimes looked down to see black folks out in the cotton fields not far from here—the same fields where decades before, their ancestors [were] slaves. And he knew that he was taking to the skies for them—to give them and their children something more to hope for, something to aspire to.

And in so many ways, that never-failing miracle—the constant work to rise above the bumps in our path to greater freedom for our brothers and sisters—that has always been the story of African Americans here at Tuskegee. (Applause.)

Just think about the arc of this university's history. Back in the late 1800s, the school needed a new dormitory, but there was no money to pay for it. So Booker T. Washington pawned his pocket watch to buy a kiln, and students used their bare hands to make bricks to build that dorm—and a few other buildings along the way. (Applause.)

A few years later, when George Washington Carver first came here for his research, there was no laboratory. So he dug through trash piles and collected old bottles, and tea cups, and fruit jars to use in his first experiments.

Generation after generation, students here have shown that same grit, that same resilience to soar past obstacles and outrages—past the threat of countryside lynchings, past the humiliation of Jim Crow, past the turmoil of the Civil Rights era.

And then they went on to become scientists, engineers, nurses and teachers in communities all across the country—and continued to lift others up along the way. (Applause.)

And while the history of this campus isn't perfect, the defining story of Tuskegee is the story of rising hopes and fortunes for all African Americans.

And now, graduates, it's your turn to take up that cause. And let me tell you, you should feel so proud of making it to this day. And I hope that you're excited to get started on that next chapter. But I also imagine that you might think about all that history, all those heroes who came before you—you might also feel a little pressure, you know—pressure to live up to the legacy of those who came before you; pressure to meet the expectations of others.

And believe me, I understand that kind of pressure. (Applause.) I've experienced a little bit of it myself. You see, graduates, I didn't start out as the fully-formed First Lady who stands before you today. No, no, I had my share of bumps along the way.

Back when my husband first started campaigning for President, folks had all sorts of questions of me: What kind of First Lady would I be? What kinds of issues would I take on? Would I be more like Laura Bush, or Hillary Clinton, or Nancy Reagan? And the truth is, those same questions would have been posed to any candidate's spouse. That's just the way the process works. But, as potentially the first African American First Lady, I was also the focus of another set of questions and speculations; conversations sometimes rooted in the fears and misperceptions of others. Was I too loud, or too angry, or too emasculating? (Applause.) Or was I too soft, too much of a mom, not enough of a career woman?

Then there was the first time I was on a magazine cover—it was a cartoon drawing of me with a huge afro and machine gun. Now, yeah, it was satire, but if I'm really being honest, it knocked me back a bit. It made me wonder, just how are people seeing me.

Or you might remember the on-stage celebratory fist bump between me and my husband after a primary win that was referred to as a "terrorist fist jab." And over the years, folks have used plenty of interesting words to describe me. One said I exhibited "a little bit of uppity-ism." Another noted that I was one of my husband's "cronies of color." Cable news once charmingly referred to me as "Obama's Baby Mama."

And of course, Barack has endured his fair share of insults and slights. Even today, there are still folks questioning his citizenship.

And all of this used to really get to me. Back in those days, I had a lot of sleepless nights, worrying about what people thought of me, wondering if I might be hurting my husband's chances of winning his election, fearing how my girls would feel if they found out what some people were saying about their mom.

But eventually, I realized that if I wanted to keep my sanity and not let others define me, there was only one thing I could do, and that was to have faith in God's plan for me. (Applause.) I had to ignore all of the noise and be true to myself—and the rest would work itself out. (Applause.)

So throughout this journey, I have learned to block everything out and focus on my truth. I had to answer some basic questions for myself: Who am I? No, really, who am I? What do I care about?

And the answers to those questions have resulted in the woman who stands before you today. (Applause.) A woman who is, first and foremost, a mom. (Applause.) Look, I love our daughters more than anything in the world, more than life itself. And while that may not be the first thing that some folks want to hear from an Ivy-league educated lawyer, it is truly who I am. (Applause.) So for me, being Mom-in-Chief is, and always will be, job number one.

Next, I've always felt a deep sense of obligation to make the biggest impact possible with this incredible platform. So I took on issues that were personal to me—issues like helping families raise healthier kids, honoring the incredible military families I'd met on the campaign trail, inspiring our young people to value their education and finish college. (Applause.)

Now, some folks criticized my choices for not being bold enough. But these were my choices, my issues. And I decided to tackle them in the way that felt most authentic to me—in a way that was both substantive and strategic, but also fun and, hopefully, inspiring.

So I immersed myself in the policy details. I worked with Congress on legislation, gave speeches to CEOs, military generals and Hollywood executives. But I also worked to ensure that my efforts would resonate with kids and families—and that meant doing things in a creative and unconventional way. So, yeah, I planted a garden, and hula-hooped on the White House Lawn with kids. I did some Mom Dancing on TV. I celebrated military kids with Kermit the Frog. I asked folks across the country to wear their alma mater's T-shirts for College Signing Day.

And at the end of the day, by staying true to the me I've always known, I found that this journey has been incredibly freeing. Because no matter what happened, I had the peace of mind of knowing that all of the chatter, the name calling, the doubting—all of it was just noise. (Applause.) It did not define me. It didn't change who I was. And most importantly, it couldn't hold me back. I have learned that as long as I hold fast to my beliefs and values—and follow my own moral compass—then the only expectations I need to live up to are my own.

So, graduates, that's what I want for all of you. I want you all to stay true to the most real, most sincere, most authentic parts of yourselves. I want you to ask those basic questions: Who do you want to be? What inspires you? How do you want to give back? And then I want you to take a deep breath and trust yourselves to chart your own course and make your mark on the world.

Maybe it feels like you're supposed to go to law school—but what you really want to do is to teach little kids. Maybe your parents are expecting you to come back home after you graduate—but you're feeling a pull to travel the world. I want you to listen to those thoughts. I want you to act with both your mind, but also your heart. And no matter what path you choose, I want you to make sure it's you choosing it, and not someone else. (Applause.)

Because here's the thing—the road ahead is not going to be easy. It never is, especially for folks like you and me. Because while we've come so far, the truth is that those age-old problems are stubborn and they haven't fully gone away. So there will be times, just like for those Airmen, when you feel like folks look right past you, or they see just a fraction of who you really are.

The world won't always see you in those caps and gowns. They won't know how hard you worked and how much you sacrificed to make it to this day—the countless hours you spent studying to get this diploma, the multiple jobs you worked to pay for school, the times you had to drive home and take care of your grandma, the evenings you gave up to volunteer at a food bank or organize a campus fundraiser. They don't know that part of you.

Instead they will make assumptions about who they think you are based on their limited notion of the world. And my husband and I know how frustrating that experience can be. We've both felt the sting of those daily slights throughout our entire lives—the folks who crossed the street in fear of their safety; the clerks who kept a close eye on us in all those department stores, the people at formal events who assumed we were the "help"—and those who have questioned our intelligence, our honesty, even our love of this country.

And I know that these little indignities are obviously nothing compared to what folks across the country are dealing with every single day—those nagging worries that you're going to get stopped or pulled over for absolutely no reason; the fear that your job application will be overlooked because of the way your name sounds; the agony of sending your kids to schools that may no longer be separate, but are far from equal; the realization that no matter how far you rise in life, how hard you work to be a good person, a good parent, a good citizen—for some folks, it will never be enough. (Applause.)

And all of that is going to be a heavy burden to carry. It can feel isolating. It can make you feel like your life somehow doesn't matter—that you're like the invisible man that Tuskegee grad Ralph Ellison wrote about all those years ago. And as we've seen over the past few years, those feelings are real. They're rooted in decades of structural challenges that have made too many folks feel frustrated and invisible. And those feelings are playing out in communities like Baltimore and Ferguson and so many others across this country. (Applause.)

But, graduates, today, I want to be very clear that those feelings are not an excuse to just throw up our hands and give up. (Applause.) Not an excuse. They are not an excuse to lose hope. To succumb to feelings of despair and anger only means that in the end, we lose.

But here's the thing—our history provides us with a better story, a better blueprint for how we can win. It teaches us that when we pull ourselves out of those lowest emotional depths, and we channel our frustrations into studying and organizing and banding together—then we can build ourselves and our communities up. We can take on those deep-rooted problems, and together—together—we can overcome anything that stands in our way.

And the first thing we have to do is vote. (Applause.) Hey, no, not just once in a while. Not just when my husband or somebody you like is on the ballot. But in every election at every level, all of the time. (Applause.) Because here is the truth—if you want to have a say in your community, if you truly want the power to control your own destiny, then you've got to be involved. You got to be at the table. You've got to vote, vote, vote, vote. That's it; that's the way we move forward. That's how we make progress for ourselves and for our country.

That's what's always happened here at Tuskegee. Think about those students who made bricks with their bare hands. They did it so that others could follow them and learn on this campus, too. Think about that brilliant scientist who made his lab from a trash pile. He did it because he ultimately wanted to help sharecroppers feed their families. Those Airmen who rose above brutal discrimination—they did it so the whole world could see just how high black folks could soar. That's the spirit we've got to summon to take on the challenges we face today. (Applause.)

And you don't have to be President of the United States to start addressing things like poverty, and education, and lack of opportunity. Graduates, today—today, you can mentor a young person and make sure he or she takes the right path. Today, you can volunteer at an after-school program or food pantry. Today, you can help your younger cousin fill out her college financial aid form so that she could be sitting in those chairs one day. (Applause.) But just like all those folks who came before us, you've got to do something to lay the groundwork for future generations.

That pilot I mentioned earlier—Charles DeBow—he didn't rest on his laurels after making history. Instead, after he left the Army, he finished his education. He became a high school English teacher and a college lecturer. He kept lifting other folks up through education. He kept fulfilling his "double duty" long after he hung up his uniform.

And, graduates, that's what we need from all of you. We need you to channel the magic of Tuskegee toward the challenges of today. And here's what I really want you to know—you have got everything you need to do this. You've got it in you. Because even if you're nervous or unsure about what path to take in the years ahead, I want you to realize that you've got everything you need right now to succeed. You've got it.

You've got the knowledge and the skills honed here on this hallowed campus. You've got families up in the stands who will support you every step of the way. And most of all, you've got yourselves—and all of the heart, and grit, and smarts that got you to this day.

And if you rise above the noise and the pressures that surround you, if you stay true to who you are and where you come from, if you have faith in God's plan for you, then you will keep fulfilling your duty to people all across this country. And as the years pass, you'll feel the same freedom that Charles DeBow did when he was taking off in that airplane. You will feel the bumps smooth off. You'll take part in that "never-failing miracle" of progress. And you'll be flying through the air, out of this world—free.

God bless you, graduates. (Applause.) I can't wait to see how high you soar. Love you all. Very proud. Thank you. (Applause.)

Climate Change Is a Crisis We Can Only Solve Together

By Naomi Klein

In this address to the graduating class of the College of the Atlantic, Naomi Klein emphasizes the importance of collective action, saying we can only solve the world's greatest challenges if we organize together to bring about change on both a local and global level. In her remarks, she exposes the fallacy behind the notion so widespread in wealthy western countries that our individual, personal choices are all that matter. Unless people work collectively, Klein notes, individual choices cannot have an impact on major world-wide problems like climate change and wealth inequality. At the same time, she encourages individuals and activists not to put an inordinate amount of pressure on themselves, as any one individual can only do so much. Klein is a contributing editor for Harper's, *a reporter for* Rolling Stone, *and she writes a regular column for* The Nation *and* The Guardian. *She is a member of the board at 350.org, a global grassroots movement devoted to solving the climate crisis, a Puffin Foundation Writing Fellow at The Nation Institute, and a former Miliband Fellow at the London School of Economics.*

First of all, a huge congratulations to all the graduates—and to the parents who raised you, and the teachers who guided you. It's a true privilege to be included in this special day.

Mine is not going to be your average commencement address, for the simple reason that College of the Atlantic is not your average college. I mean, what kind of college lets students vote on their commencement speaker—as if this is their day or something? What's next? Women choosing whom they are going to marry?

Usually, commencement addresses try to equip graduates with a moral compass for their post-university life. You hear stories that end with clear lessons like: "Money can't buy happiness." "Be kind." "Don't be afraid to fail."

But my sense is that very few of you are flailing around trying to sort out right from wrong. Quite remarkably, you knew you wanted to go not just to an excellent college, but to an excellent socially and ecologically engaged college. A school surrounded by tremendous biological diversity and suffused with tremendous human diversity, with a student population that spans the globe. You also knew that strong community mattered more than almost anything. That's more self-awareness and

Delivered June 6, 2015, at the College of the Atlantic commencement, Bar Harbor, Maine, by Naomi Klein.

self-direction than most people have when they leave graduate school—and somehow you had it when you were still in high school.

Which is why I am going to skip the homilies and get down to business: the historical moment into which you graduate—with climate change, wealth concentration, and racialized violence all reaching breaking points.

How do we help most? How do we best serve this broken world? And we know that time is short, especially when it comes to climate change. We all hear the clock ticking loudly in the background.

But that doesn't mean that climate change trumps everything else. It means we need to create integrated solutions—ones that radically bring down emissions, while closing the inequality gap and making life tangibly better for the majority.

This is no pipe dream. We have living examples from which to learn. Germany's energy transition has created 400,000 jobs in just over a decade, and not just cleaned up energy but made it fairer—so that energy systems are owned and controlled by hundreds and hundreds of cities, towns, and cooperatives. The mayor of New York just announced a climate plan that would bring 800,000 people out of poverty by 2025, by investing massively in transit and affordable housing and raising the minimum wage.

The holistic leap we need is within our grasp. And know that there is no better preparation for that grand project than your deeply interdisciplinary education in human ecology. You were made for this moment. No, that's not quite right: You somehow knew to make yourselves for this moment.

But much rests on the choices we make in the next few years. "Don't be afraid to fail" may be a standard commencement-address life lesson. Yet it doesn't work for those of us who are part of the climate-justice movement, where being afraid of failure is perfectly rational.

Because, let's face it: The generations before you used up more than your share of atmospheric space. We used up your share of big failures too. The ultimate intergenerational injustice. That doesn't mean that we all can't still make mistakes. We can and we will. But Alicia Garza, one of the amazing founders of Black Lives Matter, talks about how we have to "make new mistakes."

Sit with that one for a minute. Let's stop making the same old mistakes. Here are a few, but I trust that you will silently add your own. Projecting messianic fantasies onto politicians. Thinking the market will fix it. Building a movement made up entirely of upper-middle-class white people and then wondering why people of color don't want to join "our movement." Tearing each other to bloody shreds because it's easier to do that than go after the forces most responsible for this mess. These are social-change clichés, and they are getting really boring.

We don't have the right to demand perfection from each other. But we do have the right to expect progress. To demand evolution. So let's make some new mistakes. Let's make new mistakes as we break through our silos and build the kind of beautifully diverse and justice-hungry movement that actually has a chance of winning—winning against the powerful interests that want us to keep failing.

With this in mind, I want talk about an old mistake that I see reemerging. It has to do with the idea that since attempts at big systemic change have failed, all we can do is act small. Some of you will relate. Some of you won't. But I suspect all of you will have to deal with this tension in your future work.

A story: When I was 26, I went to Indonesia and the Philippines to do research for my first book, *No Logo*. I had a simple goal: to meet the workers making the clothes and electronics that my friends and I purchased. And I did. I spent evenings on concrete floors in squalid dorm rooms where teenage girls—sweet and giggly—spent their scarce nonworking hours. Eight or even 10 to a room. They told me stories about not being able to leave their machines to pee. About bosses who hit. About not having enough money to buy dried fish to go with their rice.

They knew they were being badly exploited—that the garments they were making were being sold for more than they would make in a month. One 17-year-old said to me: "We make computers, but we don't know how to use them."

So one thing I found slightly jarring was that some of these same workers wore clothing festooned with knockoff trademarks of the very multinationals that were responsible for these conditions: Disney characters or Nike check marks. At one point, I asked a local labor organizer about this. Wasn't it strange—a contradiction?

It took a very long time for him to understand the question. When he finally did, he looked at me like I was nuts. You see, for him and his colleagues, individual consumption wasn't considered to be in the realm of politics at all. Power rested not in what you did as one person, but what you did as many people, as one part of a large, organized, and focused movement. For him, this meant organizing workers to go on strike for better conditions, and eventually it meant winning the right to unionize. What you ate for lunch or happened to be wearing was of absolutely no concern whatsoever.

This was striking to me because it was the mirror opposite of my culture back home in Canada. Where I came from, you expressed your political beliefs—firstly and very often lastly—through personal lifestyle choices. By loudly proclaiming your vegetarianism. By shopping fair trade and local and boycotting big, evil brands.

These very different understandings of social change came up again and again a couple of years later, once my book came out. I would give talks about the need for international protections for the right to unionize. About the need to change our global trading system so it didn't encourage a race to the bottom. And yet at the end of those talks, the first question from the audience was: "What kind of sneakers are OK to buy?" "What brands are ethical?" "Where do you buy your clothes?" "What can I do, as an individual, to change the world?"

Fifteen years after I published *No Logo*, I still find myself facing very similar questions. These days, I give talks about how the same economic model that superpowered multinationals to seek out cheap labor in Indonesia and China also supercharged global greenhouse-gas emissions. And, invariably, the hand goes up: "Tell me what I can do as an individual." Or maybe "as a business owner."

The hard truth is that the answer to the question "What can I, as an individual, do to stop climate change?" is: nothing. You can't do anything. In fact, the very idea that we—as atomized individuals, even lots of atomized individuals—could play a significant part in stabilizing the planet's climate system, or changing the global economy, is objectively nuts. We can only meet this tremendous challenge together. As part of a massive and organized global movement.

The irony is that people with relatively little power tend to understand this far better than those with a great deal more power. The workers I met in Indonesia and the Philippines knew all too well that governments and corporations did not value their voice or even their lives as individuals. And because of this, they were driven to act not only together, but to act on a rather large political canvas. To try to change the policies in factories that employ thousands of workers, or in export zones that employ tens of thousands. Or the labor laws in an entire country of millions. Their sense of individual powerlessness pushed them to be politically ambitious, to demand structural changes.

In contrast, here in wealthy countries, we are told how powerful we are as individuals all the time. As consumers. Even individual activists. And the result is that, despite our power and privilege, we often end up acting on canvases that are unnecessarily small—the canvas of our own lifestyle, or maybe our neighborhood or town. Meanwhile, we abandon the structural changes—the policy and legal work—to others.

This is not to belittle local activism. Local is critical. Local organizing is winning big fights against fracking and tar-sands pipelines. Local is showing us what the post-carbon economy looks and feels like.

And small examples inspire bigger examples. College of the Atlantic was one of the first schools to divest from fossil fuels. And you made the decision, I am told, in a week. It took that kind of leadership from small schools that knew their values to push more, shall we say, insecure institutions to follow suit. Like Stanford University. Like Oxford University. Like the British royal family. Like the Rockefeller family. So local matters, but local is not enough.

I got a vivid reminder of this when I visited Red Hook, Brooklyn, in the immediate aftermath of Superstorm Sandy. Red Hook was one of the hardest-hit neighborhoods and is home to an amazing community farm—a place that teaches kids from nearby housing projects how to grow healthy food, provides composting for a huge number of residents, hosts a weekly farmers' market, and runs a terrific CSA [community-supported agriculture] program. In short, it was doing everything right: reducing food miles, staying away from petroleum inputs, sequestering carbon in the soil, reducing landfill by composting, fighting inequality and food insecurity.

But when the storm came, none of that mattered. The entire harvest was lost, and the fear was the storm water would make the soil toxic. They could buy new soil and start over. But the farmers I met there knew that unless other people were out there fighting to lower emissions on a systemic and global level, then this kind of loss would occur again and again.

It's not that one sphere is more important than the other. It's that we have to do both: the local and the global. The resistance and the alternatives. The "no" to what we cannot survive and "yeses" that we need to thrive.

* * *

Before I leave you, I want to stress one other thing. And please listen because it's important. It is true that we have to do it all. That we have to change everything. But you personally do not have to do everything. This is not all on you.

One of the real dangers of being brilliant, sensitive young people who hear the climate clock ticking loudly is the danger of taking on too much. Which is another manifestation of that inflated sense of our own importance.

It can seem that every single life decision—whether to work at a national NGO or a local permaculture project or a green start-up, whether to work with animals or with people, whether to be a scientist or an artist, whether to go to grad school or have kids—carries the weight of the world.

I was struck by this impossible burden some of you are placing on yourselves when I was contacted recently by a 21-year-old Australian science student named Zoe Buckley Lennox. At the time she reached me, she was camped out on top of Shell's Arctic drilling rig in the middle of the Pacific. She was one of six Greenpeace activists who had scaled the giant rig to try to slow its passage and draw attention to the insanity of drilling for oil in the Arctic. They lived up there in the howling winds for a week.

While they were still up there, I arranged to call Zoe on the Greenpeace satellite phone—just to personally thank her for her courage. Do you know what she did? She asked me: "How do you know you are doing the right thing? I mean, there is divestment. There is lobbying. There's the Paris climate conference."

And I was touched by her seriousness, but I also wanted to weep. Here she was, doing one of the more incredible things imaginable—freezing her butt off trying to physically stop Arctic drilling with her body. And up there in her seven layers of clothing and climbing gear, she was still beating herself up, wondering whether she should be doing something else.

What I told her is what I will tell you. What you are doing is amazing. And what you do next will be amazing too. Because you are not alone. You are part of a movement. And that movement is organizing for Paris and getting their schools to divest and trying to block Arctic drilling in Congress and the courts. And on the open water. All at the same time.

And, yes, we need to grow faster and do more. But the weight of the world is not on any one person's shoulders—not yours. Not Zoe's. Not mine. It rests in the strength of the project of transformation that millions are already a part of.

That means we are free to follow our passions. To do the kind of work that will sustain us for the long run. It even means we can take breaks—in fact, we have a duty to take them. And to make sure our friends do too.

Which is why I am going to skip yet another commencement-address tradition—the one that somberly tells graduates that they have finally become adults. Because my strong sense is that most of you have been adults since your early teens.

So what I really want to say to you is something else entirely. Make sure to give yourself time to be a kid.

And make sure to truly enjoy this tremendous accomplishment. Congratulations.

On Free Speech

By Ian McEwan

In this commencement address, Ian McEwan meditates on the importance of free speech. In January 2015 two Islamist gunman opened fire and killed twelve staff members at the headquarters of French satirical newspaper Charlie Hebdo, *which had repeatedly lampooned the Prophet Mohammed and Islam more broadly. Although* Charlie Hebdo *had satirized many religions, McEwan recalls how at the time, some American writers were reluctant to speak out against these attacks for fear of seeming critical of Islam or seeming to support the "War on Terror." Critiquing this thinking, McEwan insists that politics must never get in the way of defending free speech, and he encourages the graduating class to remember this and always seek out the "mental freedom" and pluralism of thought encouraged by the novels they may have read throughout their education. Ian McEwan, the award-winning author of more than twenty novels and short stories, has been shortlisted for the Man Booker Prize for Fiction numerous times and won the award for* Amsterdam *in 1998. His novel* Atonement *received several awards, including the 2003 National Book Critics' Circle Fiction Award, and he was named the 2010 Peggy V. Helmerich Distinguished Author.*

My most sincere congratulations to all the graduates here. You made it through. You have a degree from a truly excellent institution. A lot of reading, writing, lying in bed (thinking, of course). And now you stand on one of life's various summits. As you know, there's only one way off a summit—but that's another story. Don't be taken in by those who tell you that life is short. It's inordinately long. I was into my twenties when my mother astonished me by saying wistfully, "I'd give anything to be forty-five again." Forty-five sounded like old age to me then. Now I see what she meant. Most of you have more than 20 years before you peak. Barring all-out nuclear war or a catastrophic meteor collision, a substantial minority of you will get a toe in the door of the next century—a very wrinkled, arthritic toe, but the same toe you're wearing now. You have a lot of years in the bank—but don't worry, I'm not here to tell you how to spend them.

Instead, I would like to share a few thoughts with you about free speech (and speech here includes writing and reading, listening and thinking)—free speech—the life blood, the essential condition of the liberal education you've just received. Let's begin on a positive note: there is likely more free speech, free thought, free inquiry on earth now than at any previous moment in recorded history (even taking into account the golden age of the so-called "pagan" philosophers). And you've come

Delivered May 18, 2015, at the Dickinson College commencement, Carlisle, Pennsylvania, by Ian McEwan.

of age in a country where the enshrinement of free speech in the First Amendment is not an empty phrase, as it is in many constitutions, but a living reality.

But free speech was, it is and always will be, under attack—from the political right, the left, the center. It will come from under your feet, from the extremes of religion as well as from unreligious ideologies. It's never convenient, especially for entrenched power, to have a lot of free speech flying around.

The words associated with Voltaire (more likely, his sentiments but not his actual phrasing) remain crucial and should never be forgotten: I disapprove of what you say, but I will defend to the death your right to say it. It's only rarely appropriate to suppress the speech of those you disagree with. As my late friend Christopher Hitchens used to say, when you meet a flat-earther or a creationist, it can be useful to be made to remember just why you think the earth is round or whether you're capable of making the case for natural selection. For that reason, it's a poor principle, adopted in some civilized countries, to imprison the deniers of the Holocaust or the Armenian massacres, however contemptible they might be.

It's worth remembering this: freedom of expression sustains all the other freedoms we enjoy. Without free speech, democracy is a sham. Every freedom we possess or wish to possess (of habeas corpus and due process, of universal franchise and of assembly, union representation, sexual equality, of sexual preference, of the rights of children, of animals—the list goes on) has had to be freely thought and talked and written into existence. No single individual can generate these rights alone. The process is cumulative. It was a historical context of relative freedom of speech that made possible the work of those who were determined to extend that liberty. John Milton, Tom Paine, Mary Wollstonecraft, George Washington, Thomas Jefferson, John Stuart Mill, Oliver Wendell Holmes—the roll call is long and honorable—and that is why an education in the liberal arts is so vital to the culture you are about to contribute to.

Take a long journey from these shores as I'm sure many of you will, and you will find the condition of free expression to be desperate. Across almost the entire Middle East, free thought can bring punishment or death, from governments or from street mobs or motivated individuals. The same is true in Bangladesh, Pakistan, across great swathes of Africa. These past years the public space for free thought in Russia has been shrinking. In China, state monitoring of free expression is on an industrial scale. To censor daily the internet alone, the Chinese government employs as many as fifty thousand bureaucrats—a level of thought repression unprecedented in human history.

Paradoxically, it's all the more important to be vigilant for free expression wherever it flourishes. And nowhere has it been more jealously guarded than under the First Amendment of the U.S. Constitution. Which is why it has been so puzzling lately, when we saw scores of American writers publicly disassociating themselves from a PEN gala to honor the murdered journalists of the French satirical magazine, *Charlie Hebdo*. American PEN exists to defend and promote free speech. What a disappointment that so many American authors could not stand with courageous fellow writers and artists at a time of tragedy. The magazine has been scathing about racism. It's also scathing about organized religion and politicians and it might not be to your taste—but that's when you should remember your Voltaire.

Hebdo's offices were fire-bombed in 2011, and the journalists kept going. They received constant death threats—and they kept going. In January nine colleagues were murdered, gunned down, in their office—the editorial staff kept going and within days they had produced an edition whose cover forgave their attackers. *Tout est pardonne*, all is forgiven. All this, when in the U.S. and U.K. one threatening phone call can be enough to stop a major publishing house in its tracks.

The attack on *Charlie Hebdo* came from religious fanatics whose allegiances became clear when one of the accomplices made her way from France, through Turkey to ISIS in Syria. Remember, this is a form of fanaticism whose victims, across Africa and the Middle East, are mostly Muslims—Muslim gays and feminists, Muslim reformists, bloggers, human rights activists, dissidents, apostates, novelists, and ordinary citizens, including children, murdered in or kidnapped from their schools.

There's a phenomenon in intellectual life that I call bipolar thinking. Let's not side with *Charlie Hebdo* because it might seem as if we're endorsing George Bush's "war on terror". This is a suffocating form of intellectual tribalism and a poor way of thinking for yourself. As a German novelist friend wrote to me in anguish about the PEN affair—"It's the Seventies again: Let's not support the Russian dissidents, because it would get 'applause from the wrong side.' That terrible phrase."

But note the end of the *Hebdo* affair: the gala went ahead, the surviving journalists received a thunderous and prolonged standing ovation from American PEN.

Timothy Garton Ash reminds us in a new book on free speech that "the U.S. Supreme Court has described academic freedom as a 'special concern of the First Amendment.'" Worrying too, then, is the case of Ayaan Hirsi Ali, an ex-Muslim, highly critical of Islam, too critical for some. As a victim herself, she has campaigned against female genital mutilation. She has campaigned for the rights of Muslim women. In a recent book she has argued that for Islam to live more at ease in the modern world it needs to rethink its attitudes to homosexuality, to the interpretation of the Koran as the literal word of God, to blasphemy, to punishing severely those who want to leave the religion. Contrary to what some have suggested, such arguments are neither racist nor driven by hatred. But she has received death threats. Crucially, on many American campuses she is not welcomed, and, notoriously, Brandeis withdrew its offer of an honorary degree. Islam is worthy of respect, as indeed is atheism. We want respect flowing in all directions. But religion and atheism, and all thought systems, all grand claims to truth, must be open to criticism, satire, even, sometimes, mockery. Surely, we have not forgotten the lessons of the Salman Rushdie affair.

Campus intolerance of inconvenient speakers is hardly new. Back in the sixties my own university blocked a psychologist for promoting the idea of a hereditable component to intelligence. In the seventies, the great American biologist EO Wilson was drowned out for suggesting a genetic element in human social behavior. As I remember, both men were called fascists. The ideas of these men did not fit prevailing ideologies, but their views are unexceptionable today.

More broadly—the internet has, of course, provided extraordinary possibilities for free speech. At the same time, it has taken us onto some difficult and unexpected terrain. It has led to the slow decline of local newspapers, and so removed a sceptical and knowledgeable voice from local politics. Privacy is an essential element of free expression; the Snowden files have revealed an extraordinary and unnecessary level of email surveillance by government agencies. Another essential element of free expression is access to information; the internet has concentrated huge power over that access into the hands of private companies like Google, Facebook and Twitter. We need to be careful that such power is not abused. Large pharmaceutical companies have been known to withhold research information vital to the public interest. On another scale, the death of young black men in police custody could be framed as the ultimate sanction against free expression. As indeed is poverty and poor educational resources.

All these issues need the input of men and women with a liberal arts education and you, graduates, are well placed to form your own conclusions. And you may reasonably conclude that free speech is not simple. It's never an absolute. We don't give space to proselytizing paedophiles, to racists (and remember, race is not identical to religion) or to those who wish to incite violence against others. Wendell Holmes's hypothetical "shouting fire in a crowded theatre" is still relevant. But it can be a little too easy sometimes to dismiss arguments you don't like as "hate speech" or to complain that this or that speaker makes you feel "disrespected." Being offended is not to be confused with a state of grace; it's the occasional price we all pay for living in an open society. Being robust is no bad thing. Either engage, with arguments—not with banishments and certainly not with guns —or, as an American Muslim teacher said recently at Friday prayers, ignore the entire matter.

In making your mind up on these issues, I hope you'll remember your time at Dickinson and the novels you may have read here. It would prompt you, I hope, in the direction of mental freedom. The novel as a literary form was born out of the Enlightenment, out of curiosity about and respect for the individual. Its traditions impel it toward pluralism, openness, a sympathetic desire to inhabit the minds of others. There is no man, woman or child, on earth whose mind the novel cannot reconstruct. Totalitarian systems are right with regard to their narrow interests when they lock up novelists. The novel is, or can be, the ultimate expression of free speech.

I hope you'll use your fine liberal education to preserve for future generations the beautiful and precious but also awkward, sometimes inconvenient and even offensive culture of freedom of expression we have. Take with you these celebrated words of George Washington: "If the freedom of speech is taken away then, dumb and silent, we may be led like sheep to the slaughter."

We may be certain that Dickinson has not prepared you to be sheep. Good luck 2015 graduates in whatever you choose to do in life.

Commencement Address: Vassar College

By Arianna Huffington

In this commencement address to the Vassar College Class of 2015, Arianna Huffington advises the graduates on the importance of cultivating three healthy relationships: with technology, with themselves, and with the world around them. Inflecting her speech with both humor and sincerity, Huffington discusses the dangers of being addicted to smart phones and the distraction that comes with it. She suggests that people need to be able to master technology rather than being enslaved by it and should make time for themselves to focus on what is important in this life—enjoying the present moment, developing a meaningful inner life, cultivating relationships with significant people, and effecting positive change in the world. Founder, chair, president and editor-in-chief of the Huffington Post Media Group, Arianna Huffington has been named in the Time *magazine list of the world's 100 most influential people and the* Forbes *list of "Most Powerful Women." She is also the author of fourteen books, most recently* Thrive: The Third Metric to Redefining Success, *which debuted at #1 on* The New York Times *bestseller list in 2014.*

Thank you so much, President Hill, Members of the Board of Trustees, distinguished alumni, members of the faculty, devoted parents and friends, and especially the fabulous Vassar College Class of 2015. I am deeply grateful to have been invited to be part of such a special moment in your lives. Commencement is one of my favorite rituals—coming together for one last time, dressed alike before you head off into your singular and unique lives. When I was deciding what to wear under my gown, I asked Siri what the weather was in Poughkeepsie. And Siri responded with a list of mixed drinks with whiskey. I think I'm going to wait until Siri comes up with an update for Greek accents.

Today is the culmination of your time at Vassar. And it's also a mini-culmination for me. Because I've spent a lot of time in recent weeks getting to know you—following you and your activities on social media, on Vassar's website, in*The Miscellany News*, and in other ways I'm not prepared to disclose that will remain between me and the folks at the NSA. It feels a little like I've been checking out your online dating profile, and now we're finally meeting. And when I saw you walk in, all 611 of you, I breathed a huge sigh of relief. Because let's face it, you look fantastic. If we were on Tinder, I would definitely be ready to swipe right. Or is it left? Actually, at my age, it doesn't matter, as long as you're swiping.

Delivered May 31, 2015, at the Vassar College commencement, Poughkeepsie, New York, by Arianna Huffington.

One of the things I learned from my cyber-stalking is that the Vassar College seal shows the goddess Athena in front of the Parthenon, which I love. Though it occurs to me that I'm probably here because Athena couldn't be booked, so you settled for another Greek lady from Athens. And to really sell it, I'll be delivering my speech in a thick, sometimes-hard-to-understand Greek accent, instead of the crystal clear, accentless voice I use at all other times. In my private detective work, I also learned that your former motto "purity and wisdom" was abandoned in 1930, which was probably a good idea given that when *The Miscellany News*—or the *Misc*as I understand you call it—sent out an email to seniors asking what was on their bucket list, most of the answers had to do with sex. One replied, "Have sex under the sex tree!" Another said, "Have sex in the circle couches near the Art Library." A third wrote back, "Sex in the meditation room or the roof of the library." Aren't you glad I'm not disclosing your names in front of your parents? You owe me!

What was clear from all my private detective work is that you belong to a community. And for the rest of your lives, you'll essentially have a language you speak that no one else understands. . . sort of a more fun version of how I've been feeling my whole life. Chili Wednesdays at The Retreat. The Bell Ringing. Founder's Day. Mug Nights. A Quidditch team, The Butterbeer Brooers. The Deece. Running naked through the library the night before final exams. The Vassar Devil, which I understand to be some sort of ice cream sensation I'm definitely planning to sample before I leave. The a cappella groups—all 3,475 of them.

And what a treasure trove of stories you're leaving Vassar with. Not just from your years here but from Vassar's incredibly colorful past: Way back in the 1880s, you invented fudge—maybe. Some of you actually believe that the squirrels around campus are the slightly deranged reincarnations of English majors who couldn't get jobs after graduation. But, hey, at least the squirrels aren't living at home, right, mom and dad? And here is my favorite: before your time, Vassar students were given the emblem of an acorn to display on their doors when they did not wish to be disturbed. The custom was apparently discontinued, but I want to urge you to revive it as something to use physically and spiritually for the rest of your lives. It's actually central to the three relationships I want to talk to you about today. And those are: your relationship with technology, your relationship with yourself, and your relationship with the world.

Let's start with your relationship with technology. No generation has been as liberated and as connected by technology as yours. But also, no generation has been as enslaved and as distracted by technology. So bring on that acorn because as the writer Eric Barker said, "Those who can sit in a chair, undistracted for hours, mastering subjects and creating things will rule the world—while the rest of us frantically and futilely try to keep up with texts, tweets and other incessant interruptions." Sadly, we have become not just distracted by our devices, our texts, emails, constant notifications, and social media, but addicted to them. And when it comes to social media, let me break it to you: our addiction is not a bug, but a feature. This isn't some unforeseen side effect, it was always the intention, that social media would consume as much of our time and attention—as much of our lives—as possible.

To your credit, many of you have already recognized this and have taken steps to curb this addiction. As senior Justin Mitchell told the *Misc,* "I was mindlessly going through people's profiles and being an idiot. So I cut it out. There's just not enough time to do that with school." And having graduated just a few years before you, I can tell you there is even less time to do that with life.

But the addiction is so powerful that, according to a recent survey, 20 percent of millennials actually use their smartphones during sex. Maybe I should have read the instructions on my phone more carefully, but I'm not even sure what that means. Indeed, a recent study shows that more than half of women would rather go a month with no sex than a month with no smartphone—although I am sure this survey did not include any women with access to the Vassar Sex Tree.

Contrary to what many of you may think, not only is multitasking not very efficient, it doesn't actually exist. It's actually rapid task switching—instead of doing two things at once, we simply switch between doing two things badly. It's one of the most stressful ways we can use our time, and it robs us of our capacity to notice and appreciate every moment of our lives. I live in New York, and you hardly ever see anybody simply walking down the street who's not also staring at a screen, talking on the phone, or, even worse, texting while walking. It's like being in a really boring zombie movie. I used to be exactly like that myself. I remember one day, I left my apartment with a friend. I looked up and said, "What a gorgeous building! I wonder when that went up?" "1890" my friend said. I'd never noticed it. As Vassar alum Mary Oliver put it, "Instructions for living a life: Pay attention. Be Astonished. Tell about it." And by the way, when you do, please tell about it on *The Huffington Post.* I'm going to make it super easy for you by giving you my email so you can bypass the growing *HuffPost* blogging bureaucracy: arianna@huffingtonpost.com.

As someone who runs a 24/7 digital media company and who uses every form of social media ever invented, I hope I have some street cred when I urge you to build boundaries, introduce digital detoxes into your life, and learn to regularly disconnect from the jumble and the cacophony and make time to reconnect with yourself. There will be many profound and fulfilling relationships ahead of you, but the relationship with yourself is the most important relationship you'll ever have. And, like any relationship, it can't be taken for granted—without care and attention, it will atrophy and, ultimately, break down.

If there is one thing I wish I knew when I was sitting where you are today—and by the way, there are many—it's that the Delphic admonition "Know Thyself" and Socrates' admonition that "the unexamined life is not worth living" are not ancient philosophical platitudes, but in fact the most relevant and important guiding truths for our lives. In the well-earned rush and excitement of your new life that's about to begin, it's remarkably easy to forget that most important relationship. That's because the ever-increasing creep of technology—into our bedrooms, our brains, and our lives—makes it much harder to connect with ourselves.

Indeed, for so many of us, connecting with ourselves has been so neglected that we will do anything to avoid it. Researchers from Harvard and the University of Virginia did an experiment in which they gave people a choice to be alone in a room, without anything—no devices, no papers, no phones—or get an electric shock. A whopping 67 percent of men chose the electric shock. I'm very happy to say that only 25 percent of women chose the shock. Seriously guys—and a quarter of women—what is wrong with you? It's not like you have to go shopping with your own thoughts or move in with them and pick out drapes, just be alone with them for fifteen minutes. Is it that bad?

In fact most of us actually know more about the state of our smartphones than we do about the state of ourselves. I bet pretty much everyone here knows approximately how much battery remains in your smartphone right now. And when it gets below twenty percent, giving us the dreaded red low power alert, we begin to get anxious and desperately look around for one of the little recharging shrines we meticulously maintain everywhere around us, lest anything should happen to our precious phone. But how much do you know, how aware are you, how mindful are you, of the state of your own being? Of your own energy and alertness and reserves? How quickly do you spring into action when you go into the low power zone?

I was fascinated to read about Vassar's Maria Mitchell, America's first female astronomer, and to see the gorgeous building that used to house her observatory. And while I completely understand the sense of wonder that has led men and women through the ages to explore outer space, I'm personally much more fascinated with exploring inner space. As Thomas Merton put it, "What can we gain by sailing to the moon if we are not able to cross the abyss that separates us from ourselves? This is the most important of all voyages of discovery, and without it all the rest are not only useless but disastrous." In other words, it's the quality of our inner journeys that allows us to make sense of our outer journeys.

There is now a collective longing to stop living in the shallows and recognize that life is actually shaped from the inside out—a truth that has been celebrated by spiritual teachers, poets and philosophers throughout the ages and has now been unambiguously validated by modern science. And you, Vassar graduates, can lead the way, and chart a new path forward. You're the first generation born into the digital world. And you can be the first generation to master it, to make it serve you, instead of the other way around. And when you do, you'll find that you have the wind at your back because that's what the times are calling for.

One of the things that's so special about Vassar is that at the heart of your education is a deep and profound sense of responsibility for the world and those around us. You've been taught to use your considerable talents, and your drive and your dedication to make a difference in the world. I was moved and inspired by all the projects you've started and been involved in: The Vassar Prison Initiative, The Vassar Haiti Project, The College Committee on Sustainability, Operation Donation, et cetera, et cetera. You've already made a difference in the world you're about to enter.

And it's no accident that Vassar has recognized the crisis of growing inequality in our country. In fact, congratulations for being the number one college to enroll high-performing, low-income students and support them through successful graduation. The concern about growing inequality has become almost universal—transcending political parties and ideologies. The statistics are staggering: Student loan debt is at 1.2 trillion dollars, the number of Americans in poverty has grown by 15 million since 2000, the number of high-poverty neighborhoods has tripled since 1970, while America is now home to more prisoners than any other country in the world, with more than 2 million people behind bars.

As we see this happening, I keep being reminded of my visit to Pompeii, whose people were wiped out in the first century by a violent volcanic eruption. There had been many warning signs, including a severe earthquake, tremors, springs and wells that dried up, dogs that ran away, and birds that no longer sang. And then the most obvious warning sign: columns of smoke belching out of Mount Vesuvius before the volcano blew its top, burying the city and its inhabitants under sixty feet of ash and volcanic rock. But the warning signs had been dismissed as "not particularly alarming." The warning signs are all around us today, too, pointing out the gulf between what we know we should be doing and what we're choosing to do instead.

It's not that we don't have enough data—in fact, we're drowning in data. What we're lacking is wisdom. Indeed ninety percent of the data now available to us has been created in the last two years. But how much of our collective wisdom has been made available in that time? That's what's missing from our leaders and from our public discourse. Could our political debate, dominated as it is by meaningless head-to-head polls, manufactured controversies, horse-race sound-bites, and news of Hillary Clinton asking for extra guacamole at Chipotle and Ted Cruz suddenly liking country music after 9/11—be any more trivialized?

In fact, at *The Huffington Post* we've started a "Who Cares?" section to cover all these non-issues and hopefully leave more room for the real ones. And for those of you going into journalism, our goal at *HuffPost* is to reimagine the craft. There's an old saying in the news business, one that's guided editorial thinking for decades: "If it bleeds, it leads." But it turns out this is just lousy journalism. As journalists, our job is to provide an accurate picture—and that means the full picture—of what's going on in the world. Just showing tragedy, violence, and mayhem—just focusing on what's broken and what's not working—misses too much of what is really happening all around us. What about how people are responding to these challenges, how they're coming together, even in the midst of violence, poverty and loss? And what about all the stories of innovation, creativity, ingenuity, compassion and grace? By shining a light on these stories, we can scale up these solutions and create a positive contagion that can expand and broaden their reach. Instead of just producing copycat crimes, we can start to produce copycat solutions.

And you can be a part of those solutions. There is an invisible but very real and inescapable connection between our relationship with ourselves and our relationship with the world. As Alexander Solzhenitsyn put it, "If you wanted to put the world to rights, who should you begin with: yourself or others?" I know everyone here wants to help put the world to rights. But please remember, it begins with yourself. . . as they say on airplanes, secure your own oxygen mask first.

So regularly hang that virtual acorn on your door because while the world will provide plenty of insistent, pleading, flashing, high-volume signals directing you to distract yourself, to not be in the moment, to burn out in order to climb higher up the ladder of what the world defines as success, there will be almost no worldly signals reminding you to stay connected to the essence of who you are, to pause to wonder, and to connect to that place of wisdom in you—that place from which everything is possible. The world will keep coming at you with its incessant demands, beeps, blinking lights, and alerts. "Every day," Iain Thomas wrote, "the world will drag you by the hand, yelling, 'This is important! And this is important! And this is important! You need to worry about this! And This! And This!' And each day, it's up to you to yank your hand back, put it on your heart and say, 'No. This is what's important.'"

It's from this sacred place that life is transformed from struggle to grace, from information to wisdom. We have, if we're lucky, about 30,000 days to play the game of life. And trust me, that's not morbid. In fact, it's wisdom that will put all the inevitable failures and rejections and disappointments and heartbreaks into perspective. Because as the great *Onion* headline summed it up, "Death Rate Holding Steady at 100%." So let's stop sweeping it under the rug. That's a modern impulse. Ancient Romans would carve "MM," Memento Mori, Remember Death, on statues and trees—to put every victory and every defeat into its proper perspective. I'm not sure if you want to carve it on the sex tree, though, because things could get weird.

And if you've been to a memorial service recently, you'll have noticed that our eulogies have very little to do with our resumes and our LinkedIn profiles. For instance, here's the sort of thing you don't hear in a eulogy: "George was amazing, he increased market share by one-third." Or "her PowerPoint slides were always meticulously prepared." Or "she ate lunch at her desk every single day." Our eulogies are always about the other stuff: what we gave, how we connected, how much we meant to our family and friends, small kindnesses, lifelong passions, and the things that made us laugh. So why do we spend so much of our lives chasing things we don't value and that don't ultimately matter?

As you leave this magical campus, don't let technology wrap you up in a perpetually harried existence. Don't be so connected to everybody that you're not truly connected to anybody. Or to yourself. And don't get so caught up in your busy life that life's mystery passes you by. Bring joy and gratitude into every moment—even the tough ones—and start displaying that acorn on your door. Thank you so much.

The Goddess is in the Connections

By Gloria Steinem

In an address to the graduating class of Bennington College, Gloria Steinem emphasizes the importance of focusing on the connections in life—to one another, to nature, and to the world around us. If "God is in the details," she says, "the Goddess is in the connections." Through humorous and poignant anecdotes and a top-ten list, Steinem communicates the message that as the graduating students make their way in the world, they should take the time to listen to one another and make decisions, both professionally and personally, based on these connections—in a bottom-up rather than top-down fashion. Only in this way, she says, have people been able to build effective political organizations and movements over the years. Similarly, says Steinem, organizations themselves must acknowledge their common interests with one another, rather than operating as separate, atomized units. Ultimately, according to Steinem, breaking down hierarchies will lead to more equality and greater appreciation of life. Gloria Steinem is a writer, lecturer, editor, feminist activist, and recipient of the Presidential Medal of Freedom. In 1972 she co-founded Ms. *magazine, and she has written several best-selling books. Steinem helped found National Women's Political Caucus, a group that continues to work to advance the numbers of pro-equality women in elected and appointed office at a national and state level.*

In tribute to the real, let me just say that there is no way that I can live up to your expectations. Also that, listening, seeing Mariko [Silver, president of Bennington College], listening, seeing all of you, is such a gift to me. You have no idea how—you braced for my favorite word?—fan-fucking-tastic it feels.

But in real life everybody, including Lacan, is like those nests of Russian dolls in which there is the littlest person in the center and then they go like that [hands expanding outward]. I think we're all like that. So I just want to say to you that I have never escaped the moments like now in which I lose all of my saliva, each tooth acquires a little angora sweater from nervousness that catches my upper lip, and I think, "how did a writer like me ever get to be speaking in public like this?"

And the truth is that I wouldn't be here if it weren't for the fact that I couldn't get published what I wanted to publish, especially at the beginning of the women's movement. And so I began to go out with another brave co-speaker.

And I discovered something magic courtesy of that, which is that when we are in a room with all five senses, we can understand each other and empathize with each other in a way that is beyond what we do on the printed page or on the screen.

Delivered June 6, 2015, at Bennington College commencement, Bennington, Vermont, by Gloria Steinem.

It turns out, according to my friendly, brilliant neurologist, that we do not produce the same hormone that allows us to empathize. The oxytocin that floods us, both men and women, when we hold a child, when we are in each other's presence—it doesn't happen unless we are here.

That is one of the many ways, I think, in which restriction leads to liberation. If I had been able to publish what it was I wished to publish I never would have discovered the magic of being in a room like this together.

So, I hope you will forgive me if I tell you that graduations are my most favorite event of all time. I love commencements, I love the moment, the ceremony. It's all of you, it's the graduates, it's everybody – the family, the friends, the lovers, the old lovers (you know who you are), everybody who helped pay the bill. It is all of us coming together in this extraordinary moment that I am such a sucker for. These events are more permanent than weddings, right? They are more diverse than most religious ceremonies, they are more freely chosen than almost any other kind of group ritual. And I am so grateful to you that you have invited me – an outlander – to come and share this great, great occasion.

Now, of course, I have been worrying about what I could possibly say that might be helpful at a time like this of both ending and beginning. And my only comfort has been in remembering that in my case of college education, what was helpful was always completely unpredictable and often something I only realized was helpful many, many years later.

Here's one example: I took a course in geology feeling that it was the easiest way to fulfill my science requirement. And our professor took us out on a field trip to see the cut-off meander curves of the Connecticut River. I, of course, was paying no attention to his lecture because I had seen on the dirt road leading to the river a gigantic mud turtle. . . who had crawled up the dirt road and was in the muddy embankment leading to an asphalt road. It was clear to me that this turtle was about to continue onto that road and be crushed by a car.

So I picked up the enormous, snapping, angry turtle and with great difficulty I carried it down the path to the river. I had just slipped it into the water and was watching it swim away when the professor came up behind me and said, "You know, that turtle has probably spent a month crawling up that path to lay its eggs in the muddy embankment, and you have just put it back in the river."

I felt terrible but it was too late; the turtle was already swimming away.

And only in later years, when I had become a traveling organizer, only then did I realize the huge lesson I had learned: Always ask the turtle.

There are lots of corollaries of that, right? Anybody who has experience is probably more expert than the experts. Even well-meaning programs, whether they are governments or foundations, often make the mistake of making decisions up here [hand gesture] and thinking they have the solutions that they can just drop down. So even if it is the right solution, it prevents the turtle from flexing the muscles that allow us to discover who we are and to be self-determining. And now whenever I hear someone in a foundation or government position say things like, "Is it replicable?" or "Can you scale it up?," I know we're in deep shit.

Many of the things you have learned here, and hopefully even something I may say, with luck, may or may not be helpful or may or may not be something that you recognize as helpful in many years to come. But only that—only the turtle—has given me the courage to come to you today and hope that it might be useful.

I think that graduation is a time when we think about changes that we want to move us toward kindness—perhaps the most single important human quality ever—and to seek justice and to make the changes we want to make. We tend to feel that is has to be started from above, and actually that is probably opposite of the case. It depends upon what we do every day; it's those small increments that make the difference.

I think if I were to put any difference on the era into which you are graduating than the ones before you, I would say that now is the time to focus on connections. It is often said that "God is in the details," right? I think it's that "the Goddess is in the connections."

This is not to say that all the previous stages were not necessary; they were necessary. Everyone who is emerging needs to have a time in which the problem or the person or whatever it is that is unique or invisible comes forward and is identified and begins to tell their story. Nothing is more important than narrative, than stories. We haven't been sitting around campfires for a hundred thousand years telling our stories for nothing. Our brains are organized on narrative. If you tell me a fact, I will invent a story to tell you why that fact is true.

When we have been invisible unfairly in this world, for any reason—whatever that reason is—it is terribly, terribly important that we are first able to name ourselves, to come forward, to tell our story. Usually what happens is that we tell what we think is an unsayable story, a shameful story, and a story that's certainly ours alone. And then we hear six other people or a hundred or many other groups say, "That happened to you? That happened to me too." And we begin to realize that if it has happened to unique human beings—and we each are unique – then it must be political, it must be about power. And if we come together in any way, we can begin to change it.

So that is an irreplaceable step and coming together in groups is an irreplaceable step. So for good and constructive reasons, of course, this means there has been a civil rights movement based on shared experiences of lethal discrimination from voting to education and now to the unequal law enforcement that has given us a movement called Black Lives Matter. Of course we have to have that named movement.

And. . . the fact is that this contagious emotion—because justice is a very contagious idea—gave birth to a huge movement still going in Indian country where people had not been allowed to even control their own schools, were put into boarding schools with the sole purpose of "killing the Indian, saving the man," as the inventor of those boarding schools said. So that they could not control, could not teach their own language, their own spiritual ceremonies. There was a great amount of abuse and even murders in those schools.

And because of the civil rights movement and the contagion of the civil rights movement, the Indian movement was born. And because within the American Indian movement and the civil rights movement and the anti-Vietnam movement – movements we love – still the women in those movements were not playing an equal role. Really, because no one really knew what an equal role looked like. And yet the idea of equality and justice and shared humanity were so strong that it gave birth to a big and diverse and spread out women's movement. Again, by contagion.

So all of those were important steps. Becoming visible and organized at different times is crucial. But I fear that now we are seeing in silos. You know, there is the women's movement, the gay and lesbian and transgender movement, there is the peace movement. But the truth of the matter is, as we know, that every single one of these movements is inextricably connected to the next. I fear sometimes that our adversaries know this better than we do because, you may have noticed, we pretty much have the same adversaries.

I was saying earlier today that on campus that one of the questions asked me is "Why is it that the same groups are against lesbians and birth control?" It seems irrational on the surface, but it is not. Because, in fact, the opposite view of ours is that reproduction must be controlled. And that means women's bodies. If we didn't have wombs we might be fine, who knows? But reproduction must be controlled. I live for the day when every economic course starts not with production but reproduction.

They understand, from their point of view all sexuality is wrong, immoral, and should be outlawed unless it can end in reproduction. So, of course, they are against family planning and safe and legal abortion and any expression of love between two women or between two men because this all stands for non-reproductive sexuality.

And, in fact, they have been telling us for years and years a lie about human sexuality. It has always been a way we communicate with each other, a way that we bond with each other as well as procreate if we choose to. I think that human beings—although at this point I always worry that we are maligning animals in some way—I think human beings are, more or less, the only ones who experience equal sexual pleasure whether we can conceive or not. And so that tells us that the purpose of human sexuality has always been about communication. But with patriarchy, with racism, with class. . . , with the ownership of children, we have reached a point at which we have been told (and I bet in this room this sounds familiar) that sexuality is only moral and okay when it can end in reproduction and takes place inside patriarchal marriage so that children are properly owned.

So I think we begin to see that sometimes our adversaries know better what our connections are, and we have to begin to understand them. We have to begin to understand that there is no way that racism can be perpetuated without controlling reproduction. So wherever there is racism it is bad for females of that race and every race.

It may affect females differently; the females of the supposedly ruling group may be restricted, sexually and physically, and put on a pedestal. As a black suffragette said to a white suffragette sister, "A pedestal is as much a prison as any other small space." It may affect women of color differently because they become sexual possessions of everyone and the producers of cheap labor.

It isn't that it affects us all the same but it affects us. And there is no such thing as a successful feminist movement that is not anti-racist, and there is no such thing as an anti-racist movement that can be successful without also being feminist. So I think we begin to see what our connections are.

Now some of our connections we are just beginning to be able to prove. We've always known, for instance in tribal societies, that the more polarized the gender roles, the more violence in the society, [and] the more porous and chosen the gender roles, the less violence in the society. But now thanks to a book called *Sex and World Peace*, which I recommend to you—it's a greatly researched book and it is readable—how rare is that?—scholars have looked at pretty much every modern country and determined that the single greatest determinant of whether there is violence inside the country or whether that country will be willing to use military violence against another country is not actually poverty, it is not lack of natural resources, it is not religion, it is not even degree of democracy—it is degree of violence against females.

Not because females are any more valuable than males, no, but because patriarchy demands control of reproduction and that becomes the model we see first. We see the controller and the controlled; we see the dominant and the passive. It normalizes that for everything else—for race, for class, for hierarchy in general.

So I hope that we, as women, in seeing the connection 'cause sometimes we've been so trained to not fight for ourselves, it is tough to fight for ourselves—if we see it as the root cause of hierarchy and domination and violence, I hope we are more likely to understand that we are not only fighting for ourselves but fighting for a greater purpose. And we are also helping to point out that masculinity is a prison too. It may be a better prison, with wall-to-wall carpeting and people to serve you coffee, but. . . .

We once at *Ms.*magazine tried to figure out if you backed out the statistics on why men die, if you backed out those things that could be reasonably attributed to the masculine role (accidents and gun-related violence, tension, disease. . .). It turned out that men lived four or five years longer without the masculine role.

So, what other movement can offer you that? So I hope, I hope, I hope that we can begin to see the connections.

With this in mind, I have followed the advice of David Letterman, who was still doing it when I worked on this, and I have tried to do ten top pieces of advice that I give to myself just in case they might be useful to you as graduates. See if any of these help you, and don't feel you have to take any of them or all of them because some are quite controversial.

Okay:

Number 10: If it looks like a duck and walks like a duck and quacks like a duck but you think it's a pig, it's a pig. Trust your instinct. Your instinct is like a computer and the facts are like long division on a piece of old paper. Trust your instinct.

Number 9: Marx and Engels were smart about a lot of things (mainly because they were inspired by the Iroquois confederacy, incidentally. Inspired by what was on this ground). But not about the end justifying the means. Actually, the means dictates the ends. We won't have laughter and kindness and poetry and pleasure at the end of any revolution unless we have laughter and kindness and poetry and pleasure along the way.

Number 8: Laughter is the most revolutionary emotion because it is free. It is the only emotion that is free. Fear can be compelled, as we know. Even love can be compelled if we are kept isolated and dependent for long enough. In order to survive, we enmesh with our captor and believe we are in love. The Stockholm Syndrome—it happens to men too, right? But laughter is an "aha" of understanding that comes when known things coincide and make something brand new. It's an orgasm of the mind, I think. Einstein said—Einstein could not possibly have said everything he is claimed to have said—but Einstein said he had to be careful while shaving because when he suddenly had an "aha"—he had thought of something new—he would laugh and cut himself.

Do not go anyplace they won't let you laugh. Big, important rule. Including religious places. It's the difference actually between spirituality and religion. Religion doesn't let you laugh; spirituality does.

Number 7: There's more variation among groups than between groups. As we can see, we know that masculine and feminine are creations, very powerful cultural creations, but still creations. Just as the ideas of race and class are creations. So when making any generalized statement about women and men substitute, say, Gentiles and Jews, blacks and whites, rich and poor. If it is still acceptable okay. But if not, it's not acceptable.

Number 6: For 95% of human history, spirituality saw God in all living things. Then God was gradually withdrawn over millennia from women and nature. Have any of you taken the trip down or up the Nile? Because you can see it in the carvings in the Nile. You can see that in the oldest African part God is present in papyrus and men and women and flowers and everything; then, you get back in the boat and it's a thousand years later and the goddess has a son but no daughter and there's less nature; then you get back in the boat and it's another thousand years and finally the son goes up to be a consort; and then a male pharaoh sits on a throne, a male pharaoh sits on a throne that is the goddess; and then it gets to mosques, which, like Christian churches and others, are built on top of the ancient ruins, and no representations of women or nature is allowed. As James Henry Breasted, a very smart Egyptologist, said, "Monotheism is but imperialism in religion." Think about it.

Number 5: This follows 6, you'll see. Religion is often politics in the sky, and we have to say so. It is the only politics that has managed to put itself off limits and continue to be powerful. When God looks like the ruling class, it's a problem. When all the priesthood is guys, it's an even deeper problem. When we're told to obey in order to get a reward after death—I mean, even corporations only do it for after retirement. And, incidentally, heaven didn't exist in the very specific form, you know in that way as it does now in various monotheisms in great detail. In egalitarian cultures you went to join your ancestors but there wasn't this elaborate system of punishment and reward.

I am feeling really tempted to do something I probably shouldn't do.

Okay, well one day I was reading a historian of religious architecture and he said, like everybody knows it, that the structures of patriarchal religions are built to resemble the body of a woman because the central ceremony they house is one of men giving birth. Yes, they've taken over reproduction and controlled reproduction but it is still a big mythic thing, giving birth. So, as he explains (and you can find it easily thanks to Google) there is always an outer entrance and an inner entrance—labia majora and labia minora—and a vestibule in between. The same word physically. A vaginal aisle up the center; two curved ovarian structures on either sides; and the womb—I knew I shouldn't do this—and the altar in the center which is the womb where the miracle takes place. Where men say, "Yes you were born of woman—inferior creature, sex, dirty stuff, nasty break—but if you obey the rules of the patriarchy we will sprinkle imitation birth food over your head, give you a new name and you will be reborn through the patriarchy." In skirts, they have the nerve!

But, I mean, I'm actually serious. When you were a kid, didn't you wonder why Jesus was blond and blue eyed? A Jewish guy in the middle of the Middle East? It's about sex and race and class and, you know, if God looks like the ruling class, the ruling class is God. And we have to do something about this.

I had to go for a very minor test in a hospital, and they gave me one of those forms to fill out where it asks your religion because in case you drop dead they want to know who to call. And at first I put "none" but then I am always a little negative. So I wrote "pagan." And the nurse said to me, "What does that mean?" I said, "It just means you believe there is an essence of godliness in all living things. All living things."

I converted her on the spot.

Okay, now here's a more practical one –

Number 4: The Golden Rule was written by smart folks for those who were kind of superior or controlling their own lives, and it is very important. Treat others as you would want to be treated. Very important. But women and men who have been treated as inferior need to reverse it: You need to treat yourself as well as you treat other people.

Number 3: Labeling, as I was saying, makes the invisible visible. So, naming ourselves is all very important—but it's limiting. We've had a Declaration of Independence; I think now we need a Declaration of Interdependence, about the connections. So, categories are the enemy of connecting. Here's what I think we can use as an image instead. We are linked, we are not ranked. We are linked with each other, we are linked with nature. And the paradigm becomes a circle not a pyramid. And the paradigm of the old culture, the original cultures was, as we know, a circle, not a pyramid. Whether they were in Africa or here, they shared the idea of the circle.

[*Number 2:*] Because we only have all of our five senses in the present, we can't live in the past or the future. For this one I am really talking to myself because I live in the future. And you can't, as it happens. You can only be alive in the present. Right now is all there is.

1: This is the last one. . . . This is to say that not only did it exist before, not only, might you say thateverything we want was once here in some form. It's not human nature to be hierarchical and divided.

So this is my last and hopeful one: If even one generation were born without ranking and without violence and without shaming, and raised without shaming or violence or ranking, we have no idea what might be possible on this fragile spaceship Earth that we love so much. And you, the graduates of 2015 are part of that future, so part of that future. And I and so many of us here—well, I am going to live to 100, so I'll be with you for a while—but eventually, I and the parents and everybody here, we won't be with you. And yet we will. We'll always be with you.

Thank you so much for letting me be part of this celebration.

2
Civil Rights and Social Justice

United Nations Secretary General Ban Ki-moon addresses attendees during the 70th session of the United Nations General Assembly at the U.N. Headquarters in New York, September 28, 2015.

Amazing Grace

By Barack Obama

President Barack Obama delivers a eulogy for Reverend Clementa Pinckney, one of the nine people killed in the June 17, 2015 racially-charged shooting at Emanuel African Methodist Episcopal Church in Charleston, South Carolina. In this speech, held on June 26 at the College of Charleston, President Obama remembers a life of faith and service but also discusses the historical significance of the church in the African-American community and in the long struggle for equality and human rights. The words here reflect on how the violent act that killed Reverend Pinckney is but one in a history of violence and oppression. The president further meditates on the nature of grace and forgiveness amidst injustice, exploring how the state of grace allows people to recognize and begin to correct past and ongoing sins in order to change as individuals and as a nation. President Obama is the forty-fourth president of the United States, having been elected to office in 2008 and reelected in 2012. Prior to becoming president, Obama was a United States senator representing the state of Illinois from 2005 to 2008.

Giving all praise and honor to God. (Applause.)

The Bible calls us to hope. To persevere, and have faith in things not seen.

"They were still living by faith when they died," Scripture tells us. "They did not receive the things promised; they only saw them and welcomed them from a distance, admitting that they were foreigners and strangers on Earth."

We are here today to remember a man of God who lived by faith. A man who believed in things not seen. A man who believed there were better days ahead, off in the distance. A man of service who persevered, knowing full well he would not receive all those things he was promised, because he believed his efforts would deliver a better life for those who followed.

To Jennifer, his beloved wife; to Eliana and Malana, his beautiful, wonderful daughters; to the Mother Emanuel family and the people of Charleston, the people of South Carolina.

I cannot claim to have the good fortune to know Reverend Pinckney well. But I did have the pleasure of knowing him and meeting him here in South Carolina, back when we were both a little bit younger. (Laughter.) Back when I didn't have visible grey hair. (Laughter.) The first thing I noticed was his graciousness, his smile, his reassuring baritone, his deceptive sense of humor—all qualities that helped him wear so effortlessly a heavy burden of expectation.

Delivered June 26, 2015, at the College of Charleston, Charleston, South Carolina, by Barack Obama.

Friends of his remarked this week that when Clementa Pinckney entered a room, it was like the future arrived; that even from a young age, folks knew he was special. Anointed. He was the progeny of a long line of the faithful—a family of preachers who spread God's word, a family of protesters who sowed change to expand voting rights and desegregate the South. Clem heard their instruction, and he did not forsake their teaching.

He was in the pulpit by 13, pastor by 18, public servant by 23. He did not exhibit any of the cockiness of youth, nor youth's insecurities; instead, he set an example worthy of his position, wise beyond his years, in his speech, in his conduct, in his love, faith, and purity.

As a senator, he represented a sprawling swath of the Lowcountry, a place that has long been one of the most neglected in America. A place still wracked by poverty and inadequate schools; a place where children can still go hungry and the sick can go without treatment. A place that needed somebody like Clem. (Applause.)

His position in the minority party meant the odds of winning more resources for his constituents were often long. His calls for greater equity were too often unheeded, the votes he cast were sometimes lonely. But he never gave up. He stayed true to his convictions. He would not grow discouraged. After a full day at the capitol, he'd climb into his car and head to the church to draw sustenance from his family, from his ministry, from the community that loved and needed him. There he would fortify his faith, and imagine what might be.

Reverend Pinckney embodied a politics that was neither mean nor small. He conducted himself quietly, and kindly, and diligently. He encouraged progress not by pushing his ideas alone, but by seeking out your ideas, partnering with you to make things happen. He was full of empathy and fellow feeling, able to walk in somebody else's shoes and see through their eyes. No wonder one of his senate colleagues remembered Senator Pinckney as "the most gentle of the 46 of us—the best of the 46 of us."

Clem was often asked why he chose to be a pastor and a public servant. But the person who asked probably didn't know the history of the AME church. (Applause.) As our brothers and sisters in the AME church know, we don't make those distinctions. "Our calling," Clem once said, "is not just within the walls of the congregation, but. . . the life and community in which our congregation resides." (Applause.)

He embodied the idea that our Christian faith demands deeds and not just words; that the "sweet hour of prayer" actually lasts the whole week long—(applause)—that to put our faith in action is more than individual salvation, it's about our collective salvation; that to feed the hungry and clothe the naked and house the homeless is not just a call for isolated charity but the imperative of a just society.

What a good man. Sometimes I think that's the best thing to hope for when you're eulogized—after all the words and recitations and resumes are read, to just say someone was a good man. (Applause.)

You don't have to be of high station to be a good man. Preacher by 13. Pastor by 18. Public servant by 23. What a life Clementa Pinckney lived. What an example he set. What a model for his faith. And then to lose him at 41—slain in his sanctuary with eight wonderful members of his flock, each at different stages in life but bound together by a common commitment to God.

Cynthia Hurd. Susie Jackson. Ethel Lance. DePayne Middleton-Doctor. Tywanza Sanders. Daniel L. Simmons. Sharonda Coleman-Singleton. Myra Thompson. Good people. Decent people. God-fearing people. (Applause.) People so full of life and so full of kindness. People who ran the race, who persevered. People of great faith.

To the families of the fallen, the nation shares in your grief. Our pain cuts that much deeper because it happened in a church. The church is and always has been the center of African-American life—(applause)—a place to call our own in a too often hostile world, a sanctuary from so many hardships.

Over the course of centuries, black churches served as "hush harbors" where slaves could worship in safety; praise houses where their free descendants could gather and shout hallelujah—(applause)—rest stops for the weary along the Underground Railroad; bunkers for the foot soldiers of the Civil Rights Movement. They have been, and continue to be, community centers where we organize for jobs and justice; places of scholarship and network; places where children are loved and fed and kept out of harm's way, and told that they are beautiful and smart—(applause)—and taught that they matter. (Applause.) That's what happens in church.

That's what the black church means. Our beating heart. The place where our dignity as a people is inviolate. When there's no better example of this tradition than Mother Emanuel—(applause)—a church built by blacks seeking liberty, burned to the ground because its founder sought to end slavery, only to rise up again, a Phoenix from these ashes. (Applause.)

When there were laws banning all-black church gatherings, services happened here anyway, in defiance of unjust laws. When there was a righteous movement to dismantle Jim Crow, Dr. Martin Luther King, Jr. preached from its pulpit, and marches began from its steps. A sacred place, this church. Not just for blacks, not just for Christians, but for every American who cares about the steady expansion—(applause)—of human rights and human dignity in this country; a foundation stone for liberty and justice for all. That's what the church meant. (Applause.)

We do not know whether the killer of Reverend Pinckney and eight others knew all of this history. But he surely sensed the meaning of his violent act. It was an act that drew on a long history of bombs and arson and shots fired at churches, not random, but as a means of control, a way to terrorize and oppress. (Applause.) An act that he imagined would incite fear and recrimination; violence and suspicion. An act that he presumed would deepen divisions that trace back to our nation's original sin.

Oh, but God works in mysterious ways. (Applause.) God has different ideas. (Applause.)

He didn't know he was being used by God. (Applause.) Blinded by hatred, the alleged killer could not see the grace surrounding Reverend Pinckney and that Bible study group—the light of love that shone as they opened the church doors and invited a stranger to join in their prayer circle. The alleged killer could have never anticipated the way the families of the fallen would respond when they saw him in court—in the midst of unspeakable grief, with words of forgiveness. He couldn't imagine that. (Applause.)

The alleged killer could not imagine how the city of Charleston, under the good and wise leadership of Mayor Riley—(applause)—how the state of South Carolina, how the United States of America would respond—not merely with revulsion at his evil act, but with big-hearted generosity and, more importantly, with a thoughtful introspection and self-examination that we so rarely see in public life.

Blinded by hatred, he failed to comprehend what Reverend Pinckney so well understood—the power of God's grace. (Applause.)

This whole week, I've been reflecting on this idea of grace. (Applause.) The grace of the families who lost loved ones. The grace that Reverend Pinckney would preach about in his sermons. The grace described in one of my favorite hymnals—the one we all know: Amazing grace, how sweet the sound that saved a wretch like me. (Applause.) I once was lost, but now I'm found; was blind but now I see. (Applause.)

According to the Christian tradition, grace is not earned. Grace is not merited. It's not something we deserve. Rather, grace is the free and benevolent favor of God—(applause)—as manifested in the salvation of sinners and the bestowal of blessings. Grace.

As a nation, out of this terrible tragedy, God has visited grace upon us, for he has allowed us to see where we've been blind. (Applause.) He has given us the chance, where we've been lost, to find our best selves. (Applause.) We may not have earned it, this grace, with our rancor and complacency, and short-sightedness and fear of each other—but we got it all the same. He gave it to us anyway. He's once more given us grace. But it is up to us now to make the most of it, to receive it with gratitude, and to prove ourselves worthy of this gift.

For too long, we were blind to the pain that the Confederate flag stirred in too many of our citizens. (Applause.) It's true, a flag did not cause these murders. But as people from all walks of life, Republicans and Democrats, now acknowledge—including Governor Haley, whose recent eloquence on the subject is worthy of praise—(applause)—as we all have to acknowledge, the flag has always represented more than just ancestral pride. (Applause.) For many, black and white, that flag was a reminder of systemic oppression and racial subjugation. We see that now.

Removing the flag from this state's capitol would not be an act of political correctness; it would not be an insult to the valor of Confederate soldiers. It would simply be an acknowledgment that the cause for which they fought—the cause of slavery—was wrong—(applause)—the imposition of Jim Crow after the Civil War, the resistance to civil rights for all people was wrong. (Applause.) It would be one step in an honest accounting of America's history; a modest but meaningful balm for so many unhealed wounds. It would be an expression of the amazing changes that have transformed this state and this country for the better, because of the work of so many people of goodwill, people of all races striving to form a more perfect union. By taking down that flag, we express God's grace. (Applause.)

But I don't think God wants us to stop there. (Applause.) For too long, we've been blind to the way past injustices continue to shape the present. Perhaps we see that now. Perhaps this tragedy causes us to ask some tough questions about how we can permit so many of our children to languish in poverty, or attend dilapidated schools, or grow up without prospects for a job or for a career. (Applause.)

Perhaps it causes us to examine what we're doing to cause some of our children to hate. (Applause.) Perhaps it softens hearts towards those lost young men, tens and tens of thousands caught up in the criminal justice system—(applause)—and leads us to make sure that that system is not infected with bias; that we embrace changes in how we train and equip our police so that the bonds of trust between law enforcement and the communities they serve make us all safer and more secure. (Applause.)

Maybe we now realize the way racial bias can infect us even when we don't realize it, so that we're guarding against not just racial slurs, but we're also guarding against the subtle impulse to call Johnny back for a job interview but not Jamal. (Applause.) So that we search our hearts when we consider laws to make it harder for some of our fellow citizens to vote. (Applause.) By recognizing our common humanity by treating every child as important, regardless of the color of their skin or the station into which they were born, and to do what's necessary to make opportunity real for every American—by doing that, we express God's grace. (Applause.)

For too long —

AUDIENCE: For too long!

THE PRESIDENT: For too long, we've been blind to the unique mayhem that gun violence inflicts upon this nation. (Applause.) Sporadically, our eyes are open: When eight of our brothers and sisters are cut down in a church basement, 12 in a movie theater, 26 in an elementary school. But I hope we also see the 30 precious lives cut short by gun violence in this country every single day; the countless more whose lives are forever changed—the survivors crippled, the children traumatized and fearful every day as they walk to school, the husband who will never feel his wife's warm touch, the entire communities whose grief overflows every time they have to watch what happened to them happen to some other place.

The vast majority of Americans—the majority of gun owners—want to do something about this. We see that now. (Applause.) And I'm convinced that by acknowledging the pain and loss of others, even as we respect the traditions and ways of life that make up this beloved country—by making the moral choice to change, we express God's grace. (Applause.)

We don't earn grace. We're all sinners. We don't deserve it. (Applause.) But God gives it to us anyway. (Applause.) And we choose how to receive it. It's our decision how to honor it.

None of us can or should expect a transformation in race relations overnight. Every time something like this happens, somebody says we have to have a conversation about race. We talk a lot about race. There's no shortcut. And we don't need more talk. (Applause.) None of us should believe that a handful of gun safety measures will prevent every tragedy. It will not. People of goodwill will continue to debate the merits of various policies, as our democracy requires—this is a big, raucous place, America is. And there are good people on both sides of these debates. Whatever solutions we find will necessarily be incomplete.

But it would be a betrayal of everything Reverend Pinckney stood for, I believe, if we allowed ourselves to slip into a comfortable silence again. (Applause.) Once the eulogies have been delivered, once the TV cameras move on, to go back to business as usual—that's what we so often do to avoid uncomfortable truths about the prejudice that still infects our society. (Applause.) To settle for symbolic gestures without following up with the hard work of more lasting change—that's how we lose our way again.

It would be a refutation of the forgiveness expressed by those families if we merely slipped into old habits, whereby those who disagree with us are not merely wrong but bad; where we shout instead of listen; where we barricade ourselves behind preconceived notions or well-practiced cynicism.

Reverend Pinckney once said, "Across the South, we have a deep appreciation of history—we haven't always had a deep appreciation of each other's history." (Applause.) What is true in the South is true for America. Clem understood that justice grows out of recognition of ourselves in each other. That my liberty depends on you being free, too. (Applause.) That history can't be a sword to justify injustice, or a shield against progress, but must be a manual for how to avoid repeating the mistakes of the past—how to break the cycle. A roadway toward a better world. He knew that the path of grace involves an open mind—but, more importantly, an open heart.

That's what I've felt this week—an open heart. That, more than any particular policy or analysis, is what's called upon right now, I think—what a friend of mine, the writer Marilyn Robinson, calls "that reservoir of goodness, beyond, and of another kind, that we are able to do each other in the ordinary cause of things."

That reservoir of goodness. If we can find that grace, anything is possible. (Applause.) If we can tap that grace, everything can change. (Applause.)

Amazing grace. Amazing grace.

(Begins to sing)—Amazing grace—(applause)—how sweet the sound, that saved a wretch like me; I once was lost, but now I'm found; was blind but now I see. (Applause.)

Clementa Pinckney found that grace.

Cynthia Hurd found that grace.

Susie Jackson found that grace.

Ethel Lance found that grace.

DePayne Middleton-Doctor found that grace.

Tywanza Sanders found that grace.

Daniel L. Simmons, Sr. found that grace.

Sharonda Coleman-Singleton found that grace.

Myra Thompson found that grace.

Through the example of their lives, they've now passed it on to us. May we find ourselves worthy of that precious and extraordinary gift, as long as our lives endure. May grace now lead them home. May God continue to shed His grace on the United States of America. (Applause.)

On Civil Rights

By Elizabeth Warren

At the Edward M. Kennedy Institute for the United States Senate, Senator Elizabeth Warren delivers a speech on the long history of racial injustice in this country, from legal segregation to state-sanctioned violence and lynchings to discriminatory economic practices that inhibited the growth of wealth among African American communities, and despite some real progress over the years, continue to do so to this day. She proceeds to discuss how the growing economic disparities between the rich and poor in the United States, which impact lower income populations of all races and backgrounds, disproportionately affect blacks and Latinos. Remembering the work of the original civil rights movement of the 1960s and 1970s, Warren notes that Americans still have work to do. Recognized as one of the nation's top experts on bankruptcy and the financial pressures facing middle class families, Elizabeth Warren was elected to the United States Senate by the people of Massachusetts in 2012.

Thank you. I'm grateful to be here at the Edward M. Kennedy Institute for the United States Senate. This place is a fitting tribute to our champion, Ted Kennedy. A man of courage, compassion, and commitment, who taught us what public service is all about. Not a day goes by that we don't miss his passion, his enthusiasm, and—most of all—his dedication to all of our working families.

As the Senior Senator from Massachusetts, I have the great honor of sitting at Senator Kennedy's desk—right over there. The original, back in Washington, is a little more dented and scratched, but it has something very special in the drawer. Ted Kennedy carved his name in it. When I sit at my desk, sometimes when I'm waiting to speak or to vote, I open the drawer and run my thumb across his name. It reminds me of the high expectations of the people of Massachusetts, and I try, every day, to live up to the legacy he left behind.

Senator Kennedy took office just over fifty years ago, in the midst of one of the great moral and political debates in American history—the debate over the Civil Rights Act. In his first speech on the floor of the Senate, just four months after his brother's assassination, he stood up to support equal rights for all Americans. He ended that speech with a powerful personal message about what the civil rights struggle meant to the late President Kennedy:

Delivered September 27, 2015, at the Edward M. Kennedy Institute for the United States Senate, Boston, Massachusetts, by Elizabeth Warren.

> His heart and soul are in this bill. If his life and death had a meaning, it was that we should not hate but love one another; we should use our powers not to create conditions of oppression that lead to violence, but conditions of freedom that lead to peace.

"We should use our powers not to create conditions of oppression that lead to violence, but conditions of freedom that lead to peace." That's what I'd like to talk about today.

A half-century ago, when Senator Kennedy spoke of the Civil Rights Act, entrenched, racist power did everything it could to sustain oppression of African-Americans, and violence was its first tool. Lynchings, terrorism, intimidation. The 16th Street Baptist Church. Medgar Evers. Emmett Till. When Alabama Governor George Wallace stood before the nation and declared during his 1963 inaugural address that he would defend "segregation now, segregation tomorrow, segregation forever," he made clear that the state would stand with those who used violence.

But violence was not the only tool. African Americans were effectively stripped of citizenship when they were denied the right to vote. The tools varied—literacy tests, poll taxes, moral character tests, grandfather clauses—but the results were the same. They were denied basic rights of citizenship and the chance to participate in self-government.

The third tool of oppression was to deliberately deny millions of African Americans economic opportunities solely because of the color of their skin.

I have often spoken about how America built a great middle class. Coming out of the Great Depression, from the 1930s to the late 1970s, as GDP went up, wages went up for most Americans. But there's a dark underbelly to that story. While median family income in America was growing—for both white and African-American families—African-American incomes were only a fraction of white incomes. In the mid-1950s, the median income for African-American families was just a little more than half the income of white families.

And the problem went beyond just income. Look at housing: For most middle class families in America, buying a home is the number one way to build wealth. It's a retirement plan—pay off the house and live on Social Security. An investment option—mortgage the house to start a business. It's a way to help the kids get through college, a safety net if someone gets really sick, and, if all goes well and Grandma and Grandpa can hang on to the house until they die, it's a way to give the next generation a boost—extra money to move the family up the ladder.

For much of the twentieth century, that's how it worked for generation after generation of white Americans—but not black Americans. Entire legal structures were created to prevent African Americans from building economic security through home ownership. Legally-enforced segregation. Restrictive deeds. Redlining. Land contracts. Coming out of the Great Depression, America built a middle class, but systematic discrimination kept most African-American families from being part of it.

State-sanctioned discrimination wasn't limited to homeownership. The government enforced discrimination in public accommodations, discrimination in schools, discrimination in credit—it was a long and spiteful list.

Economic justice is not—and has never been—sufficient to ensure racial justice. Owning a home won't stop someone from burning a cross on the front lawn. Admission to a school won't prevent a beating on the sidewalk outside. But when Dr. King led hundreds of thousands of people to march on Washington, he talked about an end to violence, access to voting AND economic opportunity. As Dr. King once wrote, "the inseparable twin of racial injustice was economic injustice.

The tools of oppression were woven together, and the civil rights struggle was fought against that oppression wherever it was found—against violence, against the denial of voting rights, and against economic injustice."

The battles were bitter and sometimes deadly. Firehoses turned on peaceful protestors. Police officers setting their dogs to attack black students. Bloody Sunday at the Edmund Pettus Bridge.

But the civil rights movement pushed this country in a new direction.

- The federal government cracked down on state-sponsored violence. Presidents Eisenhower, Kennedy and Johnson all called out the National Guard, and, in doing so, declared that everyone had a right to equal protection under the law, guaranteed by the Constitution. Congress protected the rights of all citizens to vote with the Voting Rights Act.
- And economic opportunities opened up when Congress passed civil rights laws that protected equal access to employment, public accommodations, and housing.

In the same way that the tools of oppression were woven together, a package of civil rights laws came together to protect black people from violence, to ensure access to the ballot box, and to build economic opportunity. Or to say it another way, these laws made three powerful declarations: Black lives matter. Black citizens matter. Black families matter.

Fifty years later, we have made real progress toward creating the conditions of freedom—but we have not made ENOUGH progress.

Fifty years later, violence against African Americans has not disappeared. Consider law enforcement. The vast majority of police officers sign up so they can protect their communities. They are part of an honorable profession that takes risks every day to keep us safe. We know that. But we also know—and say—the names of those whose lives have been treated with callous indifference. Sandra Bland. Freddie Gray. Michael Brown. We've seen sickening videos of unarmed, black Americans cut down by bullets, choked to death while gasping for air—their lives ended by those who are sworn to protect them. Peaceful, unarmed protestors have been beaten. Journalists have been jailed. And, in some cities, white vigilantes with weapons freely walk the streets. And it's not just about law enforcement either. Just look to the terrorism this summer at Emanuel AME Church. We must be honest: Fifty years after John Kennedy and Martin Luther King, Jr. spoke out, violence against African Americans has not disappeared.

And what about voting rights? Two years ago, five conservative justices on the Supreme Court gutted the Voting Rights Act, opening the floodgates ever wider for measures designed to suppress minority voting. Today, the specific tools of oppression have changed—voter ID laws, racial gerrymandering, and mass disfranchisement through a criminal justice system that disproportionately incarcerates black citizens. The tools have changed, but black voters are still deliberately cut out of the political process.

Violence. Voting. And what about economic injustice? Research shows that the legal changes in the civil rights era created new employment and housing opportunities. In the 1960s and the 1970s, African-American men and women began to close the wage gap with white workers, giving millions of black families hope that they might build real wealth.

But then, Republicans' trickle-down economic theory arrived. Just as this country was taking the first steps toward economic justice, the Republicans pushed a theory that meant helping the richest people and the most powerful corporations get richer and more powerful. I'll just do one statistic on this: From 1980 to 2012, GDP continued to rise, but how much of the income growth went to the 90% of America—everyone outside the top 10%—black, white, Latino? None. Zero. Nothing. One hundred percent of all the new income produced in this country over the past 30 years has gone to the top 10%.

Today, 90% of Americans see no real wage growth. For African-Americans, who were so far behind earlier in the twentieth century, this means that since the 1980s they have been hit particularly hard. In January of this year, African-American unemployment was 10.3%—more than twice the rate of white unemployment. And, after beginning to make progress during the civil rights era to close the wealth gap between black and white families, in the 1980s the wealth gap exploded, so that from 1984 to 2009, the wealth gap between black and white families tripled.

The 2008 housing collapse destroyed trillions in family wealth across the country, but the crash hit African-Americans like a punch in the gut. Because middle-class black families' wealth was disproportionately tied up in homeownership and not other forms of savings, these families were hit harder by the housing collapse. But they also got hit harder because of discriminatory lending practices—yes, discriminatory lending practices in the twenty-first century. Recently several big banks and other mortgage lenders paid hundreds of millions in fines, admitting that they illegally steered black and Latino borrowers into more expensive mortgages than white borrowers who had similar credit. Tom Perez, who at the time was the Assistant Attorney General for Civil Rights, called it a "racial surtax." And it's still happening—earlier this month, the National Fair Housing Alliance filed a discrimination complaint against real estate agents in Mississippi after an investigation showed those agents consistently steering white buyers away from interracial neighborhoods and black buyers away from affluent ones. Another investigation showed similar results across our nation's cities. Housing discrimination alive and well in 2015.

Violence, voting, economic justice.

We have made important strides forward. But we are not done yet. And now, it is our time.

I speak today with the full knowledge that I have not personally experienced and can never truly understand the fear, the oppression, and the pain that confronts African Americans every day. But none of us can ignore what is happening in this country. Not when our black friends, family, neighbors literally fear dying in the streets.

Listen to the brave, powerful voices of today's new generation of civil rights leaders. Incredible voices. Listen to them say: "If I die in police custody, know that I did not commit suicide." Watch them march through the streets, "hands up don't shoot"—not to incite a riot, but to fight for their lives. To fight for their lives.

This is the reality all of us must confront, as uncomfortable and ugly as that reality may be. It comes to us to once again affirm that black lives matter, that black citizens matter, that black families matter.

Once again, the task begins with safeguarding our communities from violence. We have made progress, but it is a tragedy when any American cannot trust those who have sworn to protect and serve. This pervasive and persistent distrust isn't based on myths. It is grounded in the reality of unjustified violence.

Policing must become a truly community endeavor—not in just a few cities, but everywhere. Police forces should look like, and come from, the neighborhoods they serve. They should reach out to support and defend the community—working with people in neighborhoods before problems arise. All police forces—not just some—must be trained to de-escalate and to avoid the likelihood of violence. Body cameras can help us know what happens when someone is hurt.

We honor the bravery and sacrifice that our law enforcement officers show every day on the job—and the noble intentions of the vast majority of those who take up the difficult job of keeping us safe. But police are not occupying armies. This is America, not a war zone-and policing practices in all cities—not just some—need to reflect that.

Next, voting.

It's time to call out the recent flurry of new state law restrictions for what they are: an all-out campaign by Republicans to take away the right to vote from poor and black and Latino American citizens who probably won't vote for them. The push to restrict voting is nothing more than a naked grab to win elections that they can't win if every citizen votes.

Two years ago the Supreme Court eviscerated critical parts of the Voting Rights Act. Congress could easily fix this, and Democrats in the Senate have called for restoration of voting rights. Now it is time for Republicans to step up to support a restoration of the Voting Rights Act—or to stand before the American people and explain why they have abandoned America's most cherished liberty, the right to vote.

And while we're at it, we need to update the rules around voting. Voting should be simple. Voter registration should be automatic. Get a driver's license, get registered automatically. Nonviolent, law-abiding citizens should not lose the right to vote because of a prior conviction. Election Day should be a holiday, so no one has to choose between a paycheck and a vote. Early voting and vote by mail would give fast food and retail workers who don't get holidays day off a chance to proudly cast their votes. The hidden discrimination that comes with purging voter rolls and short-staffing polling places must stop. The right to vote remains essential to protect all other rights, and no candidate for president or for any other elected office—Republican or Democrat—should be elected if they will not pledge to support full, meaningful voting rights.

Finally, economic justice. Our task will not be complete until we ensure that every family—regardless of race—has a fighting chance to build an economic future for themselves and their families. We need less talk and more action about reducing unemployment, ending wage stagnation and closing the income gap between white and nonwhite workers.

And one more issue, dear to my heart: It's time to come down hard on predatory practices that allow financial institutions to systematically strip wealth out of communities of color. One of the ugly consequences of bank deregulation was that there was no cop on the beat when too many financial institutions figured out that they could make great money by tricking, trapping, and defrauding targeted families. Now we have a Consumer Financial Protection Bureau, and we need to make sure it stays strong and independent so that it can do its job and make credit markets work for black families, Latino families, white families—all families.

Yes, there's work to do.

Back in March, I met an elderly man at the First Baptist Church in Montgomery, Alabama. We were having coffee and donuts in the church basement before the service started. He told me that more than 50 years earlier—in May of 1961—he had spent 11 hours in that same basement, along with hundreds of people, while a mob outside threatened to burn down the church because it was a sanctuary for civil rights workers. Dr. King called Attorney General Bobby Kennedy, desperately asking for help. The Attorney General promised to send the Army, but the closest military base was several hours away. So the members of the church and the civil rights workers waited in the sweltering basement, crowded together, listening to the mob outside and hoping the U.S. Army would arrive in time.

After the church service, I asked Congressman John Lewis about that night. He had been right there in that church back in 1961 while the mob gathered outside. He had been in the room during the calls to the Attorney General. I asked if he had been afraid that the Army wouldn't make it in time. He said that he was "never, ever afraid. You come to that point where you lose all sense of fear." And then he said something I'll never forget. He said that his parents didn't want him to get involved in civil rights. They didn't want him to "cause trouble." But he had done it anyway. He told me: "Sometimes it is important to cause necessary trouble."

The first civil rights battles were hard fought. But they established that Black Lives Matter. That Black Citizens Matter. That Black Families Matter. Half a century later, we have made real progress, but we have not made ENOUGH progress. As Senator Kennedy said in his first floor speech, "This is not a political issue. It is a moral issue, to be resolved through political means." So it comes to us to continue the fight, to make, as John Lewis said, the "necessary trouble" until we can truly say that in America, every citizen enjoys the conditions of freedom.

Thank you.

10 Years after Katrina

By Barack Obama

In a speech before a New Orleans crowd, President Barack Obama addresses the renewal of the city in the aftermath of Hurricane Katrina, which devastated the city and surrounding areas ten years ago. Linking the recovery of the city and other areas hit by the storm to the regrowth of the country's economy following the collapse of the market in 2008, Obama attributes both rebounds to the investment of federal recovery programs. Providing impressive statistics on the growth of schools, health care, business, and jobs in both the public and private sector in New Orleans, Obama holds up the city as an example of what strong, empowered government can accomplish. President Obama is the forty-fourth president of the United States, having been elected to office in 2008 and reelected in 2012.

Everybody, have a seat. Hello, everybody! Where y'at? It is good to be back in the Big Easy. And this is the weather in August all the time, right? (Laughter.) As soon as I land in New Orleans, the first thing I do is get hungry. When I was here with the family a few years ago, I had a shrimp po-boy at Parkway Bakery and Tavern. I still remember it—that's how good it was. And one day, after I leave office, maybe I'll finally hear Rebirth at the Maple Leaf on Tuesday night. (Applause.) I'll get a chance to "see the Mardi Gras," and somebody will tell me what's Carnival for. (Laughter.) But right now, I just go to meetings.

I want to thank Michelle for the introduction and, more importantly, for the great work she's doing, what she symbolizes, and what she represents in terms of the city bouncing back. I want to acknowledge a great friend and somebody who has been working tirelessly on behalf of this city, and he's following a family legacy of service—your mayor, Mitch Landrieu. (Applause.) Proud of him. And his beautiful wife, Cheryl. Senator Bill Cassidy is here. Where did Senator Cassidy go? There he is. (Applause.) Congressman Cedric Richmond. (Applause.) Where's the Congressman? There he is over there. We've got a lifelong champion of Louisiana in your former senator, Mary Landrieu in the house. Mary! (Applause.) I want to acknowledge a great supporter to the efforts to recover and rebuild, Congressman Hakeem Jeffries from New York, who has traveled down here with us. (Applause.)

To all the elected officials from Louisiana and Mississippi who are here today, thank you so much for your reception.

I'm here to talk about a specific recovery. But before I begin to talk just about New Orleans, I want to talk about America's recovery, take a little moment of

Delivered August 27, 2015, at the Andrew Sanchez Community Center, New Orleans, Louisiana, by Barack Obama.

presidential privilege to talk about what's been happening in our economy. This morning, we learned that our economy grew at a stronger and more robust clip back in the spring than anybody knew at the time. The data always lags. We already knew that over the past five and a half years, our businesses have created 13 million new jobs. (Applause.) These new numbers that came out, showing that the economy was growing at a 3.7 percent clip, means that the United States of America remains an anchor of global strength and stability in the world—that we have recovered faster, more steadily, stronger than just about any economy after the worst financial crisis since the Great Depression.

And it's important for us to remember that strength. It's been a volatile few weeks around the world. And there's been a lot of reports in the news, and the stock market swinging, and worries about China and about Europe. But the United States of America, for all the challenges that we still have, continue to have the best cards. We just got to play them right.

Our economy has been moving, and continues to grow. And unemployment continues to come down. And our work is not yet done, but we have to have that sense of steadiness and vision and purpose in order to sustain this recovery so that it reaches everybody and not just some. It's why we need to do everything we can in government to make sure our economy keeps growing. That requires Congress to protect our momentum—not kill it. Congress is about to come back from a six-week recess. The deadline to fund the government is, as always, the end of September. And so I want everybody just to understand that Congress has about a month to pass a budget that helps our economy grow. Otherwise, we risk shutting down the government and services that we all count on for the second time in two years. That would not be responsible. It does not have to happen.

Congress needs to fund America in a way that invests in our growth and our security, and not cuts us off at the knees by locking in mindless austerity or short-sighted sequester cuts to our economy or our military. I've said I will veto a budget like that. I think most Americans agree we've got to invest in, rather than cut, things like military readiness, infrastructure, schools, public health, the research and development that keeps our companies on the cutting edge.

That's what great nations do. (Applause.) That's what great nations do. And you know, eventually, we're going to do it anyway, so let's just do it without too much drama. (Laughter.) Let's do it without another round of threats to shut down the government. (Applause.) Let's not introduce unrelated partisan issues. Nobody gets to hold the American economy hostage over their own ideological demands. You, the people who send us to Washington, expect better. Am I correct? (Applause.)

So my message to Congress is: Pass a budget. Prevent a shutdown. Don't wait until the last minute. Don't worry our businesses or our workers by contributing unnecessarily to global uncertainty. Get it done, and keep the United States of America the anchor of global strength that we are and always should be.

Now, that's a process of national recovery that from coast to coast we've been going through. But there's been a specific process of recovery that is perhaps unique in my lifetime, right here in the state of Louisiana, right here in New Orleans. (Applause.)

Not long ago, our gathering here in the Lower Ninth probably would have seemed unlikely. As I was flying here today with a homegirl from Louisiana, Donna Brazile, she was—she saved all the magazines, and she was whipping them out, and one of them was a picture of the Lower Ninth right after the storm had happened. And the notion that there would be anything left seemed unimaginable at the time.

Today, this new community center stands as a symbol of the extraordinary resilience of this city, the extraordinary resilience of its people, the extraordinary resilience of the entire Gulf Coast and of the United States of America. You are an example of what is possible when, in the face of tragedy and in the face of hardship, good people come together to lend a hand, and, brick by brick, block by block, neighborhood by neighborhood, you build a better future.

And that, more than any other reason, is why I've come back here today—plus, Mitch Landrieu asked me to. (Laughter.) It's been 10 years since Katrina hit, devastating communities in Louisiana and Mississippi, across the Gulf Coast. In the days following its landfall, more than 1,800 of our fellow citizens—men, women and children—lost their lives. Some folks in this room may have lost a loved one in that storm.

Thousands of people saw their homes destroyed, livelihoods wiped out, hopes and dreams shattered. Many scattered in exodus to cities across the country, and too many still haven't returned. Those who stayed and lived through that epic struggle still feel the trauma sometimes of what happened. As one woman from Gentilly recently wrote me, "A deep part of the whole story is the grief." So there's grief then and there's still some grief in our hearts.

Here in New Orleans, a city that embodies a celebration of life, suddenly seemed devoid of life. A place once defined by color and sound—the second line down the street, the crawfish boils in backyards, the music always in the air—suddenly it was dark and silent. And the world watched in horror. We saw those rising waters drown the iconic streets of New Orleans. Families stranded on rooftops. Bodies in the streets. Children crying, crowded in the Superdome. An American city dark and under water.

And this was something that was supposed to never happen here—maybe somewhere else. But not here, not in America. And we came to realize that what started out as a natural disaster became a manmade disaster—a failure of government to look out for its own citizens. And the storm laid bare a deeper tragedy that had been brewing for decades because we came to understand that New Orleans, like so many cities and communities across the country, had for too long been plagued by structural inequalities that left too many people, especially poor people, especially people of color, without good jobs or affordable health care or decent housing. Too many kids grew up surrounded by violent crime, cycling through substandard schools where few had a shot to break out of poverty. And so like a body weakened already, undernourished already, when the storm hit, there was no resources to fall back on.

Shortly after I visited—shortly after the storm, I visited with folks not here because we couldn't distract local recovery efforts. Instead, I visited folks in a shelter in Houston—many who had been displaced. And one woman told me, "We had nothing before the hurricane. And now we have less than nothing." We had nothing before the hurricane—now we had less than nothing.

And we acknowledge this loss, and this pain, not to dwell on the past, not to wallow in grief; we do it to fortify our commitment and to bolster our hope, to understand what it is that we've learned, and how far we've come.

Because this is a city that slowly, unmistakably, together, is moving forward. Because the project of rebuilding here wasn't just to restore the city as it had been. It was to build a city as it should be—a city where everyone, no matter what they look like, how much money they've got, where they come from, where they're born has a chance to make it. (Applause.)

And I'm here to say that on that larger project of a better, stronger, more just New Orleans, the progress that you have made is remarkable. The progress you've made is remarkable. (Applause.)

That's not to say things are perfect. Mitch would be the first one to say that. We know that African Americans and folks in hard-hit parishes like Plaquemines and St. Bernard are less likely to feel like they've recovered. Certainly we know violence still scars the lives of too many youth in this city. As hard as rebuilding levees are, as hard as—

PARTICIPANT: (Inaudible) mental health.

THE PRESIDENT: I agree with that. But I'll get to that. Thank you, ma'am.

As hard as rebuilding levees is, as hard as rebuilding housing is, real change—real lasting, structural change—that's even harder. And it takes courage to experiment with new ideas and change the old ways of doing things. That's hard. Getting it right, and making sure that everybody is included and everybody has a fair shot at success—that takes time. That's not unique to New Orleans. We've got those challenges all across the country.

But I'm here to say, I'm here to hold up a mirror and say because of you, the people of New Orleans, working together, this city is moving in the right direction. And I have never been more confident that together we will get to where we need to go. You inspire me. (Applause.)

Your efforts inspire me. And no matter how hard it's been and how hard and how long the road ahead might seem, you're working and building and striving for a better tomorrow. I see evidence of it all across this city. And, by the way, along the way, the people of New Orleans didn't just inspire me, you inspired all of America. Folks have been watching what's happened here, and they've seen a reflection of the very best of the American spirit.

As President, I've been proud to be your partner. Across the board, I've made the recovery and rebuilding of the Gulf Coast a priority. I made promises when I was a senator that I'd help. And I've kept those promises. (Applause.)

We're cutting red tape to help you build back even stronger. We're taking the lessons we've learned here, we've applied them across the country, including places like New York and New Jersey after Hurricane Sandy.

If Katrina was initially an example of what happens when government fails, the recovery has been an example of what's possible when government works together—(applause)—state and local, community—everybody working together as true partners.

Together, we've delivered resources to help Louisiana, Mississippi, Alabama, and Florida rebuild schools and hospitals, roads, police and fire stations, restore historic buildings and museums. And we're building smarter, doing everything from elevating homes to retrofitting buildings to improving drainage, so that our communities are better prepared for the next storm.

Working together, we've transformed education in this city. Before the storm, New Orleans public schools were largely broken, leaving generations of low-income kids without a decent education. Today, thanks to parents and educators, school leaders, nonprofits, we're seeing real gains in achievement, with new schools, more resources to retain and develop and support great teachers and principals. We have data that shows before the storm, the high school graduation rate was 54 percent. Today, it's up to 73 percent. (Applause.) Before the storm, college enrollment was 37 percent. Today, it's almost 60 percent. (Applause.) We still have a long way to go, but that is real progress. New Orleans is coming back better and stronger.

Working together, we're providing housing assistance to more families today than before the storm, with new apartments and housing vouchers. And we will keep working until everybody who wants to come home can come home. (Applause.)

Together, we're building a New Orleans that is as entrepreneurial as any place in the country, with a focus on expanding job opportunities and making sure that more people benefit from a growing economy here. We're creating jobs to rebuild the city's transportation infrastructure, expanding training programs for industries like high-tech manufacturing, but also water management, because we've been building some good water management around here and we want to make sure everybody has access to those good, well-paying jobs. Small businesses like Michelle's are growing. It's small businesses like hers that are helping to fuel 65 straight months of private-sector job growth in America. That's the longest streak in American history. (Applause.)

Together, we're doing more to make sure that everyone in this city has access to great health care. More folks have access to primary care at neighborhood clinics so that they can get the preventive care that they need. We're building a brand new VA Medical Center downtown, alongside a thriving biosciences corridor that's attracting new jobs and investment. We are working to make sure that we have additional mental health facilities across the city and across the country, and more people have access to quality, affordable health care—some of the more than 16 million Americans who have gained health insurance over the past few years. (Applause.)

All of this progress is the result of the commitment and drive of the people of this region. I saw that spirit today. Mitch and I started walking around a little bit. Such a nice day outside. And we went to Faubourg Lafitte, we were in Tremé, and we saw returning residents living in brand new homes, mixed income—new homes near schools and clinics and parks, child care centers; more opportunities for working families.

We saw that spirit today at Willie Mae's Scotch House. After Katrina had destroyed that legendary restaurant, some of the best chefs from the country decided America could not afford to lose such an important place. So they came down here to help—helped rebuild. And I just sampled some of her fried chicken. (Laughter.) It was really good. (Laughter.) Although I did get a grease spot on my suit. (Laughter.) But that's okay. If you come to New Orleans and you don't have a grease spot somewhere—(applause)—then you didn't enjoy the city. Just glad I didn't get it on my tie. (Laughter.)

We all just heard that spirit of New Orleans in the remarkable young people from Roots of Music. (Applause.) When the storm washed away a lot of middle school music programs, Roots of Music helped fill that gap. And today, it's building the next generation of musical talent—the next Irma Thomas, or the next Trombone Shorty, or the next Dr. John. (Applause.) There's a Marsalis kid in here somewhere. How you doing?

And I saw it in the wonderful young men I met earlier who are part of "NOLA for Life," which is focused on reducing the number of murders in the city of New Orleans. (Applause.) This is a program that works with the White House's My Brother's Keeper initiative to make sure that all young people, and particularly our boys and young men of color who so disproportionately are impacted by crime and violence, have the opportunity to fulfill their full potential.

In fact, after the storm, this city became a laboratory for urban innovation across the board. And we've been tackling with you, as a partner, all sorts of major challenges—fighting poverty, supporting our homeless veterans. And as a result, New Orleans has become a model for the nation as the first city, the first major city to end veterans' homelessness—(applause)—which is a remarkable achievement.

You're also becoming a model for the nation when it comes to disaster response and resilience. We learned lessons from Katrina. The U.S. Army Corps of Engineers developed stricter standards, more advanced techniques for levees. Here in Louisiana, we built a $14 billion system of improved levees and pump stations and gates—a system that stood the test of Hurricane Isaac.

We've revamped FEMA—and I just have to say, by the way, there's a man named Craig Fugate who runs FEMA—(applause)—and has been doing extraordinary work, and his team, all across the country, every time there's a disaster. I love me some Craig Fugate. (Laughter.) Although it's a little disturbing—he gets excited when there are disasters—(laughter)—because he gets restless if everything is just quiet. But under his leadership, we've revamped FEMA into a stronger, more efficient agency. In fact, the whole federal government has gotten smarter at preventing and recovering from disasters, and serving as a better partner to local and state governments.

And as I'll talk about next week, when I visit Alaska, making our communities more resilient is going to be increasingly important, because we're going to see more extreme weather events as the result of climate change—deeper droughts, deadlier wildfires, stronger storms. That's why, in addition to things like new and better levees, we've also been investing in restoring wetlands and other natural systems that are just as critical for storm protection.

So we've made a lot of progress over the past 10 years. You've made a lot of progress. That gives us hope. But it doesn't allow for complacency. It doesn't mean we can rest. Our work here won't be done when almost 40 percent of children still live in poverty in this city. That's not a finished job. That's not a full recovery. Our work won't be done when a typical black household earns half the income of white households in this city. The work is not done yet. (Applause.)

Our work is not done when there's still too many people who have yet to find good, affordable housing, and too many people—especially African American men—who can't find a job. Not when there are still too many people who haven't been able to come back home; folks who, around the country, every day, live the words sung by Louis Armstrong, "Do you know what it means to miss New Orleans?"

But the thing is, the people of New Orleans, there's something in you guys that is just irrepressible. You guys have a way of making a way out of no way. (Applause.) You know the sun comes out after every storm. You've got hope—especially your young people reflect hope—young people like Victor York-Carter. Where's Victor? Victor York-Carter. Stand up, Victor. I was just talking to Victor. I had some lunch with him. He's this fine young man that I just met with. (Applause.) Stand up—everybody. See, these are the guys who I ate chicken with. (Applause.) Really impressive—have overcome more than their fair share of challenges, but are still focused on the future. Yes, sit down. I don't want you to start getting embarrassed. (Laughter.)

So I'll just give you one example. Victor grew up in the Eighth Ward. Gifted art student, loved math. He was 13 when Katrina hit. And he remembers waking up to what looked like something out of a disaster movie. He and his family waded across the city, towing his younger brother in a trash can to keep him afloat.

They were eventually evacuated to Texas. Six months later, they returned, and the city was almost unrecognizable. Victor saw his peers struggling to cope, many of them still traumatized, their lives still disordered. So he joined an organization called Rethink to help young people get more involved in rebuilding New Orleans. And recently, he finished a coding bootcamp at Operation Spark; today, he's studying to earn a high-tech job. He wants to introduce more young people to science and technology and civics so that they have the tools to change the world.

And so Victor and these young men that I just met with, they've overcome extraordinary odds. They've lived through more than most of us will ever have to endure. (Applause.) They've made some mistakes along the way. But for all that they've been through, they have been just as determined to improve their own lives, to take responsibility for themselves, but also to try to see if they can help others along the way.

So when I talk to young men like that, that gives me hope. It's still hard. I told them they can't get down on themselves. Tough stuff will happen along the way. But if they've come this far, they can keep on going. (Applause.)

And Americans like you—the people of New Orleans, young men like this—you're what recovery has been all about. You're why I'm confident that we can recover from crisis and start to move forward. You've helped this country recover from a crisis and helped it move forward. You're the reason 13 million new jobs have been created. You're the reason the unemployment rate fell from 10 percent to 5.3. You're the reason that layoffs are near an all-time low. You're the reason the uninsured rate is at an all-time low and the high school graduation rate is at an all-time high, and the deficit has been cut by two-thirds, and two wars are over. (Applause.) And nearly 180,000 American troops who were serving in Iraq and Afghanistan have now gone down to 15,000. And a clean energy revolution is helping to save this planet.

You're the reason why justice has expanded and now we're focused on making sure that everybody is treated fairly under the law, and why people have the freedom to marry whoever they love from sea to shining sea. (Applause.)

I tell you, we're moving into the next presidential cycle and the next political season, and you will hear a lot of people telling you everything that's wrong with America. And that's okay. That's a proper part of our democracy. One of the things about America is we're never satisfied. We keep pushing forward. We keep asking questions. We keep challenging our government. We keep challenging our leaders. We keep looking for the next set of challenges to tackle. We find what's wrong because we have confidence that we can fix it.

But it's important that we remember what's right, and what's good, and what's hopeful about this country. It's worth remembering that for all the tragedy, for all the images of Katrina in those first few days, in those first few months, look at what's happened here. It's worth remembering the thousands of Americans like Michelle, and Victor, and Mrs. Willie Mae and the folks who rallied around her—Americans all across this country who, when they saw neighbors and friends or strangers in need, came to help. And people who today still spend their time every day helping others—rolling up their sleeves, doing the hard work of changing this country without the need for credit or the need for glory; don't get their name in the papers, don't see their day in the sun, do it because it's right.

These Americans live the basic values that define this country—the value we've been reminded of in these past 10 years as we've come back from a crisis that changed this city, and an economic crisis that spread throughout the nation—the basic notion that I am my brother's keeper, and I am my sister's keeper, and that we look out for each other and that we're all in this together.

That's the story of New Orleans—but that's also the story of America—a city that, for almost 300 years, has been the gateway to America's soul. Where the jazz makes you cry, the funerals make you dance—(laughter)—the bayou makes you believe all kinds of things. (Laughter.) A place that has always brought together people of all races and religions and languages. And everybody adds their culture and their flavor into this city's gumbo. You remind our nation that for all of our differences, in the end, what matters is we're all in the same boat. We all share a similar destiny.

If we stay focused on that common purpose, if we remember our responsibility to ourselves but also our responsibilities and obligations to one another, we will not just rebuild this city, we will rebuild this country. We'll make sure not just these young men, but every child in America has a structure and support and love and the kind of nurturing that they need to succeed. We'll leave behind a city and a nation that's worthy of generations to come.

That's what you've gotten started. Now we got to finish the job.

Thank you. God bless you. God bless America. (Applause.)

Four Representatives of the American People

By Pope Francis

On September 24, 2015, Pope Francis became the first pope to speak before a joint meeting of Congress. In his address, he evokes the names of four Americans—Abraham Lincoln, Martin Luther King, Jr., Dorothy Day, and Thomas Merton—who represent for the pope important aspects of the American Dream, including liberty, equality, social justice, and openness to dialogue. Pope Francis implores Americans to allow these principles to guide their treatment of refugees, other immigrants, and the poor. The same principles, he contends, should be considered in confronting the global environmental crisis as well as other important issues of our time. Born Jorge Mario Bergoglio in Buenos Aires, Argentina, Pope Francis is the 266th pope of the Roman Catholic Church and the first to hail from the Americas.

Mr. Vice President, Mr. Speaker, Honorable Members of Congress, dear friends, I am most grateful for your invitation to address this Joint Session of Congress in "the land of the free and the home of the brave." I would like to think that the reason for this is that I too am a son of this great continent, from which we have all received so much and toward which we share a common responsibility.

Each son or daughter of a given country has a mission, a personal and social responsibility. Your own responsibility as members of Congress is to enable this country, by your legislative activity, to grow as a nation. You are the face of its people, their representatives. You are called to defend and preserve the dignity of your fellow citizens in the tireless and demanding pursuit of the common good, for this is the chief aim of all politics.

A political society endures when it seeks, as a vocation, to satisfy common needs by stimulating the growth of all its members, especially those in situations of greater vulnerability or risk. Legislative activity is always based on care for the people. To this you have been invited, called and convened by those who elected you.

Yours is a work which makes me reflect in two ways on the figure of Moses. On the one hand, the patriarch and lawgiver of the people of Israel symbolizes the need of peoples to keep alive their sense of unity by means of just legislation. On the other, the figure of Moses leads us directly to God and thus to the transcendent dignity of the human being. Moses provides us with a good synthesis of your work:

Delivered September 24, 2015, to the U.S. Congress, Washington D.C., by Pope Francis.

you are asked to protect, by means of the law, the image and likeness fashioned by God on every human face.

Today I would like not only to address you, but through you the entire people of the United States. Here, together with their representatives, I would like to take this opportunity to dialogue with the many thousands of men and women who strive each day to do an honest day's work, to bring home their daily bread, to save money and—one step at a time—to build a better life for their families.

These are men and women who are not concerned simply with paying their taxes, but in their own quiet way sustain the life of society. They generate solidarity by their actions, and they create organizations which offer a helping hand to those most in need.

I would also like to enter into dialogue with the many elderly persons who are a storehouse of wisdom forged by experience, and who seek in many ways, especially through volunteer work, to share their stories and their insights. I know that many of them are retired, but still active; they keep working to build up this land.

I also want to dialogue with all those young people who are working to realize their great and noble aspirations, who are not led astray by facile proposals, and who face difficult situations, often as a result of immaturity on the part of many adults. I wish to dialogue with all of you, and I would like to do so through the historical memory of your people.

My visit takes place at a time when men and women of good will are marking the anniversaries of several great Americans. The complexities of history and the reality of human weakness notwithstanding, these men and women, for all their many differences and limitations, were able by hard work and self-sacrifice—some at the cost of their lives—to build a better future. They shaped fundamental values which will endure forever in the spirit of the American people.

A people with this spirit can live through many crises, tensions and conflicts, while always finding the resources to move forward, and to do so with dignity. These men and women offer us a way of seeing and interpreting reality. In honoring their memory, we are inspired, even amid conflicts, and in the here and now of each day, to draw upon our deepest cultural reserves.

I would like to mention four of these Americans: Abraham Lincoln, Martin Luther King, Dorothy Day and Thomas Merton.

This year marks the one hundred and fiftieth anniversary of the assassination of President Abraham Lincoln, the guardian of liberty, who labored tirelessly that "this nation, under God, [might] have a new birth of freedom." Building a future of freedom requires love of the common good and cooperation in a spirit of subsidiarity and solidarity.

All of us are quite aware of, and deeply worried by, the disturbing social and political situation of the world today. Our world is increasingly a place of violent conflict, hatred and brutal atrocities, committed even in the name of God and of religion. We know that no religion is immune from forms of individual delusion or ideological extremism.

This means that we must be especially attentive to every type of fundamentalism, whether religious or of any other kind. A delicate balance is required to combat violence perpetrated in the name of a religion, an ideology or an economic system, while also safeguarding religious freedom, intellectual freedom and individual freedoms.

But there is another temptation which we must especially guard against: the simplistic reductionism which sees only good or evil, or, if you will, the righteous and sinners. The contemporary world, with its open wounds which affect so many of our brothers and sisters, demands that we confront every form of polarization which would divide it into these two camps.

We know that in the attempt to be freed of the enemy without, we can be tempted to feed the enemy within. To imitate the hatred and violence of tyrants and murderers is the best way to take their place. That is something which you, as a people, reject.

Our response must instead be one of hope and healing, of peace and justice. We are asked to summon the courage and the intelligence to resolve today's many geopolitical and economic crises. Even in the developed world, the effects of unjust structures and actions are all too apparent.

Our efforts must aim at restoring hope, righting wrongs, maintaining commitments, and thus promoting the well-being of individuals and of peoples. We must move forward together, as one, in a renewed spirit of fraternity and solidarity, cooperating generously for the common good.

The challenges facing us today call for a renewal of that spirit of cooperation, which has accomplished so much good throughout the history of the United States. The complexity, the gravity and the urgency of these challenges demand that we pool our resources and talents, and resolve to support one another, with respect for our differences and our convictions of conscience.

In this land, the various religious denominations have greatly contributed to building and strengthening society. It is important that today, as in the past, the voice of faith continue to be heard, for it is a voice of fraternity and love, which tries to bring out the best in each person and in each society. Such cooperation is a powerful resource in the battle to eliminate new global forms of slavery, born of grave injustices which can be overcome only through new policies and new forms of social consensus.

Politics is, instead, an expression of our compelling need to live as one, in order to build as one the greatest common good: that of a community which sacrifices particular interests in order to share, in justice and peace, its goods, its interests, its social life. I do not underestimate the difficulty that this involves, but I encourage you in this effort.

Here too I think of the march which Martin Luther King led from Selma to Montgomery fifty years ago as part of the campaign to fulfill his "dream" of full civil and political rights for African Americans. That dream continues to inspire us all. I am happy that America continues to be, for many, a land of "dreams." Dreams which lead to action, to participation, to commitment. Dreams which awaken what is deepest and truest in the life of a people.

In recent centuries, millions of people came to this land to pursue their dream of building a future in freedom. We, the people of this continent, are not fearful of foreigners, because most of us were once foreigners. I say this to you as the son of immigrants, knowing that so many of you are also descended from immigrants.

Tragically, the rights of those who were here long before us were not always respected. For those peoples and their nations, from the heart of American democracy, I wish to reaffirm my highest esteem and appreciation. Those first contacts were often turbulent and violent, but it is difficult to judge the past by the criteria of the present.

Nonetheless, when the stranger in our midst appeals to us, we must not repeat the sins and the errors of the past. We must resolve now to live as nobly and as justly as possible, as we educate new generations not to turn their back on our "neighbors" and everything around us. Building a nation calls us to recognize that we must constantly relate to others, rejecting a mindset of hostility in order to adopt one of reciprocal subsidiarity, in a constant effort to do our best. I am confident that we can do this.

Our world is facing a refugee crisis of a magnitude not seen since the Second World War. This presents us with great challenges and many hard decisions. On this continent, too, thousands of persons are led to travel north in search of a better life for themselves and for their loved ones, in search of greater opportunities. Is this not what we want for our own children? We must not be taken aback by their numbers, but rather view them as persons, seeing their faces and listening to their stories, trying to respond as best we can to their situation. To respond in a way which is always humane, just, and fraternal. We need to avoid a common temptation nowadays: to discard whatever proves troublesome. Let us remember the Golden Rule: "Do unto others as you would have them do unto you" (Mt 7:12).

This Rule points us in a clear direction. Let us treat others with the same passion and compassion with which we want to be treated. Let us seek for others the same possibilities which we seek for ourselves. Let us help others to grow, as we would like to be helped ourselves. In a word, if we want security, let us give security; if we want life, let us give life; if we want opportunities, let us provide opportunities. The yardstick we use for others will be the yardstick which time will use for us.

The Golden Rule also reminds us of our responsibility to protect and defend human life at every stage of its development. This conviction has led me, from the beginning of my ministry, to advocate at different levels for the global abolition of the death penalty. I am convinced that this way is the best, since every life is sacred, every human person is endowed with an inalienable dignity, and society can only benefit from the rehabilitation of those convicted of crimes.

Recently my brother bishops here in the United States renewed their call for the abolition of the death penalty. Not only do I support them, but I also offer encouragement to all those who are convinced that a just and necessary punishment must never exclude the dimension of hope and the goal of rehabilitation.

In these times when social concerns are so important, I cannot fail to mention the Servant of God Dorothy Day, who founded the Catholic Worker Movement. Her social activism, her passion for justice and for the cause of the oppressed were inspired by the Gospel, her faith, and the example of the saints.

How much progress has been made in this area in so many parts of the world! How much has been done in these first years of the third millennium to raise people out of extreme poverty! I know that you share my conviction that much more still needs to be done, and that in times of crisis and economic hardship a spirit of global solidarity must not be lost.

At the same time, I would encourage you to keep in mind all those people around us who are trapped in a cycle of poverty. They too need to be given hope. The fight against poverty and hunger must be fought constantly and on many fronts, especially in its causes. I know that many Americans today, as in the past, are working to deal with this problem.

It goes without saying that part of this great effort is the creation and distribution of wealth. The right use of natural resources, the proper application of technology, and the harnessing of the spirit of enterprise are essential elements of an economy which seeks to be modern, inclusive and sustainable. "Business is a noble vocation, directed to producing wealth and improving the world. It can be a fruitful source of prosperity for the area in which it operates, especially if it sees the creation of jobs as an essential part of its service to the common good." This common good also includes the earth, a central theme of the encyclical which I recently wrote in order to "enter into dialogue with all people about our common home." "We need a conversation which includes everyone, since the environmental challenge we are undergoing, and its human roots, concern and affect us all."

In Laudato Si', I call for a courageous and responsible effort to "redirect our steps," and to avert the most serious effects of the environmental deterioration caused by human activity. I am convinced that we can make a difference and I have no doubt that the United States—and this Congress—have an important role to play. Now is the time for courageous actions and strategies, aimed at implementing a "culture of care" and "an integrated approach to combating poverty, restoring dignity to the excluded, and at the same time protecting nature." "We have the freedom needed to limit and direct technology, to devise intelligent ways of. . . developing and limiting our power," and to put technology "at the service of another type of progress, one which is healthier, more human, more social, more integral." In this regard, I am confident that America's outstanding academic and research institutions can make a vital contribution in the years ahead.

A century ago, at the beginning of the Great War, which Pope Benedict XV termed a "pointless slaughter," another notable American was born: the Cistercian monk Thomas Merton. He remains a source of spiritual inspiration and a guide for many people. In his autobiography he wrote: "I came into the world. Free by nature, in the image of God, I was nevertheless the prisoner of my own violence and my own selfishness, in the image of the world into which I was born. That world was the picture of Hell, full of men like myself, loving God, and yet hating him; born to love him, living instead in fear of hopeless self-contradictory hungers." Merton was above all a man of prayer, a thinker who challenged the certitudes of his time and opened new horizons for souls and for the Church. He was also a man of dialogue, a promoter of peace between peoples and religions.

From this perspective of dialogue, I would like to recognize the efforts made in recent months to help overcome historic differences linked to painful episodes of the past. It is my duty to build bridges and to help all men and women, in any way possible, to do the same. When countries which have been at odds resume the path of dialogue—a dialogue which may have been interrupted for the most legitimate of reasons—new opportunities open up for all. This has required, and requires, courage and daring, which is not the same as irresponsibility. A good political leader is one who, with the interests of all in mind, seizes the moment in a spirit of openness and pragmatism. A good political leader always opts to initiate processes rather than possessing spaces.

Being at the service of dialogue and peace also means being truly determined to minimize and, in the long term, to end the many armed conflicts throughout our world. Here we have to ask ourselves: Why are deadly weapons being sold to those who plan to inflict untold suffering on individuals and society? Sadly, the answer, as we all know, is simply for money: money that is drenched in blood, often innocent blood. In the face of this shameful and culpable silence, it is our duty to confront the problem and to stop the arms trade.

Three sons and a daughter of this land, four individuals and four dreams: Lincoln, liberty; Martin Luther King, liberty in plurality and non-exclusion; Dorothy Day, social justice and the rights of persons; and Thomas Merton, the capacity for dialogue and openness to God. Four representatives of the American people.

I will end my visit to your country in Philadelphia, where I will take part in the World Meeting of Families. It is my wish that throughout my visit the family should be a recurrent theme. How essential the family has been to the building of this country! And how worthy it remains of our support and encouragement! Yet I cannot hide my concern for the family, which is threatened, perhaps as never before, from within and without. Fundamental relationships are being called into question, as is the very basis of marriage and the family. I can only reiterate the importance and, above all, the richness and the beauty of family life.

In particular, I would like to call attention to those family members who are the most vulnerable, the young. For many of them, a future filled with countless possibilities beckons, yet so many others seem disoriented and aimless, trapped in a hopeless maze of violence, abuse and despair. Their problems are our problems. We cannot avoid them. We need to face them together, to talk about them and to seek effective solutions rather than getting bogged down in discussions. At the risk of oversimplifying, we might say that we live in a culture which pressures young people not to start a family, because they lack possibilities for the future. Yet this same culture presents others with so many options that they too are dissuaded from starting a family.

A nation can be considered great when it defends liberty as Lincoln did; when it fosters a culture which enables people to "dream" of full rights for all their brothers and sisters, as Martin Luther King sought to do; when it strives for justice and the cause of the oppressed, as Dorothy Day did by her tireless work; the fruit of a faith which becomes dialogue and sows peace in the contemplative style of Thomas Merton.

In these remarks I have sought to present some of the richness of your cultural heritage, of the spirit of the American people. It is my desire that this spirit continue to develop and grow, so that as many young people as possible can inherit and dwell in a land which has inspired so many people to dream.

God bless America!

Address to the UN General Assembly

By Ban Ki-moon

In an address to the 70th session of the General Assembly of the United Nations, Secretary General Ban Ki-moon discusses the most pressing issues of the day, including climate change, a grave concern that requires immediate attention and concentrated effort, and other humanitarian issues such as the global refugee crisis, childhood poverty, women's rights, and international peacekeeping more broadly. Remedying these causes requires more funding which, he notes, must be diverted from other areas such as military spending. Ban Ki-moon has been the eighth secretary general of the United Nations since January 1, 2007 and was unanimously re-elected on June 21, 2011. Prior to holding this position, Ban spent thirty-seven years at South Korea's foreign ministry and held a number of high-ranking positions, including the minister of Foreign Affairs and Trade (2004-2006).

The 70th session of the General Assembly has opened with a towering achievement: the adoption of the 2030 Agenda, including 17 inspiring Sustainable Development Goals, the SDGs.

Our aim is clear. Our mission is possible. And our destination is in our sights: an end to extreme poverty by 2030; a life of peace and dignity for all.

What counts now is translating promises on paper into change on the ground.

We owe this and much more to the vulnerable, the oppressed, the displaced and the forgotten people in our world.

We owe this to a world where inequality is growing, trust is fading, and impatience with leadership can be seen and felt far and wide.

We owe this to "succeeding generations," in the memorable words the Charter.

In this year in which we mark the 70th anniversary of the United Nations, we must heed the call of the Charter, and hear the voices of "we the peoples." That is how we can overcome the grim realities of the present—and seize the remarkable opportunities of our era.

The Millennium Development Goals made poverty history for hundreds of millions of people.

Now we are poised to continue the job while reaching higher, broader and deeper.

The new framework does not just add goals. It weaves the goals together, with human rights, the rule of law and women's empowerment as crucial parts of an integrated whole.

The global goals are universal.

You, the world's leaders, have committed to leave no one behind—and to reach those farthest behind, first.

We can build on the momentum this December [2015] in Paris with a robust agreement on climate change. Remarkable changes are under way to reduce harmful greenhouse emissions. I have seen and visited vast solar power installations bringing a new energy future into being. There is wind in the sails of climate action.

Yet it is clear that the national targets submitted by the member states will not be enough. We face a choice: either raise ambition—or risk raising temperatures above the 2-degree Celsius threshold, which science tells us we must not cross.

Reaching our sustainable development goals means organizing ourselves better. Let there be no more walls or boxes; no more ministries or agencies working at cross purposes. Let us move from silos to synergy, supported by data, long-term planning and a will to do things differently.

Financing will be a key test.

I welcome the Addis Ababa Action Agenda, and the renewed pledge by developed countries to invest 0.7 percent of gross national income in official development assistance. Aid works—but few countries have met this target. I salute those that have, and urge others to follow their example.

Climate finance will be crucial. I urge developed countries to meet the agreed goal of $100 billion per year by 2020. We must also get the Green Climate Fund up and running.

The world continues to squander trillions in wasteful military spending. Why is it easier to find the money to destroy people and planet than it is to protect them?

Succeeding generations depend on us to finally get our priorities right.

Suffering today is at heights not seen in a generation. One hundred million people require immediate humanitarian assistance. At least 60 million people have been forced to flee their homes or their countries. The United Nations has asked for nearly $20 billion to meet this year's needs—six times the level of a decade ago.

UN humanitarian agencies and our partners are braving difficult conditions to reach people.

Member States have been generous, but demands continue to dwarf funding.

The World Humanitarian Summit in May 2016 in Istanbul is a critical moment to reaffirm solidarity and explore how to better build resilience and address emergencies.

But the global humanitarian system is not broken; it is broke.

We are not receiving enough money to save enough lives.

We have about half of what we need to help the people of Iraq, South Sudan and Yemen – and just a third for Syria.

Our response plan for Ukraine is just 39 percent funded.

And the appeal for Gambia, where one in four children suffers from stunting, has been met with silence.

Numbers this low raise suffering to new highs.

People need emergency assistance, but what they want even more is lasting solutions. They may appreciate a tent, but they deserve to go home.

Our aim is not just to keep people alive, but to give them a life—a decent life.

Lebanon, Jordan and Turkey are generously hosting several million Syrian and Iraqi refugees. Countries across the developing world continue to host and receive large numbers of refugees despite their own limited means.

People are on the move as never before, in the Americas and the Sahel, in the Mediterranean and Andaman Seas.

These flows raise complex issues, and rouse strong passions.

Certain touchstones must guide our response: international law, human rights, basic compassion.

All countries need to do more to shoulder their responsibilities. I commend those in Europe that are upholding the Union's values and providing asylum. At the same time, I urge Europe to do more. After the Second World War, it was Europeans seeking the world's assistance.

I will convene a high-level meeting on September 30, the day after tomorrow, aimed at promoting a comprehensive approach to the refugee and migration crisis.

We must crack down on traffickers and address the pressures being faced by countries of destination.

We must combat discrimination. In the twenty-first century, we should not be building fences or walls.

But above all, we must look at root causes in countries of origin.

Syrians are leaving their country and their homes because of oppression, extremism, destruction and fear.

Four years of diplomatic paralysis by the Security Council and others have allowed the crisis to spin out of control.

The responsibility for ending the conflict lies first and foremost with the Syrian warring parties. They are the ones turning their country to ruins.

But it is not enough to look only within Syria for a solution. The battle is also being driven by regional powers and rivalries. Weapons and money flowing into the country are fueling the fire.

My Special Envoy is doing everything he can to forge the basis for a peaceful settlement.

It is time now for others, primarily the Security Council and key regional actors, to step forward.

Five countries in particular hold the key: the Russian Federation, the United States, Saudi Arabia, Iran and Turkey. But as long as one side will not compromise with the other, it is futile to expect change on the ground.

Innocent Syrians pay the price of more barrel bombs and terrorism. There must be no impunity for atrocious crimes. Our commitment to justice should lead us to refer the situation to the International Criminal Court.

In Yemen, 21 million people—80 percent of the population—need humanitarian assistance.

All sides are showing disregard for human life—but most of the casualties are being caused by air-strikes. I call for an end to the bombings, which are also destroying Yemeni cities, infrastructure and heritage.

Here, too, the proxy battles of others are driving the fighting. I once again urge the parties to return to the table, negotiate in good faith and resolve this crisis through dialogue facilitated by my Special Envoy. Let me be clear: There is no military solution to this conflict.

We must also guard against the dangerous drift in the Middle East Peace Process. With settlements expanding and incitement and provocations on the rise, it is essential for—5—Israelis and Palestinians to re-engage—and for the international community to pressure the parties to do so. The world can no longer wait for leaders to finally choose a path to peace.

Da'esh, Boko Haram and Al-Shabab remain major threats, especially to the women and girls who have been systematically targeted. The world must unite against the blatant brutality of these groups. We must also counter the exclusion and hopelessness on which extremists feed. Moreover, States must never violate human rights in the fight against terror; such abuses only perpetuate the cycle.

Early next year, I will present to the General Assembly a comprehensive plan of action on how to counter violent extremism and terrorism.

I commend the landmark nuclear agreement between the Islamic Republic of Iran and the P5+1 countries. Dialogue and patient diplomacy have paid dividends. I hope this spirit of solidarity among the Permanent Members of the Security Council can be demonstrated in other conflict areas, such as Syria, Yemen and Ukraine.

Let us build on the recent agreements in South Sudan, finalize the agreement in Libya, and spare those countries further suffering.

Now is the time for renewed dialogue to address continuing tension on the Korean peninsula. I call on the parties to refrain from taking any action that may increase mistrust, and urge them to instead promote reconciliation and efforts toward a peaceful, de-nuclearized peninsula. I am ready to support inter-Korean cooperation. We also need to step up our work for the well-being of the people of the Democratic People's Republic of Korea.

I am deeply troubled by growing restrictions on media freedoms and civil society across the world. It is not a crime for journalists, human rights defenders and others to exercise their basic rights. We must preserve the space for civil society and the press to do their vital work without fear of attack and imprisonment.

Democratic backsliding is a threat in too many places, as leaders seek to stay in office beyond their mandated limits. We see rallies and petitions being engineered to look like the spontaneous will of the people. Those manufactured groundswells of support only lay the groundwork for instability. I urge leaders to abide by the constitutional limits on their terms.

Collectively, these crises have stretched to the limits our vital tools for conflict resolution and humanitarian response.

Earlier this month, I put forward my vision for strengthening UN peace operations, building on the recommendations of an independent panel.

Our peacekeeping and political missions need enhanced capabilities and clear objectives.

We need a renewed commitment to prevention, stronger regional partnerships, and sustained engagement on peacebuilding.

And we must unlock the potential of women to advance peace, as envisaged in Security Council resolution 1325.

I hope the General Assembly will take early action as a signal of its commitment to this effort.

People today, and succeeding generations, need us to make the most of this rare opportunity for comprehensive progress.

Founded in a fractured world, the United Nations brought hope that collective action could avoid another global catastrophe.

Over the past 70 years, we have helped to liberate millions of people from colonialism and supported the successful struggle against apartheid. We have defeated deadly diseases, defended human rights and deepened the rule of law.

This and more we have done—but that is far from enough.

We are living through a time of severe test—but also one of great opportunity.

Today, we are more connected than ever, better informed than ever, and have better tools than ever. The recipes for positive change are on the table; the ingredients for success are in our hands.

We continue to reform the United Nations—although we know we must do much more, both managerially and politically.

We can draw strength from the empowerment of women—but we still need to step it up for gender equality on the way to Planet 50/50.

I am inspired by the world's young people, who make up half the world's population—and whose voices we must integrate more fully in decision-making everywhere.

And I am impressed with the way we, all of us, can unite behind vital causes—like the 2030 Development Agenda.

One year ago, when we gathered for the general debate, the Ebola crisis in West Africa was claiming lives daily. Families were being devastated. Fear was rife. Forecasts suggested frightening losses in the months ahead.

Today, thanks to collective action by communities and their governments and others all around the world, cases of Ebola have declined dramatically. The outbreak is not over, and we must remain vigilant. But the response is working, with lessons pointing to a safer future for all.

When we stand together, there is no limit to what we can achieve.

Three days ago, young people from many nations stood together in the balcony of this Hall. They asked for one thing above all: change.

There is nothing we can say to the world's children that can convince them the world needs to be the way it is.

That means we must do everything we can to close the gap between the world as it is and the world as it should be. That is the mission of the United Nations.

Let's work together to make this world better for all, where everybody can live with dignity and prosperity.

I thank you for your leadership.

3
Rethinking Criminal Justice

Official White House Photo by Pete Souza

President Barack Obama delivers remarks at the NAACP Convention in Philadelphia, Pennsylvania, July 14, 2015.

Hard Truths: Law Enforcement and Race

By James Comey

In this speech at Georgetown University, FBI Director James Comey addresses the rising tensions around law enforcement particularly in communities of color, pointing out that there is much more to this issue than discriminatory policing practices. In order to move past the surface of this discussion, Comey says, we have to acknowledge some "hard truths." These hard truths include not only the troubled past of law enforcement carrying out racist laws of the land under slavery but also the role of unconscious bias in the present day which, Comey asserts, is no more common among police than the rest of the country. In proposing a solution, he suggests that our country needs to fix the deep structural inequities that disproportionately affect communities of color and lead to higher crime rates, which then exacerbate police bias. Comey suggests that only by addressing the hard truths of greater social inequities—not simply by blaming racist police—can we begin to fix the problems plaguing criminal justice in this country. James B. Comey was sworn in as the seventh Director of the FBI on September 4, 2013. Comey served as an assistant United States attorney for both the Southern District of New York and the Eastern District of Virginia and also served as the U.S. attorney for the Southern District of New York before becoming the deputy attorney general at the Department of Justice in 2003.

Thank you, President DeGioia. And good morning, ladies and gentlemen. Thank you for inviting me to Georgetown University. I am honored to be here. I wanted to meet with you today, as President DeGioia said, to share my thoughts on the relationship between law enforcement and the diverse communities we serve and protect. Like a lot of things in life, that relationship is complicated. Relationships often are.

Beautiful Healy Hall—part of, and all around where we sit now—was named after this great university's twenty-ninth President, Patrick Francis Healy. Healy was born into slavery, in Georgia, in 1834. His father was an Irish immigrant plantation owner and his mother, a slave. Under the laws of that time, Healy and his siblings were considered to be slaves. Healy is believed to be the first African-American to earn a Ph.D., the first to enter the Jesuit order, and the first to be president of Georgetown University or any predominantly white university.

Given Georgetown's remarkable history, and that of President Healy, this struck me as an appropriate place to talk about the difficult relationship between law enforcement and the communities we are sworn to serve and protect.

Delivered February 12, 2015, at Georgetown University, Washington, D.C., by James Comey.

With the death of Michael Brown in Ferguson, the death of Eric Garner in Staten Island, the ongoing protests throughout the country, and the assassinations of NYPD Officers Wenjian Liu and Rafael Ramos, we are at a crossroads. As a society, we can choose to live our everyday lives, raising our families and going to work, hoping that someone, somewhere, will do something to ease the tension—to smooth over the conflict. We can roll up our car windows, turn up the radio and drive around these problems, or we can choose to have an open and honest discussion about what our relationship is today—what it should be, what it could be, and what it needs to be—if we took more time to better understand one another.

Current Issues Facing Law Enforcement

Unfortunately, in places like Ferguson and New York City, and in some communities across this nation, there is a disconnect between police agencies and many citizens—predominantly in communities of color.

Serious debates are taking place about how law enforcement personnel relate to the communities they serve, about the appropriate use of force, and about real and perceived biases, both within and outside of law enforcement. These are important debates. Every American should feel free to express an informed opinion—to protest peacefully, to convey frustration and even anger in a constructive way. That's what makes our democracy great. Those conversations—as bumpy and uncomfortable as they can be—help us understand different perspectives, and better serve our communities. Of course, these are only conversations in the true sense of that word if we are willing not only to talk, but to listen, too.

I worry that this incredibly important and incredibly difficult conversation about race and policing has become focused entirely on the nature and character of law enforcement officers, when it should also be about something much harder to discuss. Debating the nature of policing is very important, but I worry that it has become an excuse, at times, to avoid doing something harder.

The Hard Truths

Let me start by sharing some of my own hard truths.

First, all of us in law enforcement must be honest enough to acknowledge that much of our history is not pretty. At many points in American history, law enforcement enforced the status quo, a status quo that was often brutally unfair to disfavored groups. It was unfair to the Healy siblings and to countless others like them. It was unfair to too many people.

I am descended from Irish immigrants. A century ago, the Irish knew well how American society—and law enforcement—viewed them: as drunks, ruffians, and criminals. Law enforcement's biased view of the Irish lives on in the nickname we still use for the vehicles we use to transport groups of prisoners. It is, after all, the "paddy wagon."

The Irish had tough times, but little compares to the experience on our soil of black Americans. That experience should be part of every American's consciousness, and law enforcement's role in that experience—including in recent times—must be remembered. It is our cultural inheritance.

There is a reason that I require all new agents and analysts to study the FBI's interaction with Dr. Martin Luther King, Jr., and to visit his memorial in Washington as part of their training. And there is a reason I keep on my desk a copy of Attorney General Robert Kennedy's approval of J. Edgar Hoover's request to wiretap Dr. King. It is a single page. The entire application is five sentences long, it is without fact or substance, and is predicated on the naked assertion that there is "communist influence in the racial situation." The reason I do those things is to ensure that we remember our mistakes and that we learn from them.

One reason we cannot forget our law enforcement legacy is that the people we serve and protect cannot forget it, either. So we must talk about our history. It is a hard truth that lives on.

A second hard truth: Much research points to the widespread existence of unconscious bias. Many people in our white-majority culture have unconscious racial biases and react differently to a white face than a black face. In fact, we all, white and black, carry various biases around with us. I am reminded of the song from the Broadway hit, *Avenue Q*: "Everyone's a Little Bit Racist." Part of it goes like this:

Look around and you will find
No one's really color blind.
Maybe it's a fact
We all should face
Everyone makes judgments
Based on race.

You should be grateful I did not try to sing that.

But if we can't help our latent biases, we can help our behavior in response to those instinctive reactions, which is why we work to design systems and processes that overcome that very human part of us all. Although the research may be unsettling, it is what we do next that matters most.

But racial bias isn't epidemic in law enforcement any more than it is epidemic in academia or the arts. In fact, I believe law enforcement overwhelmingly attracts people who want to do good for a living—people who risk their lives because they want to help other people. They don't sign up to be cops in New York or Chicago or L.A. to help white people or black people or Hispanic people or Asian people. They sign up because they want to help all people. And they do some of the hardest, most dangerous policing to protect people of color.

But that leads me to my third hard truth: something happens to people in law enforcement. Many of us develop different flavors of cynicism that we work hard to resist because they can be lazy mental shortcuts. For example, criminal suspects routinely lie about their guilt, and nearly everybody we charge is guilty. That makes it easy for some folks in law enforcement to assume that everybody is lying and that no suspect, regardless of their race, could be innocent. Easy, but wrong.

Likewise, police officers on patrol in our nation's cities often work in environments where a hugely disproportionate percentage of street crime is committed by young men of color. Something happens to people of good will working in that environment. After years of police work, officers often can't help but be influenced by the cynicism they feel.

A mental shortcut becomes almost irresistible and maybe even rational by some lights. The two young black men on one side of the street look like so many others the officer has locked up. Two white men on the other side of the street—even in the same clothes—do not. The officer does not make the same association about the two white guys, whether that officer is white or black. And that drives different behavior. The officer turns toward one side of the street and not the other. We need to come to grips with the fact that this behavior complicates the relationship between police and the communities they serve.

So why has that officer—like his colleagues—locked up so many young men of color? Why does he have that life-shaping experience? Is it because he is a racist? Why are so many black men in jail? Is it because cops, prosecutors, judges, and juries are racist? Because they are turning a blind eye to white robbers and drug dealers?

The answer is a fourth hard truth: I don't think so. If it were so, that would be easier to address. We would just need to change the way we hire, train, and measure law enforcement and that would substantially fix it. We would then go get those white criminals we have been ignoring. But the truth is significantly harder than that.

The truth is that what really needs fixing is something only a few, like President Obama, are willing to speak about, perhaps because it is so daunting a task. Through the "My Brother's Keeper" initiative, the President is addressing the disproportionate challenges faced by young men of color. For instance, data shows that the percentage of young men not working or not enrolled in school is nearly twice as high for blacks as it is for whites. This initiative, and others like it, is about doing the hard work to grow drug-resistant and violence-resistant kids, especially in communities of color, so they never become part of that officer's life experience.

So many young men of color become part of that officer's life experience because so many minority families and communities are struggling, so many boys and young men grow up in environments lacking role models, adequate education, and decent employment—they lack all sorts of opportunities that most of us take for granted. A tragedy of American life—one that most citizens are able to drive around because it doesn't touch them—is that young people in "those neighborhoods" too often inherit a legacy of crime and prison. And with that inheritance, they become part of a police officer's life, and shape the way that officer—whether white or black—sees the world. Changing that legacy is a challenge so enormous and so complicated that it is, unfortunately, easier to talk only about the cops. And that's not fair.

Let me be transparent about my affection for cops. When you dial 911, whether you are white or black, the cops come, and they come quickly, and they come quickly whether they are white or black. That's what cops do, in addition to all of the other hard and difficult and dangerous and frightening things that they do. They respond to homes in the middle of the night where a drunken father, wielding a gun, is threatening his wife and children. They pound up the back stairs of an apartment building, not knowing whether the guys behind the door they are about to enter are armed, or high, or both.

I come from a law enforcement family. My grandfather, William J. Comey, was a police officer. Pop Comey is one of my heroes. I have a picture of him on my wall in my office at the FBI, reminding me of the legacy I've inherited and that I must honor.

He was the child of immigrants. When he was in the sixth grade, his father was killed in an industrial accident in New York. Because he was the oldest, he had to drop out of school so that he could go to work to support his mom and younger siblings. He could never afford to return to school, but when he was old enough, he joined the Yonkers, New York, Police Department.

Over the next 40 years, he rose to lead that department. Pop was the tall, strong, silent type, quiet and dignified, and passionate about the rule of law. Back during Prohibition, he heard that bootleggers were running beer through fire hoses between Yonkers and the Bronx.

Now, Pop enjoyed a good beer every now and again, but he ordered his men to cut those hoses with fire axes. Pop had to have a protective detail, because certain people were angry and shocked that someone in law enforcement would do that. But that's what we want as citizens—that's what we expect. And so I keep that picture of Pop on my office wall to remind me of his integrity, and his pride in the integrity of his work.

Law enforcement ranks are filled with people like my grandfather. But, to be clear, although I am from a law enforcement family, and have spent much of my career in law enforcement, I'm not looking to let law enforcement off the hook. Those of us in law enforcement must redouble our efforts to resist bias and prejudice. We must better understand the people we serve and protect—by trying to know, deep in our gut, what it feels like to be a law-abiding young black man walking on the street and encountering law enforcement. We must understand how that young man may see us. We must resist the lazy shortcuts of cynicism and approach him with respect and decency.

We must work—in the words of New York City Police Commissioner Bill Bratton—to really see each other. Perhaps the reason we struggle as a nation is because we've come to see only what we represent, at face value, instead of who we are. We simply must see the people we serve.

But the "seeing" needs to flow in both directions. Citizens also need to really see the men and women of law enforcement. They need to see what police see through the windshields of their squad cars, or as they walk down the street. They need to see the risks and dangers law enforcement officers encounter on a typical late-night shift. They need to understand the difficult and frightening work they do to keep us safe. They need to give them the space and respect to do their work, well and properly.

If they take the time to do that, what they will see are officers who are human, who are overwhelmingly doing the right thing for the right reasons, and who are too often operating in communities—and facing challenges—most of us choose to drive around.

One of the hardest things I do as FBI Director is call the chiefs and sheriffs in departments around the nation when officers have been killed in the line of duty. I call to express my sorrow and offer the FBI's help. Officers like Wenjian Liu and Rafael Ramos, two of NYPD's finest who were gunned down by a madman who thought his ambush would avenge the deaths of Michael Brown and Eric Garner. I make far too many calls. And there are far too many names of fallen officers on the National Law Enforcement Officers Memorial and far too many names etched there each year.

Officers Liu and Ramos swore the same oath all in law enforcement do, and they answered the call to serve the people, all people. Like all good police officers, they moved toward danger, without regard for the politics or passions or race of those who needed their help—knowing the risks inherent in their work. They were minority police officers, killed while standing watch in a minority neighborhood—Bedford-Stuyvesant—one they and their fellow officers had rescued from the grip of violent crime.

Twenty years ago, Bed-Stuy was shorthand for a kind of chaos and disorder in which good people had no freedom to walk, shop, play, or just sit on the front steps and talk. It was too dangerous. But today, no more, thanks to the work of those who chose lives of service and danger to help others.

But despite this selfless service—of these two officers and countless others like them across the country—in some American communities, people view the police not as allies, but as antagonists, and think of them not with respect or gratitude, but with suspicion and distrust.

We simply must find ways to see each other more clearly. And part of that has to involve collecting and sharing better information about encounters between police and citizens, especially violent encounters.

Not long after riots broke out in Ferguson late last summer, I asked my staff to tell me how many people shot by police were African-American in this country. I wanted to see trends. I wanted to see information. They couldn't give it to me, and it wasn't their fault. Demographic data regarding officer-involved shootings is not consistently reported to us through our Uniform Crime Reporting Program. Because reporting is voluntary, our data is incomplete and therefore, in the aggregate, unreliable.

I recently listened to a thoughtful big city police chief express his frustration with that lack of reliable data. He said he didn't know whether the Ferguson police shot one person a week, one a year, or one a century, and that in the absence of good data, "all we get are ideological thunderbolts, when what we need are ideological agnostics who use information to try to solve problems." He's right.

The first step to understanding what is really going on in our communities and in our country is to gather more and better data related to those we arrest, those we confront for breaking the law and jeopardizing public safety, and those who confront us. "Data" seems a dry and boring word but, without it, we cannot understand our world and make it better.

How can we address concerns about "use of force," how can we address concerns about officer-involved shootings if we do not have a reliable grasp on the demographics and circumstances of those incidents? We simply must improve the way we collect and analyze data to see the true nature of what's happening in all of our communities.

The FBI tracks and publishes the number of "justifiable homicides" reported by police departments. But, again, reporting by police departments is voluntary and not all departments participate. That means we cannot fully track the number of incidents in which force is used by police, or against police, including nonfatal encounters, which are not reported at all.

Without complete and accurate data, we are left with "ideological thunderbolts." And that helps spark unrest and distrust and does not help us get better. Because we must get better, I intend for the FBI to be a leader in urging departments around this country to give us the facts we need for an informed discussion, the facts all of us need, to help us make sound policy and sound decisions with that information.

* * *

America isn't easy. America takes work. Today, February 12, is Abraham Lincoln's birthday. He spoke at Gettysburg about a "new birth of freedom" because we spent the first four score and seven years of our history with fellow Americans held as slaves—President Healy, his siblings, and his mother among them. We have spent the 150 years since Lincoln spoke making great progress, but along the way treating a whole lot of people of color poorly. And law enforcement was often part of that poor treatment. That's our inheritance as law enforcement and it is not all in the distant past.

We must account for that inheritance. And we—especially those of us who enjoy the privilege that comes with being the majority—must confront the biases that are inescapable parts of the human condition. We must speak the truth about our shortcomings as law enforcement, and fight to be better. But as a country, we must also speak the truth to ourselves. Law enforcement is not the root cause of problems in our hardest hit neighborhoods. Police officers—people of enormous courage and integrity, in the main—are in those neighborhoods, risking their lives, to protect folks from offenders who are the product of problems that will not be solved by body cameras.

We simply must speak to each other honestly about all these hard truths.

In the words of Dr. King, "We must learn to live together as brothers or we will all perish together as fools."

We all have work to do—hard work, challenging work—and it will take time. We all need to talk and we all need to listen, not just about easy things, but about hard things, too. Relationships are hard. Relationships require work. So let's begin that work. It is time to start seeing one another for who and what we really are.

Peace, security, and understanding are worth the effort. Thank you for listening to me today.

Reforming Criminal Justice

By Hillary Clinton

Hillary Clinton delivers a speech about the broken state of the U.S. criminal justice system and suggests that the time to repair it is now. Naming several unarmed African Americans who have been killed in recent years by police, Clinton acknowledges a glaring problem but proceeds to speak hopefully about how both Republicans and Democrats are beginning to work "across the aisle" to remedy the situation. Clinton acknowledges the good police work being done without resorting to unnecessary force but says that officials will need to be diligent in following this lead in order to restore the public's trust in law enforcement. Citing Obama's task force on policing as a step in right direction, Clinton advocates for increasing the use of police body cameras across the country, but she also endorses working in communities in order to prevent crime. She notes the startling statistic that the United States makes up only "5 percent of the world's population, yet we have almost 25 percent of the world's total prison population"—and that most of those incarcerated are low-level offenders. She goes on to discuss the social and economics implications of having so much of the population imprisoned but remains optimistic about restoring the balance and improving many social problems in the country as a result. Former First Lady, U.S. Senator for New York, and Secretary of State, Hillary Clinton, as of the publication of this book, is, for the second time, running for the office of President of the United States.

Thank you so much. I am absolutely delighted to be back here at Columbia. I want to thank President Bollinger, Dean Janow, and everyone at the School of International and Public Affairs. It is a special treat to be here with and on behalf of a great leader of this city and our country, David Dinkins. He has made such an indelible impact on New York, and I had the great privilege of working with him as First Lady and then, of course, as a new senator.

When I was just starting out as a senator, David's door was always open. He and his wonderful wife Joyce were great friends and supporters and good sounding boards about ideas that we wanted to consider to enhance the quality of life and the opportunities for the people of this city. I was pleased to address the Dinkins Leadership and Public Policy Forum in my first year as a senator, and I so appreciated then as I have in the years since David's generosity with his time and most of all his wisdom. So 14 years later, I'm honored to have this chance, once again, to help celebrate the legacy of one of New York's greatest public servants.

Delivered April 29, 2015, at Columbia University, New York, New York, by Hillary Clinton.

I'm pleased too that you will have the opportunity after my remarks to hear from such a distinguished panel, to go into more detail about some of the issues that we face. I also know that Manhattan Borough President Gale Brewer is here, along with other local and community leaders.

Because surely this is a time when our collective efforts to devise approaches to the problems that still afflict us [are] more important than ever. Indeed, it is a time for wisdom.

For yet again, the family of a young black man is grieving a life cut short.

Yet again, the streets of an American city are marred by violence. By shattered glass and shouts of anger and shows of force.

Yet again a community is reeling, its fault lines laid bare and its bonds of trust and respect frayed.

Yet again, brave police officers have been attacked in the line of duty.

What we've seen in Baltimore should, indeed does, tear at our soul.

And, from Ferguson to Staten Island to Baltimore, the patterns have become unmistakable and undeniable.

Walter Scott shot in the back in Charleston, South Carolina. Unarmed. In debt. And terrified of spending more time in jail for child support payments he couldn't afford.

Tamir Rice shot in a park in Cleveland, Ohio. Unarmed and just 12 years old.

Eric Garner choked to death after being stopped for selling cigarettes on the streets of this city.

And now Freddie Gray. His spine nearly severed while in police custody.

Not only as a mother and a grandmother but as a citizen, a human being, my heart breaks for these young men and their families.

We have to come to terms with some hard truths about race and justice in America.

There is something profoundly wrong when African American men are still far more likely to be stopped and searched by police, charged with crimes, and sentenced to longer prison terms than are meted out to their white counterparts.

There is something wrong when a third of all black men face the prospect of prison during their lifetimes. And an estimated 1.5 million black men are "missing" from their families and communities because of incarceration and premature death.

There is something wrong when more than one out of every three young black men in Baltimore can't find a job.

There is something wrong when trust between law enforcement and the communities they serve breaks down as far as it has in many of our communities.

We have allowed our criminal justice system to get out of balance. And these recent tragedies should galvanize us to come together as a nation to find our balance again.

We should begin by heeding the pleas of Freddie Gray's family for peace and unity, echoing the families of Michael Brown, Trayvon Martin, and others in the past years.

Those who are instigating further violence in Baltimore are disrespecting the Gray family and the entire community. They are compounding the tragedy of Freddie Gray's death and setting back the cause of justice. So the violence has to stop.

But more broadly, let's remember that everyone in every community benefits when there is respect *for* the law and when everyone in every community is respected *by* the law. That is what we have to work toward in Baltimore and across our country.

We must urgently begin to rebuild the bonds of trust and respect among Americans. Between police and citizens, yes, but also across society.

Restoring trust in our politics, our press, our markets. Between and among neighbors and even people with whom we disagree politically.

This is so fundamental to who we are as a nation and everything we want to achieve together.

It truly is about how we treat each other and what we value. Making it possible for every American to reach his or her God-given potential—regardless of who you are, where you were born, or who you love.

The inequities that persist in our justice system undermine this shared vision of what America can be and should be.

I learned this firsthand as a young attorney just out of law school—at one of those law schools that will remain nameless here at Columbia. One of my earliest jobs for the Children's Defense Fund, which David had mentioned—I was so fortunate to work with Marian Wright Edelman as a young lawyer and then serving on the board of the Children's Defense Fund—was studying the problem then of youth, teenagers, sometimes preteens, incarcerated in adult jails. Then, as director of the University of Arkansas School of Law's legal aid clinic, I advocated on behalf of prison inmates and poor families.

I saw repeatedly how our legal system can be and all too often is stacked against those who have the least power, who are the most vulnerable.

I saw how families could be and were torn apart by excessive incarceration. I saw the toll on children growing up in homes shattered by poverty and prison.

So, unfortunately, I know these are not new challenges by any means.

In fact they have become even more complex and urgent over time. And today they demand fresh thinking and bold action from all of us.

Today there seems to be a growing bipartisan movement for commonsense reforms in our criminal justice systems. Senators as disparate on the political spectrum as Cory Booker and Rand Paul and Dick Durbin and Mike Lee are reaching across the aisle to find ways to work together. It is rare to see Democrats and Republicans agree on anything today. But we're beginning to agreeing on this: We need to restore balance to our criminal justice system.

Now, of course, it is not enough just to agree and give speeches about it—we actually have to work together to get the job done.

We need to deliver real reforms that can be felt on our streets, in our courthouses, and our jails and prisons, in communities too long neglected.

Let me touch on two areas in particular where I believe we need to push for more progress.

First, we need smart strategies to fight crime that help restore trust between law enforcement and our communities, especially communities of color.

There's a lot of good work to build on. Across the country, there are so many police officers out there every day inspiring trust and confidence, honorably doing their duty, putting themselves on the line to save lives. There are police departments already deploying creative and effective strategies, demonstrating how we can protect the public without resorting to unnecessary force. We need to learn from those examples, build on what works.

We can start by making sure that federal funds for state and local law enforcement are used to bolster best practices, rather than to buy weapons of war that have no place on our streets.

President Obama's task force on policing gives us a good place to start. Its recommendations offer a roadmap for reform, from training to technology, guided by more and better data.

We should make sure every police department in the country has body cameras to record interactions between officers on patrol and suspects.

That will improve transparency and accountability, it will help protect good people on both sides of the lens. For every tragedy caught on tape, there surely have been many more that remained invisible. Not every problem can be or will be prevented with cameras, but this is a commonsense step we should take.

The president has provided the idea of matching funds to state and local governments investing in body cameras. We should go even further and make this the norm everywhere.

And we should listen to law enforcement leaders who are calling for a renewed focus on working with communities to prevent crime, rather than measuring success just by the number of arrests or convictions.

As your senator from New York, I supported a greater emphasis on community policing, along with putting more officers on the street to get to know those communities.

David Dinkins was an early pioneer of this policy. His leadership helped lay the foundation for dramatic drops in crime in the years that followed.

And today smart policing in communities that builds relationships, partnerships, and trust makes more sense than ever.

And it shouldn't be limited just to officers on the beat. It's an ethic that should extend throughout our criminal justice system. To prosecutors and parole officers. To judges and lawmakers.

We all share a responsibility to help re-stitch the fabric of our neighborhoods and communities.

We also have to be honest about the gaps that exist across our country, the inequality that stalks our streets. Because you cannot talk about smart policing and reforming the criminal justice system if you also don't talk about what's needed to provide economic opportunity, better educational chances for young people, more support to families so they can do the best jobs they are capable of doing to help support their own children.

Today I saw anarticleon the front page of *USA Today* that really struck me, written by a journalist who lives in Baltimore. And here's what I read three times to make sure I was reading correctly:

> "At a conference in 2013 at Johns Hopkins University, Vice Provost Jonathan Bagger pointed out that only six miles separate the Baltimore neighborhoods of Roland Park and Hollins Market. But there is a 20-year difference in the average life expectancy."

We have learned in the last few years that life expectancy, which is a measure of the quality of life in communities and countries, manifests the same inequality that we see in so many other parts of our society.

Women—white women without high school education—are losing life expectancy. Black men and black women are seeing their life expectancy go down in so many parts of our country.

This may not grab headlines, although I was glad to see it on the front page of *USA Today*. But it tells us more than I think we can bear about what we are up against.

We need to start understanding how important it is to care for every single child as though that child were our own.

David and I started our conversation this morning talking about our grandchildren; now his are considerably older than mine. But it was not just two longtime friends catching up with each other. It was so clearly sharing what is most important to us, as it is to families everywhere in our country.

So I don't want the discussion about criminal justice, smart policing, to be siloed and to permit discussions and arguments and debates about it to only talk about that. The conversation needs to be much broader. Because that is a symptom, not a cause, of what ails us today.

The second area where we need to chart a new course is how we approach punishment and prison.

It's a stark fact that the United States has less than 5 percent of the world's population, yet we have almost 25 percent of the world's total prison population. The numbers today are much higher than they were 30, 40 years ago, despite the fact that crime is at historic lows.

Of the more than 2 million Americans incarcerated today, a significant percentage are low-level offenders: people held for violating parole or minor drug crimes, or who are simply awaiting trial in backlogged courts.

Keeping them behind bars does little to reduce crime. But it is does a lot to tear apart families and communities.

One in every 28 children now has a parent in prison. Think about what that means for those children.

When we talk about one and a half million missing African American men, we're talking about missing husbands, missing fathers, missing brothers.

They're not there to look after their children or bring home a paycheck. And the consequences are profound.

Without the mass incarceration that we currently practice, millions fewer people would be living in poverty.

And it's not just families trying to stay afloat with one parent behind bars. Of the 600,000 prisoners who reenter society each year, roughly 60 percent face long-term unemployment.

And for all this, taxpayers are paying about $80 billion a year to keep so many people in prison.

The price of incarcerating a single inmate is often more than $30,000 per year—and up to $60,000 in some states. That's the salary of a teacher or police officer.

One year in a New Jersey state prison costs $44,000—more than the annual tuition at Princeton.

If the United States brought our correctional expenditures back in line with where they were several decades ago, we'd save an estimated $28 billion a year. And I believe we would not be less safe. You can pay a lot of police officers and nurses and others with $28 billion to help us deal with the pipeline issues.

It's time to change our approach. It's time to end the era of mass incarceration. We need a true national debate about how to reduce our prison population while keeping our communities safe.

I don't know all the answers. That's why I'm here—to ask all the smart people in Columbia and New York to start thinking this through with me. I know we should work together to pursue alternative punishments for low-level offenders. They do have to be in some way registered in the criminal justice system, but we don't want that to be a fast track to long-term criminal activity; we don't want to create another "incarceration generation."

I've been encouraged to see changes that I supported as Senator to reduce the unjust federal sentencing disparity between crack and powder cocaine crimes finally become law.

And last year, the Sentencing Commission reduced recommended prison terms for some drug crimes.

President Obama and former Attorney General Holder have led the way with important additional steps. And I am looking forward to our new Attorney General, Loretta Lynch, carrying this work forward.

There are other measures that I and so many others have championed to reform arbitrary mandatory minimum sentences [that] are long overdue.

We also need probation and drug diversion programs to deal swiftly with violations, while allowing low-level offenders who stay clean and stay out of trouble to stay out of prison. I've seen the positive effects of specialized drug courts and juvenile programs work to the betterment of individuals and communities. And please, please, let us put mental health back at the top of our national agenda.

You and I know that the promise of de-institutionalizing those in mental health facilities was supposed to be followed by the creation of community-based treatment centers. Well, we got half of that equation—but not the other half. Our prisons and our jails are now our mental health institutions.

I have to tell you I was somewhat surprised in both Iowa and New Hampshire to be asked so many questions about mental health. "What are we going to do with people who need help for substance abuse or mental illness?" "What are we going to do when the remaining facilities are being shut down for budget reasons?" "What are we going to do when hospitals don't really get reimbursed for providing the kind of emergency care that is needed for mental health patients?"

It's not just a problem in our cities. There's a quiet epidemic of substance abuse sweeping small-town and rural America as well. We have to do more and finally get serious about treatment.

I'll be talking about all of this in the months to come, offering new solutions to protect and strengthen our families and communities.

I know in a time when we're afflicted by short-termism, we're not looking over the horizon for the investments that we need to make in our fellow citizens, in our children. So I'm well aware that progress will not be easy, despite the emerging bipartisan consensus for certain reforms. And that we will have to overcome deep divisions and try to begin to replenish our depleted reservoirs of trust.

But I am convinced, as thecongenitaloptimist I must be to live my life, that we can rise to this challenge. We can heal our wounds. Wecan restore balance to our justice system and respect in our communities. And we can make sure that we take actions that are going to make a difference in the lives of those who for too long have been marginalized and forgotten.

Let's protect the rights of all our people. Let's take on the broader inequities in our society. You can't separate out the unrest we see in the streets from the cycles of poverty and despair that hollow out those neighborhoods.

Despite all the progress we've made in this country lifting people up—and it has been extraordinary—too many of our fellow citizens are still left out.

Twenty-five years ago, in his inaugural address as mayor, David Dinkins warned of leaving "too many lost amidst the wealth and grandeur that surrounds us."

Today, his words and the emotion behind them ring truer than ever. You don't have to look too far from this magnificent hall to find children still living in poverty or trapped in failing schools. Families who work hard but can't afford the rising prices in their neighborhood.

Mothers and fathers who fear for their sons' safety when they go off to school—or just to go buy a pack of Skittles.

These challenges are all woven together. And they all must be tackled together.

Our goal must truly be inclusive and lasting prosperity that's measured by how many families get ahead and stay ahead. . .

How many children climb out of poverty and stay out of prison. . .

How many young people can go to college without breaking the bank. . .

How many new immigrants can start small businesses. . .

How many parents can get good jobs that allow them to balance the demands of work and family.

That's how we should measure prosperity. With all due respect, that is a far better measurement than the size of the bonuses handed out in downtown office buildings.

Now even in the most painful times like those we are seeing in Baltimore. . .

When parents fear for their children. . .

When smoke fills the skies above our cities. . .

When police officers are assaulted. . .

Even then—especially then—let's remember the aspirations and values that unite us all: That every person should have the opportunity to succeed. That no one is disposable. That every life matters.

So yes, Mayor Dinkins. This is a time for wisdom.

A time for honesty about race and justice in America.

And, yes, a time for reform.

David Dinkins is a leader we can look to. We know what he stood for. Let us take the challenge and example he presents and think about what we must do to make sure that this country we love—this city we live in—are both good and great.

And please join me in saying a prayer for the family of Freddie Gray, and all the men whose names we know and those we don't who have lost their lives unnecessarily and tragically. And in particular today, include in that prayer the people of Baltimore and our beloved country.

Thank you all very much.

Criminal Justice Reform

By Barack Obama

In an address to the National Association for the Advancement of Colored People (NAACP), President Barack Obama addresses the need to reform the criminal justice system. Echoing some of the same ideas as Hillary Clinton in the preceding speech, Obama goes further to make a distinction between those who are rightfully imprisoned—such as murderers, rapists, and predators—and those lower level offenders for whom imprisonment or the length of sentences ought to be reconsidered. Considering not only both ethics and economics, Obama notes the high public cost of incarceration—$80 billion a year—and the harder to quantify cost to affected communities and society as a whole. Arguing that some money currently invested in criminal punishment ought to be redirected to such preventative measures as early education, Obama identifies three sites for reform: the community, the courtroom, and the cell block. Barack Obama is the forty-fourth president of the United States, having been elected to office in 2008 and reelected in 2012.

THE PRESIDENT: Hello, NAACP! (Applause.) Ah, it's good to be back. (Applause.) How you all doing today? (Applause.) You doing fine?

AUDIENCE: Yes!

THE PRESIDENT: You look fine. (Applause.) All right, everybody have a seat. I got some stuff to say. (Applause.) I've got some stuff to say.

AUDIENCE MEMBER: We love you!

THE PRESIDENT: I love you back. You know that. (Applause.)

So, see, now, whenever people have, like, little signs, you all got to write it bigger, because I'm getting old now. (Laughter.) And I like that picture of me. That's very nice. Thank you. (Applause.)

Let's get something out of the way up front. I am not singing today.

AUDIENCE: Awww—

Delivered July 14, 2015, at the NAACP Conference, Pennsylvania Convention Center, Philadelphia, Pennsylvania, by Barack Obama.

THE PRESIDENT: Not singing. Although I will say your board sang to me as I came in for the photograph. (Laughter.) So I know there's some good voices in the auditorium.

Let me also say what everybody knows but doesn't always want to say out loud—you all would rather have Michelle here. (Laughter.) I understand. I don't blame you. But I will do my best to fill her shoes. (Laughter.) And she sends everybody her love. And Malia and Sasha say hi, as well. (Applause.)

I want to thank your chair, Roslyn Brock. I want to thank your president, Cornell Brooks. I want to thank your Governor, Tom Wolf, who's doing outstanding work and was here. (Applause.) The Mayor of Philadelphia, Michael Nutter, who's been a great friend and ally. (Applause.) Governor Dan Malloy of Connecticut, who's here today. (Applause.) And some outstanding members of Congress who are here. I want to just say thank you to all of you for your love, for your support, but most importantly, for the work that you are doing in your communities all across the country every single day. (Applause.)

It's not always received with a lot of fanfare. Sometimes it's lonely work; sometimes it's hard work; sometimes it's frustrating work. But it's necessary work. And it builds on a tradition of this organization that reshaped the nation.

For 106 years, the NAACP has worked to close the gaps between the words of our founding that we are all created equal, endowed by our Creator with certain unalienable rights—those words try to match those with the realities that we live each and every day.

In your first century, this organization stood up to lynching and Jim Crow and segregation, helped to shepherd a Civil Rights Act and a Voting Rights Act. I would not be here, and so many others would not be here, without the NAACP. (Applause.)

In your second century, we've worked together to give more of our children a shot at a quality education, to help more families rise up out of poverty, to protect future generations from environmental damage, to create fair housing, to help more workers find the purpose of a good job. And together, we've made real progress—including a My Brother's Keeper initiative to give more young people a fair shot in life; including the passage of a law that declares health care is not a privilege for the few, but a right for all of us. (Applause.)

We made progress, but our work is not done. By just about every measure, the life chances for black and Hispanic youth still lag far behind those of their white peers. Our kids, America's children, so often are isolated, without hope, less likely to graduate from high school, less likely to earn a college degree, less likely to be employed, less likely to have health insurance, less likely to own a home.

Part of this is a legacy of hundreds of years of slavery and segregation, and structural inequalities that compounded over generations. (Applause.) It did not happen by accident. (Applause.) Partly it's a result of continuing, if sometimes more subtle, bigotry—whether in who gets called back for a job interview, or who gets suspended from school, or what neighborhood you are able to rent an apartment in—which, by the way, is why our recent initiative to strengthen the awareness and effectiveness of fair housing laws is so important. (Applause.) So we can't be satisfied or not satisfied until the opportunity gap is closed for everybody in America. Everybody. But today, I want to focus on one aspect of American life that remains particularly skewed by race and by wealth, a source of inequity that has ripple effects on families and on communities and ultimately on our nation—and that is our criminal justice system. (Applause.)

Now, this is not a new topic. I know sometimes folks discover these things like they just happened. There's a long history of inequity in the criminal justice system in America. When I was in the state legislature in Illinois, we worked to make sure that we had videotaping of interrogations because there were some problems there. We set up racial profiling laws to prevent the kind of bias in traffic stops that too many people experience. Since my first campaign, I've talked about how, in too many cases, our criminal justice system ends up being a pipeline from underfunded, inadequate schools to overcrowded jails. (Applause.)

What has changed, though, is that, in recent years the eyes of more Americans have been opened to this truth. Partly because of cameras, partly because of tragedy, partly because the statistics cannot be ignored; we can't close our eyes anymore. And the good news—and this is truly good news—is that good people of all political persuasions are starting to think we need to do something about this.

So let's look at the statistics. The United States is home to 5 percent of the world's population, but 25 percent of the world's prisoners. Think about that. Our incarceration rate is four times higher than China's. We keep more people behind bars than the top 35 European countries combined. And it hasn't always been the case—this huge explosion in incarceration rates. In 1980, there were 500,000 people behind bars in America—half a million people in 1980. I was in college in 1980. Many of you were not born in 1980—that's okay. (Laughter.) I remember 1980—500,000. Today there are 2.2 million. It has quadrupled since 1980. Our prison population has doubled in the last two decades alone.

Now, we need to be honest. There are a lot of folks who belong in prison. (Applause.) If we're going to deal with this problem and the inequities involved then we also have to speak honestly. There are some folks who need to be in jail. They may have had terrible things happen to them in their lives. We hold out the hope for redemption, but they've done some bad things. Murderers, predators, rapists, gang leaders, drug kingpins—we need some of those folks behind bars. Our communities are safer, thanks to brave police officers and hardworking prosecutors who put those violent criminals in jail. (Applause.)

And the studies show that up to a certain point, tougher prosecutors and stiffer sentences for these violent offenders contributed to the decline in violent crime over the last few decades. Although the science also indicates that you get a point of diminishing returns. But it is important for us to recognize that violence in our communities is serious and that historically, in fact, the African American community oftentimes was under-policed rather than over-policed. Folks were very interested in containing the African American community so it couldn't leave segregated areas, but within those areas there wasn't enough police presence.

But here's the thing: Over the last few decades, we've also locked up more and more nonviolent drug offenders than ever before, for longer than ever before. (Applause.) And that is the real reason our prison population is so high. In far too many cases, the punishment simply does not fit the crime. (Applause.) If you're a low-level drug dealer, or you violate your parole, you owe some debt to society. You have to be held accountable and make amends. But you don't owe 20 years. You don't owe a life sentence. (Applause.) That's disproportionate to the price that should be paid.

And by the way, the taxpayers are picking up the tab for that price. (Applause.) Every year, we spend $80 billion to keep folks incarcerated—$80 billion. Now, just to put that in perspective, for $80 billion, we could have universal preschool for every 3-year-old and 4-year-old in America. (Applause.) That's what $80 billion buys. (Applause.) For $80 billion, we could double the salary of every high school teacher in America. (Applause.) For $80 billion, we could finance new roads and new bridges and new airports, job training programs, research and development. (Applause.) We're about to get in a big budget debate in Washington—what I couldn't do with $80 billion. (Laughter.) It's a lot of money. For what we spend to keep everyone locked up for one year, we could eliminate tuition at every single one of our public colleges and universities. (Applause.)

As Republican Senator and presidential candidate Rand Paul has said—(laughter)—no, and to his credit, he's been consistent on this issue—imprisoning large numbers of nonviolent drug offenders for long periods of time, "costs the taxpayers money, without making them any safer."

Roughly one-third of the Justice Department's budget now goes toward incarceration—one-third. And there are outstanding public servants at our Justice Department, starting with our outstanding Attorney General, Loretta Lynch—(applause)—and we've got some great prosecutors here today—and they do outstanding work—so many of them. But every dollar they have to spend keeping nonviolent drug offenders in prison is a dollar they can't spend going after drug kingpins, or tracking down terrorists, or hiring more police and giving them the resources that would allow them to do a more effective job community policing.

And then, of course, there are costs that can't be measured in dollars and cents. Because the statistics on who gets incarcerated show that by a wide margin, it disproportionately impacts communities of color. African Americans and Latinos make up 30 percent of our population; they make up 60 percent of our inmates. About one in every 35 African American men, one in every 88 Latino men is serving time right now. Among white men, that number is one in 214.

The bottom line is that in too many places, black boys and black men, Latino boys and Latino men experience being treated differently under the law. (Applause.)

And I want to be clear—this is not just anecdote. This is not just barbershop talk. A growing body of research shows that people of color are more likely to be stopped, frisked, questioned, charged, detained. African Americans are more likely to be arrested. They are more likely to be sentenced to more time for the same crime. (Applause.) And one of the consequences of this is around one million fathers are behind bars. Around one in nine African American kids has a parent in prison.

What is that doing to our communities? What's that doing to those children? Our nation is being robbed of men and women who could be workers and taxpayers, could be more actively involved in their children's lives, could be role models, could be community leaders, and right now they're locked up for a non-violent offense.

So our criminal justice system isn't as smart as it should be. It's not keeping us as safe as it should be. It is not as fair as it should be. Mass incarceration makes our country worse off, and we need to do something about it. (Applause.)

But here's the good news.

AUDIENCE MEMBER: All right, good news.

THE PRESIDENT: Good news. Don't get me preaching now. (Laughter.) I am feeling more hopeful today because even now, when, let's face it, it seems like Republicans and Democrats cannot agree on anything—(laughter)—a lot of them agree on this. In fact, today, back in Washington, Republican senators from Utah and Texas are joining Democratic senators from New Jersey and Rhode Island to talk about how Congress can pass meaningful criminal justice reform this year. (Applause.) That's good news. That is good news. Good news.

That doesn't happen very often. And it's not just senators. This is a cause that's bringing people in both houses of Congress together. It's created some unlikely bedfellows. You've got Van Jones and Newt Gingrich. (Laughter.) You've got Americans for Tax Reform and the ACLU. You've got the NAACP and the Koch brothers. (Laughter.) No, you've got to give them credit. You've got to call it like you see it. (Laughter.) There are states from Texas and South Carolina to California and Connecticut who have acted to reduce their prison populations over the last five years and seen their crime rates fall. (Applause.) That's good news.

My administration has taken steps on our own to reduce our federal prison population. So I signed a bill reducing the 100–1 sentencing disparity between crack and powder cocaine. (Applause.) I've commuted the sentences of dozens of people sentenced under old drug laws that we now recognize were unfair, and yesterday I announced that I'm commuting dozens more. (Applause.)

Under the leadership of Attorney General Eric Holder—now continued by Loretta Lynch—federal prosecutors got what he called "Smart on Crime," which is refocusing efforts on the worst offenders, pursuing mandatory minimum sentences 20 percent less often than they did the year before. The idea is you don't always have to charge the max. To be a good prosecutor, you need to be proportionate. And it turns out that we're solving just as many cases and there are just as many plea bargains, and it's working. It's just that we've eliminated some of the excess.

And recently, something extraordinary happened. For the first time in 40 years, America's crime rate and incarceration rate both went down at the same time. That happened last year. (Applause.)

So there's some momentum building for reform. There's evidence mounting for why we need reform. Now I want to spend the rest of my time just laying out some basic principles, some simple ideas for what reform should look like, because we're just at the beginning of this process and we need to make sure that we stay with it. And I'm going to focus on what happens in three places—in the community, in the courtroom, and in the cell block.

So I want to begin with the community because I believe crime is like any other epidemic -- the best time to stop it is before it even starts. (Applause.) And I'm going to go ahead and say what I've said a hundred times before or a thousand times before, and what you've heard me say before, if we make investments early in our children, we will reduce the need to incarcerate those kids. (Applause.)

So one study found that for every dollar we invest in pre-K, we save at least twice that down the road in reduced crime. Getting a teenager a job for the summer costs a fraction of what it costs to lock him up for 15 years. (Applause.) Investing in our communities makes sense. It saves taxpayer money if we are consistent about it, and if we recognize that every child deserves opportunity—not just some, not just our own. (Applause.)

What doesn't make sense is treating entire neighborhoods as little more than danger zones where we just surround them. We ask police to go in there and do the tough job of trying to contain the hopelessness when we are not willing to make the investments to help lift those communities out of hopelessness. (Applause.) That's not just a police problem; that's a societal problem. (Applause.)

Places like West Philly, or West Baltimore, or Ferguson, Missouri—they're part of America, too. They're not separate. (Applause.) They're part of America like anywhere else. The kids there are American kids, just like your kids and my kids. So we've got to make sure boys and girls in those communities are loved and cherished and supported and nurtured and invested in. (Applause.) And we have to have the same standards for those children as we have for our own children.

If you are a parent, you know that there are times where boys and girls are going to act out in school. And the question is, are we letting principals and parents deal with one set of kids and we call the police on another set of kids? That's not the right thing to do. (Applause.)

We've got to make sure our juvenile justice system remembers that kids are different. Don't just tag them as future criminals. Reach out to them as future citizens. (Applause.)

And even as we recognize that police officers do one of the toughest, bravest jobs around—(applause)—and as we do everything in our power to keep those police officers safe on the job—I've talked about this—we have to restore trust between our police and some of the communities where they serve. (Applause.) And a good place to start is making sure communities around the country adopt the recommendations from the task force I set up—that included law enforcement, but also included young people from New York and from Ferguson, and they were able to arrive at a consensus around things like better training, better data collection—to make sure that policing is more effective and more accountable, but is also more unbiased. (Applause.)

So these are steps in the community that will lead to fewer folks being arrested in the first place. Now, they won't eliminate crime entirely. There's going to be crime. That's why the second place we need to change is in the courtroom. (Applause.)

For nonviolent drug crimes, we need to lower long mandatory minimum sentences—or get rid of them entirely. (Applause.) Give judges some discretion around nonviolent crimes so that, potentially, we can steer a young person who has made a mistake in a better direction.

We should pass a sentencing reform bill through Congress this year. (Applause.) We need to ask prosecutors to use their discretion to seek the best punishment, the one that's going to be most effective, instead of just the longest punishment. We should invest in alternatives to prison, like drug courts and treatment and probation programs—(applause)—which ultimately can save taxpayers thousands of dollars per defendant each year.

Now, even if we're locking up fewer people, even if we are reforming sentencing guidelines, as I've said before, some criminals still deserve to go to jail. And as Republican Senator John Cornyn has reminded us, "virtually all of the people incarcerated in our prisons will eventually someday be released." And that's why the third place we need to reform is in the cell block.

So on Thursday, I will be the first sitting president to visit a federal prison. (Applause.) And I'm going to shine a spotlight on this issue, because while the people in our prisons have made some mistakes—and sometimes big mistakes—they are also Americans, and we have to make sure that as they do their time and pay back their debt to society that we are increasing the possibility that they can turn their lives around. (Applause.)

That doesn't mean that we will turn everybody's life around. That doesn't mean there aren't some hard cases. But it does mean that we want to be in a position in which if somebody in the midst of imprisonment recognizes the error of their ways, is in the process of reflecting about where they've been and where they should be going, we've got to make sure that they're in a position to make the turn.

And that's why we should not tolerate conditions in prison that have no place in any civilized country. (Applause.) We should not be tolerating overcrowding in prison. We should not be tolerating gang activity in prison. We should not be tolerating rape in prison. And we shouldn't be making jokes about it in our popular culture. That's no joke. These things are unacceptable. (Applause.)

What's more, I've asked my Attorney General to start a review of the overuse of solitary confinement across American prisons. (Applause.) The social science shows that an environment like that is often more likely to make inmates more alienated, more hostile, potentially more violent. Do we really think it makes sense to lock so many people alone in tiny cells for 23 hours a day, sometimes for months or even years at a time? That is not going to make us safer. That's not going to make us stronger. And if those individuals are ultimately released, how are they ever going to adapt? It's not smart.

Our prisons should be a place where we can train people for skills that can help them find a job, not train them to become more hardened criminals. (Applause.)

Look, I don't want to pretend like this is all easy. But some places are doing better than others. Montgomery County, Maryland, put a job training center inside the prison walls—(applause)—to give folks a head start in thinking about what might you do otherwise than committing crime. That's a good idea.

Here's another good idea—one with bipartisan support in Congress: Let's reward prisoners with reduced sentences if they complete programs that make them less likely to commit a repeat offense. (Applause.) Let's invest in innovative new approaches to link former prisoners with employers and help them stay on track. Let's follow the growing number of our states and cities and private companies who have decided to "Ban the Box" on job applications—(applause)—so that former prisoners who have done their time and are now trying to get straight with society have a decent shot in a job interview. (Applause.) And if folks have served their time, and they've reentered society, they should be able to vote. (Applause.)

Communities that give our young people every shot at success; courts that are tough but fair; prisons that recognize eventually the majority will be released and so seek to prepare these returning citizens to grab that second chance—that's where we need to build.

But I want to add this. We can't ask our police, or our prosecutors, or our prison guards, or our judges to bear the entire burden of containing and controlling problems that the rest of us are not facing up to and willing to do something about. (Applause.)

So, yes, we have to stand up to those who are determined to slash investments in our communities at any cost—cutting preschool programs, cutting job-training programs, cutting affordable housing programs, cutting community policing programs. That's shortsighted. Those investments make this country strong. (Applause.) We've got to invest in opportunity more than ever.

An African American man born roughly 25 years ago has just a one-in-two chance of being employed today. More than one in three African American children are growing up in poverty. When America's unemployment rate was 9.5 percent, when I first came into office, as it was going up, we properly recognized this is a crisis. Right now, the unemployment rate among African Americans is 9.5 percent. What should we call that? It is a crisis. And we have to be just as concerned about continuing to lift up job opportunities for these young people. (Applause.)

So today, I've been talking about the criminal justice system, but we have to recognize that it's not something we can view in isolation. Any system that allows us to turn a blind eye to hopelessness and despair, that's not a justice system, it is an injustice system. (Applause.) But that is an extension and a reflection of some broader decisions that we're making as a society. And that has to change. That has to change.

What the marchers on Washington knew, what the marchers in Selma knew, what folks like Julian Bond knew, what the marchers in this room still know, is that justice is not only the absence of oppression, it is the presence of opportunity. (Applause.) Justice is giving every child a shot at a great education no matter what zip code they're born into. Justice is giving everyone willing to work hard the chance at a good job with good wages, no matter what their name is, what their skin color is, where they live.

Fifty years after the Voting Rights Act, justice is protecting that right for every American. (Applause.) Justice is living up to the common creed that says, I am my brother's keeper and my sister's keeper. Justice is making sure every young person knows they are special and they are important and that their lives matter—not because they heard it in a hashtag, but because of the love they feel every single day—(applause)—not just love from their parents, not just love from their neighborhood, but love from police, love from politicians. (Applause.) Love from somebody who lives on the other side of the country, but says, that young person is still important to me. (Applause.) That's what justice is. (Applause.)

And in the American tradition and in the immigrant tradition of remaking ourselves, in the Christian tradition that says none of us is without sin and all of us need redemption, justice and redemption go hand in hand. (Applause.)

Right before I came out here, I met with four former prisoners, four ex-offenders. Two of them were African American, one of them was Latino, one of them was white. All of them had amazing stories. One of them dropped out of school when he was a young kid. Now he's making film about his experience in the prison system.

One of them served 10 years in prison, then got a job at Five Guys—which is a tasty burger—(laughter)—and they gave him an opportunity, and he rose up and became a general manager there, and now is doing anti-violence work here in the community. (Applause.)

One of them, the young Latino man, he came out of prison and was given an opportunity to get trained on green jobs that are helping the environment but also gave him a marketable skill. And he talked about how the way he's staying out of trouble is he just keeps on thinking about his two daughters. And I could relate to that, because you don't want to disappoint your daughters. (Applause.) You don't want to disappoint those baby girls. And so he says, I go to work and I come home, and I grab that little baby and get a kiss, and that's keeping me focused.

And then one of them, Jeff Copeland, was arrested six times before his thirty-eighth birthday. He was drinking, using drugs, racked up DUI after DUI, sentence after sentence. And he admits that the sentences he was getting for DUI weren't reflective of all the trouble he was causing, could have been worse. And Jeff spent so much time jogging in place in his cell that inmates nicknamed him "The Running Man." And he was literally going nowhere, running in place.

And then, somehow, Jeff started examining his life. And he said, "This isn't me." So he decided to hold himself accountable. He quit drinking. He went to AA. Met a recruiter from the re-entry program at the Community College of Philadelphia, enrolled in classes once he was released—made sure to show up every day. Graduated summa cum laude—(applause)—with a 3.95 GPA. And this fall he'll graduate from Temple University with a major in criminal justice and a minor in social work. (Applause.) And he volunteers helping former inmates get their lives back on track.

And "it's sort of a cliché," he says, "but we can do anything." (Applause.) And just two years ago, "The Running Man" ran his first marathon—because he's going somewhere now. (Applause.) "You never look at crossing the finishing line," he says of his journey, "you attack it by putting one mile after the other. It takes steps." It takes steps. That's true for individuals. It's true for our nation.

Sometimes I get in debates about how to think about progress or the lack of progress when it comes to issues of race and inequality in America. And there are times where people say, "Oh, the President, he's too optimistic." Or "he's not talking enough about how bad things are." Oh, let me tell you something, I see what happens. My heart breaks when I see families who are impacted. I spend time with those families and feel their grief. I see those young men on street corners and eventually in prisons, and I think to myself, they could be me; that the main difference between me and them is I had a more forgiving environment so that when I slipped up, when I made a mistake, I had a second chance. And they've got no margin for error. (Applause.)

I know—I know—how hard things are for a lot of folks. But I also know that it takes steps. And if we have the courage to take that first step, then we take a second step. And if we have the courage to take the second step then suddenly we've taken 10 steps. The next thing you know, you've taken 100 steps. And that's true not just for us as individuals, but that is true for us as a nation.

We are not perfect, but we have the capacity to be more perfect. Mile after mile, step after step. And they pile up one after the other and pretty soon that finish line starts getting into sight, and we are not where we were. We're in a better place because we had the courage to move forward. (Applause.) So we cannot ignore the problems that we have, but we can't stop running the race. (Applause.) That's how you win the race. That's how you fix a broken system. That's how you change a country.

The NAACP understands that. (Applause.) Think about the race that you have run. Think about the race ahead. If we keep taking steps toward a more perfect union, and close the gaps between who we are and who we want to be, America will move forward. There's nothing we can't do.

Thank you. God bless you. God bless the United States of America. (Applause.)

4
Surveillance and Privacy in the Digital Age

© Pete Marovich/epa/Corbis

U.S. Senator Rand Paul speaks to the media after addressing the Senate during a rare Sunday session focused on intelligence legislation, including reforms to the National Security Agency, hours before existing legislation was to expire, on Capitol Hill in Washington, DC, May 31, 2015.

The Price of Shame

By Monica Lewinsky

In this speech before an audience in Vancouver, Canada, Monica Lewinsky delivers a powerful message on the implications of public shaming in the digital age. She discusses how the sexual scandal she was involved in with President Bill Clinton seventeen years ago became one of the first incidents to "go viral" online, leading to relentless attacks and humiliation that she has endured at the hands of strangers since then, for the majority of her adult life. Shared at a time when cyber bullying is rampant, Lewinsky's story resonates as does her plea for greater compassion and conscience in the way we treat one another. Monica Lewinsky was an intern to the president at the time the scandal broke. She went into hiding and eventually moved to London to escape the public spotlight, and in 2005 received a master's degree in social psychology from the London School of Economics.

You're looking at a woman who was publicly silent for a decade. Obviously, that's changed, but only recently.

It was several months ago that I gave my very first major public talk at the Forbes 30 Under 30 summit: 1,500 brilliant people, all under the age of 30. That meant that in 1998, the oldest among the group were only 14, and the youngest, just four. I joked with them that some might only have heard of me from rap songs. Yes, I'm in rap songs. Almost 40 rap songs. (Laughter)

But the night of my speech, a surprising thing happened. At the age of 41, I was hit on by a 27-year-old guy. I know, right? He was charming and I was flattered, and I declined. You know what his unsuccessful pickup line was? He could make me feel 22 again. (Laughter) (Applause) I realized later that night, I'm probably the only person over 40 who does not want to be 22 again.(Laughter) (Applause)

At the age of 22, I fell in love with my boss, and at the age of 24, I learned the devastating consequences.

Can I see a show of hands of anyone here who didn't make a mistake or do something they regretted at 22? Yep. That's what I thought. So like me, at 22, a few of you may have also taken wrong turns and fallen in love with the wrong person, maybe even your boss. Unlike me, though, your boss probably wasn't the president of the United States of America. Of course, life is full of surprises.

Not a day goes by that I'm not reminded of my mistake, and I regret that mistake deeply.

Delivered March 19, 2015, at Vancouver Convention Center, Vancouver, Canada, by Monica Lewinsky, TED2015.

In 1998, after having been swept up into an improbable romance, I was then swept up into the eye of a political, legal and media maelstrom like we had never seen before. Remember, just a few years earlier, news was consumed from just three places: reading a newspaper or magazine, listening to the radio, or watching television. That was it. But that wasn't my fate. Instead, this scandal was brought to you by the digital revolution. That meant we could access all the information we wanted, when we wanted it, anytime, anywhere, and when the story broke in January 1998, it broke online. It was the first time the traditional news was usurped by the Internet for a major news story, a click that reverberated around the world.

What that meant for me personally was that overnight I went from being a completely private figure to a publicly humiliated one worldwide. I was patient zero of losing a personal reputation on a global scale almost instantaneously.

This rush to judgment, enabled by technology, led to mobs of virtual stone-throwers. Granted, it was before social media, but people could still comment online, email stories, and, of course, email cruel jokes. News sources plastered photos of me all over to sell newspapers, banner ads online, and to keep people tuned to the TV. Do you recall a particular image of me, say, wearing a beret?

Now, I admit I made mistakes, especially wearing that beret. But the attention and judgment that I received, not the story, but that I personally received, was unprecedented. I was branded as a tramp, tart, slut, whore, bimbo,and, of course, that woman. I was seen by many but actually known by few. And I get it: it was easy to forget that that woman was dimensional, had a soul, and was once unbroken.

When this happened to me 17 years ago, there was no name for it. Now we call it cyberbullying and online harassment. Today, I want to share some of my experience with you, talk about how that experience has helped shape my cultural observations, and how I hope my past experience can lead to a change that results in less suffering for others.

In 1998, I lost my reputation and my dignity. I lost almost everything,and I almost lost my life.

Let me paint a picture for you. It is September of 1998. I'm sitting in a windowless office room inside the Office of the Independent Counsel underneath humming fluorescent lights. I'm listening to the sound of my voice, my voice on surreptitiously taped phone calls that a supposed friend had made the year before. I'm here because I've been legally required to personally authenticate all 20 hours of taped conversation. For the past eight months, the mysterious content of these tapes has hung like the Sword of Damocles over my head. I mean, who can remember what they said a year ago? Scared and mortified, I listen, listen as I prattle on about the flotsam and jetsam of the day; listen as I confess my love for the president, and, of course, my heartbreak; listen to my sometimes catty, sometimes churlish, sometimes silly self being cruel, unforgiving, uncouth; listen, deeply, deeply ashamed, to the worst version of myself, a self I don't even recognize.

A few days later, the Starr Report is released to Congress,and all of those tapes and transcripts, those stolen words, form a part of it. That people can read the transcripts is horrific enough, but a few weeks later, the audio tapes are aired on TV, and significant portions made available online. The public humiliation was excruciating. Life was almost unbearable.

This was not something that happened with regularity back then in 1998, and by this, I mean the stealing of people's private words, actions, conversations or photos,and then making them public—public without consent, public without context, and public without compassion.

Fast forward 12 years to 2010,and now social media has been born. The landscape has sadly become much more populated with instances like mine, whether or not someone actually make a mistake,and now it's for both public and private people. The consequences for some have become dire, very dire.

I was on the phone with my mom in September of 2010,and we were talking about the news of a young college freshman from Rutgers University named Tyler Clementi. Sweet, sensitive, creative Tyler was secretly webcammed by his roommate while being intimate with another man.When the online world learned of this incident, the ridicule and cyberbullying ignited. A few days later,Tyler jumped from the George Washington Bridge to his death. He was 18.

My mom was beside herself about what happened to Tyler and his family, and she was gutted with pain in a way that I just couldn't quite understand, and then eventually I realized she was reliving 1998, reliving a time when she sat by my bed every night, reliving a time when she made me shower with the bathroom door open, and reliving a time when both of my parents feared that I would be humiliated to death, literally.

Today, too many parents haven't had the chance to step in and rescue their loved ones. Too many have learned of their child's suffering and humiliation after it was too late. Tyler's tragic, senseless death was a turning point for me. It served to recontextualize my experiences, and I then began to look at the world of humiliation and bullying around me and see something different. In 1998, we had no way of knowing where this brave new technology called the Internet would take us. Since then, it has connected people in unimaginable ways, joining lost siblings, saving lives, launching revolutions, but the darkness, cyberbullying, and slut-shaming that I experienced had mushroomed. Every day online, people, especially young people who are not developmentally equipped to handle this, are so abused and humiliatedthat they can't imagine living to the next day, and some, tragically, don't, and there's nothing virtual about that. ChildLine, a U.K. nonprofit that's focused on helping young people on various issues, released a staggering statistic late last year: From 2012 to 2013, there was an 87 percent increase in calls and emails related to cyberbullying. A meta-analysis done out of the Netherlands showed that for the first time, cyberbullying was leading to suicidal ideations more significantly than offline bullying. And you know what shocked me, although it shouldn't have, was other research last year that determined humiliation was a more intensely felt emotion than either happiness or even anger.

Cruelty to others is nothing new, but online, technologically enhanced shaming is amplified, uncontained, and permanently accessible. The echo of embarrassment used to extend only as far as your family, village, school or community, but now it's the online community too. Millions of people, often anonymously, can stab you with their words, and that's a lot of pain, and there are no perimeters around how many people can publicly observe you and put you in a public stockade.There is a very personal priceto public humiliation, and the growth of the Internet has jacked up that price.

For nearly two decades now, we have slowly been sowing the seeds of shame and public humiliation in our cultural soil, both on- and offline. Gossip websites, paparazzi, reality programming, politics, news outlets and sometimes hackers all traffic in shame. It's led to desensitization and a permissive environment online-which lends itself to trolling, invasion of privacy, and cyberbullying. This shift has created what Professor Nicolaus Mills calls a culture of humiliation. Consider a few prominent examples just from the past six months alone. Snapchat, the service which is used mainly by younger generations and claims that its messages only have the lifespan of a few seconds. You can imagine the range of content that that gets. A third-party app which Snapchatters use to preserve the lifespan of the messages was hacked, and 100,000 personal conversations, photos, and videos were leaked online to now have a lifespan of forever. Jennifer Lawrence and several other actors had their iCloud accounts hacked, and private, intimate, nude photos were plastered across the Internet without their permission. One gossip website had over five million hits for this one story. And what about the Sony Pictures cyberhacking? The documents which received the most attention were private emails that had maximum public embarrassment value.

But in this culture of humiliation, there is another kind of price tag attached to public shaming. The price does not measure the cost to the victim, which Tyler and too many others, notably women, minorities, and members of the LGBTQ community have paid, but the price measures the profit of those who prey on them.This invasion of others is a raw material, efficiently and ruthlessly mined, packaged and sold at a profit. A marketplace has emerged where public humiliation is a commodity and shame is an industry. How is the money made? Clicks. The more shame, the more clicks.The more clicks, the more advertising dollars. We're in a dangerous cycle. The more we click on this kind of gossip, the more numb we get to the human lives behind it, and the more numb we get, the more we click. All the while, someone is making money off of the back of someone else's suffering. With every click, we make a choice. The more we saturate our culture with public shaming, the more accepted it is, the more we will see behavior like cyberbullying, trolling, some forms of hacking, and online harassment. Why? Because they all have humiliation at their cores. This behavior is a symptom of the culture we've created. Just think about it.

Changing behavior begins with evolving beliefs. We've seen that to be true with racism, homophobia, and plenty of other biases, today and in the past. As we've changed beliefs about same-sex marriage, more people have been offered equal freedoms. When we began valuing sustainability, more people began to recycle. So as far as our culture of humiliation goes, what we need is a cultural revolution. Public shaming as a blood sport has to stop, and it's time for an intervention on the Internet and in our culture.

The shift begins with something simple, but it's not easy. We need to return to a long-held value of compassion—compassion and empathy. Online, we've got a compassion deficit, an empathy crisis.

Researcher Brené Brown said, and I quote,"Shame can't survive empathy." Shame cannot survive empathy. I've seen some very dark days in my life,and it was the compassion and empathy from my family, friends, professionals,and sometimes even strangers that saved me. Even empathy from one person can make a difference. The theory of minority influence, proposed by social psychologist Serge Moscovici, says that even in small numbers, when there's consistency over time, change can happen. In the online world, we can foster minority influence by becoming upstanders. To become an upstander means instead of bystander apathy, we can post a positive comment for someone or report a bullying situation. Trust me, compassionate comments help abate the negativity. We can also counteract the culture by supporting organizations that deal with these kinds of issues, like the Tyler Clementi Foundation in the U.S. In the U.K., there's Anti-Bullying Pro, and in Australia, there's Project Rockit.

We talk a lot about our right to freedom of expression, but we need to talk more about our responsibility to freedom of expression. We all want to be heard, but let's acknowledge the difference between speaking up with intention and speaking up for attention. The Internet is the superhighway for the id, but online, showing empathy to others benefits us all and helps create a safer and better world. We need to communicate online with compassion, consume news with compassion, and click with compassion. Just imagine walking a mile in someone else's headline. I'd like to end on a personal note. In the past nine months, the question I've been asked the most is why. Why now? Why was I sticking my head above the parapet? You can read between the lines in those questions, and the answer has nothing to do with politics. The top note answer was and is because it's time: time to stop tip-toeing around my past, time to stop living a life of opprobrium, and time to take back my narrative.

It's also not just about saving myself. Anyone who is suffering from shame and public humiliation needs to know one thing: You can survive it .I know it's hard. It may not be painless, quick or easy, but you can insist on a different ending to your story. Have compassion for yourself. We all deserve compassion, and to live both online and off in a more compassionate world.

Thank you for listening.

On the Expiration of the PATRIOT Act

By Rand Paul

On the expiration of Section 215 of the PATRIOT Act, Senator Rand Paul delivers a speech on the Senate floor regarding the persisting dangers of the federal government's data collection, which, Paul contends, threaten to infringe on the rights and liberties of U.S. citizens as protected by the Four Amendment. Despite claims that the program has been used primarily to halt terrorist attacks, Paul cites evidence to the contrary showing that it has been used mostly in domestic matters unrelated to terrorism. The practice of bulk collection of metadata, Paul contends, infringes on the rights of U.S. citizens by bypassing the constitutional requirement for individualized warrants. Similarly, Paul says, while a policy proposed to replace Section 215 might stop bulk collection of data by the National Security Agency (N.S.A), this data would still be collected by telephone companies like AT&T and Verizon, which could be easily accessed by the government through a "rubber-stamped" warrant. Proposing an amendment that he claims would improve a deeply problematic program, Paul concludes with a meditation on the intent of the founding fathers when writing protections into the Constitution and considers the ethics and legality of the government's bulk data collection and the PATRIOT Act more broadly. Rand Paul is a Republican U.S. Senator for Kentucky and, as of the publication of this book, a presidential hopeful for 2016. A favorite among Tea Party conservatives for his staunchly independent tone and small-government views, Paul currently serves on the following Senate committees: Foreign Relations; Health, Education, Labor, and Pensions; Homeland Security and Government Affairs; and Small Business and Entrepreneurship.

Tonight begins the process of ending bulk collection. The bill will ultimately pass-but we always look for silver linings. I think the bill may be replacing one form of bulk collection with another, but the government after this bill passes will no longer collect your phone records. My concern is that the phone companies still may do the same thing.

Currently, my understanding is the N.S.A. is at the phone company sucking up the phone records and sending them to Utah. My concern is under the new program, that the records will still be sucked up into N.S.A. computers but the computers will be at the phone company, not in Utah.

So the question is, will it be a distinction without a difference? The question also will be, will this be individualized? One of the things about the Fourth Amendment that was the biggest part of the Fourth Amendment for our founding fathers was

Delivered May 31, 2015, on the U.S. Senate floor, Washington, D.C., by Rand Paul.

that a warrant should be individualized. General warrants were what we fought the revolution over.

James Otis fought a famous case in the 1760s and he found against the British soldiers writing their own warrants. The interesting thing is part of the PATRIOT Act allows our police to write their own warrants.We have something called national security letters. These have been done by the hundreds of thousands.

Interestingly, when the president was in the senate, he was opposed to national security letters and said that they should have judicial warrants. Now it's kind of interesting that in this bill that will pass—it's supported by the president, supported by the Director of National Intelligence and now supported in a wide bipartisan fashion.

It concerns me that the president that supports the bulk data collection and has been performing it illegally for six years now supports this bill. The devil's in the details and the question is, will the new bill still allow bulk collection by the phone companies? Will they be able to put into the search engine not an individual for whom we have suspicion but an entire corporation? This is what was revealed when we saw the warrant. . . had Verizon's name on it.

We had the Director of National Intelligence come before the American people, come before Congress, swear under oath that they weren't doing this. Part of my problem with the intelligence gathering in our country is it's hard for me to have trust. It's hard for me to have trust in the people that we're giving great power to.

They also insist that we won't be able to catch terrorists. They insist that the bulk collection allowed them to catch terrorists. But then it turned out when it was investigated, when we looked at the classified documents, when the president's bipartisan privacy and civil liberties commission looked at this, when his review board looked at this and then when the Department of Justice Inspector General looked at this, they all found that there was no unique data, there was no great discovery, there was no great breaking up of a terrorist ring.

People have brought up the Boston bomber, the Tsarnaev boy. They said we need the PATRIOT Act after the bombing to get his phone records. That's the most absurd thing I've ever heard. He's already committed a bombing. In fact, I think he was dead at the point, and you're saying we couldn't get a warrant to look at his phone records? It's absolutely absurd.

I had a meeting with somebody from the intelligence community about six months ago and I asked them this question—how do you get more information about terrorists, with a warrant with their name on it where you can go as deep into the details as you want, or this met data collection that uses a—this metadata collection thatuses a less than constitutional standard?

And he said, without question you get more information with a warrant than you do through the metadata. When someone commits an act of atrocity, there's no question we would get a warrant. But I would go even further. I would say that I want to get more warrants on people before they blow things up.

I would say that we need more money spent on F.B.I. agents analyzing data and trying to find out who we have suspicion for so we can investigate their records. I think we spend so much money on people for whom there is no suspicion that we don't have enough time and money left to go after the people who would actually harm us.

The people who argue that the world will end and we will be overrun by jihadists tonight are trying to use fear. They want to take just a little bit of your liberty but they get it by making you afraid. They want you to fear and give up your liberty. They tell you if you have nothing to hide, you have nothing to fear. That's a far cry from the standard we were founded upon—innocent until proven guilty.

One of the objections that I tried to bring forward earlier but was interrupted repeatedly was that the PATRIOT Act was originally intended to go after foreigners and terrorists. We allowed a less than constitutional standard. We didn't ask for probable cause. We just said it had to be relevent, the information had to be relevant to an investigation into terrorists.

Here's one of the problems, one of the big problems I have with the PATRIOT Act. We now use parts of the PATRIOT Act to arrest people for domestic crime.Section 213 "Sneak and peek" where the government can comeinto your house, place listening devices and never announce that they were ever in your house and then leave and then monitor your behavior and never let you know they've been there, is being used 99.5% of the time for domestic crime.

So little by little, we've allowed our freedom to slip away. We allow the Fourth Amendment to be diminished. We allowed the narrowing loss of something called probable cause. People say well, how would we get terrorists with that? The vast majority of warrants are approved in our country.

The vast majority of warrants that are Fourth Amendment warrants where we individualize them, put a name on and ask probable cause, if the police tonight are looking for a rapist or a murderer, they will go to the house, and if they suspect they're inside but nothing is imminently happening, they will stand on the curb and call the police, and they almost always get a warrant.

Do you think there's a judge in this land that would not grant a warrant, particularly after theBoston bombing, to look at the Tsarnaev boys' records. There is not a judge in the land that would say no. I would say in advance there is not much chance a judge would say no, if you went to them and said the Russians have given us indication and evidence that he has been radicalized and associated overseas with people who are training to attack us.

There's no reason why the Constitution can't be used. But we just have to not let those who are in power make us cower in fear. They use fear to take your freedom, and we have to be very, very careful of this. Now, some are saying I'm misrepresenting this, I'm saying the government is listening to your phone calls.

I'm saying they are collecting your phone records. There are programs, though, in which they may be looking at content. Emails, for example. The current law says that after six months, even the content of your email has no protection. We have a very good piece of legislation to try to fix that, but realize those who are loud, those who are really wanting you to give up your freedom, that they don't believe the Fourth Amendment protects your records at all, and this is a big debate.

We went to the court, the Second Court of Appeals, the highest court in the land just below the Supreme Court, said that what they are doing is illegal, but we don't yet have a ruling on whether it's constitutional. One of my fears about the bill that we're going to pass, the sort of in-between step that some think it may be better, is that it will moot the case.

This means that the court case may never get heard at the Supreme Court now. I have a court case against the N.S.A. There's another district court that has ruled against the N.S.A. We now have an appellate court ruling against the N.S.A. The court may well look at the activity of the Senate and say well, you guys have fixed the problem, we don't need to look at it anymore; it's no longer relevant.

My other concern about this new bill that's going to pass is the same people will judge it that judged the previous system. These people are called the rubber stamp courtroom, alsoknown as FISA. Realize that the FISA court is the court that said the collection of all American records is relevant. The appeals court basically laughed at this notion and said that it sort of destroys any meaning to the word *relevant* if you collect everybody's records.

It's not even a modifier. They should have instead of said *relevant* said you could have everyone's records all the time. One of my other concerns about the in-between solution that weare going to choose is that some are conjecturing—you have to be suspicious of a government that often lies about their purpose.

Some are conjecturing that they're going to collect more phone data under the new system. One of the complaints last week, as there was discussion about this, in the newspaper it was reported that really they were only collecting about 20% to 30% of your cell phone data.

They are trying to collect all of your landline data, but they weren't for some reason collecting all of your cellphone data. One of my concerns is that as we go to this new system, they may actually be better at collecting our phone records and they may well be able to collect all of our cell phone data.

Unless we can go to a system where we individualize the warrants, unless we can go to a system where a person's name is on the warrant, I'm going to be very, very concerned. Now, we will present amendments on this bill. We tried to negotiate to be allowed to present amendments, but there wasn't a lot of negotiating that went on in the last week. In fact, there was none.

So we will still try, we will put amendments forward and we will try to get amendments to make I think the bulk collection less bad that's going to occur. One of the things we would like to do is to say that when they search the phone records thatthey can't put the name of a corporation in there, that they would have to put an individual's name.

It's kind of tricky about the way these things are worded. The wording of this bill will say that they can only put a U.S. person into the selector term to search all the phone records. The problem is that they define U.S. person as also meaning corporation or association or grouping.

So there is a little bit of looseness to the language, and so if we are still going toallow corporation, what is to stop them from going back and putting AT&T or Verizon in the selection and then once again they are looking at all the phone records, and all we have done is transferred the phone records from government control in Utah to phone company control in another location.

Will we be trading bulk collection in Utah for bulk collection under the phone company? Now, there are good people who believe this bill will reform, and I think they are well intended. I think there are good people who really think we will end bulk collection and it won't happen. My fear, though, is that the people who interpret this work at a place known as the rubber stamp factory over at FISA. It's a secret court and it's a court in which 99.5% of the time they approve warrants. Warrants are simply rubber stamped over there. In fact, they prove that relevant meant all of your records. My question is if they put AT&T in the selector item, will we once again have the same thing, just in a different location?

I have several amendments that I'm interested in if we were to be able to amend the bill. One of the amendments would say the selector; the search would have to be an individual, which I think is more consistent with the Fourth Amendment. Another one would change the standard to the constitutional standard, which would be that it has to be probable cause, which is a higher standard than simply saying it's relevant. Then we would actually be sending a new signal to the FISA court another amendment I have which I think would go a long way towards making the PATRIOT Act less bad, I think is the best way to put it, would be to say that any information gathered under a less than constitutional standard could only be used for foreigners and terrorists.

See, that was the promise, and at the time there were people who opposed the PATRIOT Act. Not enough but there were a few. And when they opposed the PATRIOT Act, they said the fear was that it would be used against American citizens. And they said oh, no, no, we're only going after terrorists, but the law allows them to do it. We now have sections of the PATRIOT Act in which 99.5% of the time it's being used for domestic crime.

We have also seen that the Drug Enforcement Agency, it is alleged, is using information gathered under the PATRIOT Act to then go back and re-create cases against people for domestic crime. The question we have to ask ourselves is are we really willing—are we so frightened that we're willing to give upour freedoms? Are we willing to trade liberty for security?

The U.S. Court of Appeals I think had some great points that they made when they used against the government, and I think what's important to know is that the president has continued to do this illegally. You've seen him on television. The president has been saying well, Congress is just getting in the way; if Congress would just do their job and get rid of this, everything would be okay. But the truth of the matter is Congress never authorized this. Even the authors of the PATRIOT Act said that this was not something that Congress ever even contemplated.

The court is now saying that as well. This was done by the Executive Branch. Admittedly, both the Republican Executive Branch and Democratic Executive Branch, but this wasn't created by Congress. So when the president says well, Congress should just do this, the question that's never been asked by anyone in the media is why doesn't he stop it. Everybody that has given advice has said he would, he will come out and say he believes in a balanced solution, but he really is just abdicating the solution and has never discontinued the program.

Even when he has been told explicitly by the court that the program is an illegal program. This is what the U.S. Court of Appeals says in the case *A.C.L.U. versus Clapper.* We agree with the appellants that such an expansive concept of relevance is unprecedented and unwarranted. The records demanded are not those of suspects under investigation or even of people or businesses that have had contact with suspects or of people or businesses that have had contacts with others who have had contact, so even two steps removed, we're gathering records that are completely irrelevant to the investigation. We're gathering up the records of innocent Americans.

Now, the other side will say well, we're not looking at them. So I have been thinking about this. Our founders objected to the British soldiers writing warrants. They objected to them coming in their house and gathering their papers. Do you think our framers would have been happy if the British government said okay, we're just breaking your door down, we're just getting your papers, but we're not going to look at them?

Do you think that would have changed the mindset of the framers? So the fact that they say they're not looking at our records, is that any comfort or should it be comfort, the act of violation is in taking your records. The act of violation is in allowing the police or a form of the police, the F.B.I., to write warrants that are not signed by a judge.

The court goes on to say the interpretation that thegovernment asks us to adopt-defies any limiting principle. The idea of a limiting principle when the court looks at things is that the way I see it, it's a difference between something being arbitrary where there isno sort of principle that confines what can happen. If you have a law that has no limiting principle, it'sessentially arbitrary.

This is what Hayek wrote about when he wrote in *The Road to Serfdom*. He wrote about the difference between the rule of law and arbitrary and having an arbitrary interpretation of the law. The danger to having an arbitrary interpretation of the law and the danger to having general warrants is that the yhave been used in the past with bias. People have brought their own bias into this. In the 1960s, the bias was against civil rights activists; it was against Vietnam War.

In the 1940s, the bias was in incarcerating and in interning Japanese Americans. But the thing that was consistent in all of these is that there was a generalization, generalization based on the color of your skin, whether you were Asian American or African-American, and also about the shade of your ideology. There is a danger in allowing the government to generalize without suspicion and to disobey the Fourth Amendment, and that danger comes that a government could one day generalize and bias could enter into things.

We have on our records right now laws that allow an American citizen to be detained. It's not specifically part of the PATRIOT Act, but it's along the same lines of this, that you're getting rid of a process, the due process amendments and the ability of the Bill of Rights to protect the individual. When we allow an individual to be detained without a trial, what happens is there is the possibility that someone could decide we don't like those people, and when you say well, that could never happen, think about the times in our history when it has. Richard Jewel, everybody said he was the Olympic bomber.

He was convicted on TV. Within hours, people said Richard Jewel's guilty. Think about if he had been a black man in 1920 in the South what might have happened to him. Think about the possibility for bias entering into our government. Think about the fact what Madison said about government is. Madison said that, "We restrain government because we're worried that government may not becomprised of angels.If government were comprised ofangels we wouldn't have to worry about restraining government."

Patrick Henry said that the Constitution was about restraining government, not the people. It's not enough for people to say, oh, I'm a good man or I'm a good person, or the N.S.A. would never do this. The other problem that makes us doubtful is that the N.S.A. hasn't been honest with us. If they wanted to develop trust again, the president should have immediately let go the person who lied to us, the Director of National Intelligence.

The appeals court concluded by saying that the government's bulk collection of telephone metadata, metadata exceeds the scope of what Congress has authorized and therefore violates Section 215 of the PATRIOT Act. Some will try to argue that this debate was not worth the time we took on it. I could not disagree more. I'm like everybody else, you know, I prize my time with my family and being at home over the weekends. And I wish we would have done this in a more sensitive way where we had had more time on hand and had an open amendment process.

But we waited until the end, we waited until the final deadline. And this is a characteristic of government and it's a flaw in government, frankly. We lurch from deadline to deadline. People wonder why Congress is so unpopular. It's because we go from deadline to deadline and then it's hurry up, we have no time to debate, you must pass it as is.

The biggest debate against amendments is—and it finally convinced even the people who didn't like this. They so much dislike amendments and slowing down the process that they're just going to take it even though they don't like it; we'll pass what the House passed and it's unlikely anya mendments will pass. But the thing is we need to get away from lurching from deadline to deadline. What happens with budget or spending or any of these bills is we're presented with thousand-page bills with only hours to go.

About a year ago this came up and at that time we were presented with a thousand-page bill with two hours to go and I read the Senate rules and it said we're supposed to be presented with the bill for 48 hours in advance. So I raised my hand and made a motion. And the motion I made was, guys, we're breaking the rules here. Men and women, we're breaking the rules here.

So everyone just voted to amend the rules for that bill and ignore the rules. This is why the American people are so frustrated. People here in town think I'm making a huge mistake. Some of them I think secretly want there to be an attack on the

United States so they can blame it on me. One of the people in the media the other day came up to me and said, oh, when there's a great attack, aren't you going to feel guilty you caused this attack?

It's like the people who attack us are responsible for attacks on us. Do we blame the police chief for the attack of the Boston bombers? The thing is that there can be attacks even if we use the Constitution, but there have been attacks while collecting your bulk data. So the ones who say when an attack occurs it's going to be all your fault, are any of them willing to accept the blame, we have bulk collection now, are any of them willing to accept the blame for the Boston bombing, for the recent shooting in Garland?

No, but they'll be the first to point fingers and say, oh, yeah it's all your fault, we never should have given up on this great program. I'm completely convinced that we can obey the Constitution, use the Fourth Amendment as intended, spirit and letter of the law, and catch terrorists. When we look objectively at this program, when they analyzed the classified information, they found that there was no unique data.

We had to fight them tooth andnail because they started out saying 52 cases were cracked by the bulk data program. But when this president's bipartisan commission looked at it, it turned out none of that was true. This gets back to the trust issue.If we're going to be lied to by the Director of National Intelligence, it's hard for us to believe them when they come forward and they say, oh, this is protecting us; we have to have it.

But what we're hearing is, information from someone who really didn't think it was a big deal to lie to us about whether or not the program even existed. Mark my words, the battle's not over. There are some—and I talked with one of the—I would say one of the smarter people in Silicon Valley who knows this from an intimate level how things work and how the codes and programs work, and he maintains that the bulk collection of phone data is the tip of the iceberg.

That there's more information in other data pools that are classified; some of this is done through an Executive Order called 12333. I'm not sure I know everything in it. I've had no briefings on it. Anything I tell you is from the newspaper alone. But the thing is that I would like to know, are we also collecting your credit card information, are we collecting your texts, are we collecting your emails?

They've already told us the Fourth Amendment doesn't protect your emails. Even the content after six months. They've told you the Fourth Amendment doesn't apply to your records at all. So be very careful about the people who say, trust us, we'll never violate your freedoms. We'll never take advantage of things. The president's privacy and civil liberties over sightboard's conclusion was that Section 215 of the PATRIOT Act has known minimal value in safeguarding the nation from terrorism.

We not have identified a single instance involving a threat to the United States in which the program made a concrete difference in the outcome. The president's privacy board went on to say the government's collection of a person's entire telephone calling history has a significant and detrimental effect on individual privacy.

When they talked about whether or not the phone records were relevant to an investigation, the president's commission said this, "First the telephone records acquired under the program have no connection to any specific F.B.I. investigation at the time of their collection."

Second, because the records are collected in bulk, potentially encompassing all telephone calling records across the nation, they cannot be regarded as relevant to any F.B.I. investigation. Here's the continuing danger to us, though. It is I think maybe a minor success we'll prevent the government from collecting these records. But realize that theinterpretation of this will still occur in secret in theFISA court and that this is the FISA court that said that collecting everyone's records was relevant.

It completely destroys the notion that the word *relevant* has any meaning at all. This will be the question, whether or not we can trust the FISA court to make an interpretation that is at a higher degree of discernment than the one in which they said *relevant* can mean anything. The court of the original U.S. Freedom Act as patched by the House Committee was a better bill and has gradually watered down until even the Director of National Intelligence, the one who lied about the program, now supports it which gives me some misgivings.

But the records that will be collected, the question is how will we have an interpretation by the FISA court. The original bill had an advocate, and I thought this was a good part of the original bill. There would be a judicial advocate who would argue on the side of those who are having their records taken. And so there would be an adversarial court, lawyers on both sides. Many people who write about jurisprudence and trying to find justice say one of the essential functions of a court system in order to find justice is that there has to be a lawyer on both sides.There has to be an advocate on both sides. The truth isn't always easy to find.

The truth is presentation of facts by one side, presentation of contrary by the other side, and someone has to figure out which facts are more believable or which facts trump other facts. And so I think a judicial advocate would have been good. They're still going to have it; they call it by a different name now but it will be optional at the discretion of the FISA court. So the court that ruled that all of your records are relevant now will have a choice as to whether or not to give you an advocate.

That doesn't give me a great deal of comfort. There are other ways we could do this.We occasionally do look at terrorism cases in regular federal court. And when names come up that could jeopardize someone's safety and our intelligence agency or a secret, federal courts can go into secret recess. I've heard the Senator from Oregon often mention this and I think it's a great point. That no one wants to reveal the names of anyone or the code or the secrets of how we do this but if we're talking about constitutional principles, we want to do it in the open.

Law shouldn't be investigated in secret. As we move forward, the PATRIOT Act will expire tonight. It will only be temporary. They will ultimately get their way. But I think the majority of the American people actually do believe government has gone too far. In Washington it's the opposite. But I think Washington is out of touch. There will be 80 votes in order to say continue the PATRIOT Act. Maybe more.

But if you go into the general public, if you get outside the Beltway and visit America, you find it's completely the opposite. There was a poll a couple weeks ago that said over 80% of people under age 40, over 80% of them think that the government collecting your phone records is wrong. And shouldn't occur. So I think really this will be useful.

People say you're destroying yourself, you should have never done this, the American people won't side with you. And people wish me harm and wish that this will be unsuccessful. But you know what, I came here to defend the Bill of Rights and to defend the Constitution, popular or not, but I frankly think that the Bill of Rights and the Constitution are very popular, very important, and I will continue as long as I have breath and as long as I'm here to defend them and with that, Mr. President, I yield back the remainder of my time.

Privacy in the Age of Pervasive Surveillance

By David Medine

In the keynote address for the Idaho Law Review's Symposium, Privacy in the Age of Pervasive Surveillance, David Medine begins by laying out the establishment of the United States Privacy and Civil Liberties Oversight Board (PCLOB), for which he serves as Chair. As an independent organization of the executive branch, Medine says, the PCLOB maintains the necessary autonomy to oversee government operations credibly. Over the course of the speech, Medine explores the bulk collection of data, particularly under Section 215 of the PATRIOT Act, in regard to three aspects of the Fourth Amendment: "the reasonable expectation of privacy standard, … the third party doctrine, and … the foreign intelligence exception." He explains how in light of recent advances in technology and the government's ability to collect data, the PCLOB came to the conclusion of recommending increased oversight of government surveillance. David Medine started full-time as Chairman of the Privacy and Civil Liberties Oversight Board on May 27, 2013. Previously, he was an Attorney Fellow for the Security and Exchange Commission and a Special Counsel at the Consumer Financial Protection Bureau and also worked at a private law firm focused on privacy and data security.

I guess I'm the first speaker to have to give a disclaimer, which is that my views today don't necessarily represent the views of the Privacy and Civil Liberties Oversight Board or any of its other members. I want to talk a little bit about our board and following up with from what Annemarie [Bridy] said of how we got started and then turn to some topics for today.

After the 9/11 attacks, as I think you may know, a commission was formed to address what happened and how we can do a better job in protecting our country against terrorist attacks. And if you haven't read their report, I highly commend it.[1] It's extremely readable, but a very detailed account of the problems that led to the attacks on 9/11 not being thwarted. At the end of this, roughly, 500-page report there's about two or three paragraphs that say, by the way, let's not go too far in the direction—so far in the direction of protecting national security that we compromise privacy and civil liberties. Because what makes us a great country is the fact that we have both privacy and civil liberties and national security. And actually

Delivered April 3, 2015, at Idaho Law Review Annual Symposium, Boise, Idaho, by David Medine.

having both of these are strong values that complement each other and don't contradict each other.

And so the 9/11 commission recommended the creation of a board to advise the government on how to strike that balance. So shortly after that, a board was created in the White House called the Privacy and Civil Liberties Oversight Board and it started its work. But the White House felt that it could edit the board's work because it was in the White House. And so one of the board members resigned in protest, Lanny Davis, and said that the board was not sufficiently independent to exercise oversight of federal counterterrorism programs.

Congress agreed and abolished PCLOB 1.0. In 2007, Congress created PCLOB 2.0 as an independent agency in the executive branch, which is a bit of a non sequitur, but ends up working out pretty well for us. We're in the executive branch, and that's a real plus, because we have access to deliberative materials in the executive branch that, say, Congress or the courts might not get access to, privileged information, classified information. Every member of the Board and every member of our staff has to have the highest level of security clearance. So that's, I think, one of the pluses of being in the executive branch, but it's also a plus being independent because it gives us credibility and allows us to look at programs and express our own views.

And so, for instance, on the 215 program, which I'll talk about briefly later, our Board concluded that the program was not legal and also bad policy, but the White House disagreed with our conclusion about the legality of the program. We don't have to clear our views through the White House or the Office of Management and Budget; we can simply express ourselves by a vote of the board. And so I think that hopefully will give us credibility in both the national and the international context to say that we can take a look at programs, sometimes they're classified so we may not be able to discuss them in public, but knowing that we are giving a serious independent view of how those programs operate I think is really critical.

So again in 2007, legislation was created authorizing PCLOB 2.0. It took President Obama a while to get a slate of nominees together.

I noticed there's a Whole Foods across the street—and my story begins at Whole Foods as well. I was shopping at Whole Foods in September 2011, and I got a call from Peter Swire, who some of you may know, saying the White House is looking for people to chair PCLOB. "Would you be interested?"

And my first reaction is, "What's PCLOB?" And he explained it and I looked it up and I said, "Sure. I'd be happy to put my name in the ring." That was in September 2011—and after countless paperwork and background checks and interviews, finally, on December 2011 President Obama nominated me and two others to be on the Board, having previously nominated two other people, so we had a full slate of five. As Annemarie mentioned we have five members on our board, no more than three of any one political party, so we currently have three Democrats, two Republicans and we serve staggered six-year terms.

I thought the big hurdle was getting nominated and so in December 2011 I thought it'd be pretty smooth sailing after that. It turns out it took the Senate 510 days to act on and vote and confirm me as chairman of this board.

The Senate may have had some wisdom there because I started on the board on a Monday, we had no office, we had no permanent staff, two detailees, we had no website and no email system, that was on Monday. On Thursday the Snowden leaks occurred.

So the question was: Are we going to be relevant or are we irrelevant? And I thought it'd be better to be relevant. So, on Friday, I wrote a letter to the attorney general and to the Director of National Intelligence saying that we would like to be briefed on the two programs that Snowden initially leaked, the 215 and 702 programs, and p.s., I don't have a security clearance.

On Monday I had a security clearance. On Tuesday we were briefed at the Justice Department by the NSA, FBI, and DOJ, and so forth, on how these programs operated. And then about two weeks after that we met with the President in the Situation Room to discuss surveillance issues. So it was quite a busy couple of weeks on the job, and it's been quite a busy year and a half or so on the job as well.

Since then, as I think as you may know, we've issued two reports and we've embarked on an additional project, as well as some smaller things. But in looking at the agenda for today on [private and public] surveillance, my former life with the FTC would have been from the private-sector side, and my current job is focused on the government side. And so—I think that naturally brings to mind the Fourth Amendment.

I really want to focus today on the Fourth Amendment's application in this context, particularly government surveillance. And I wanted to give you three aspects of it. Two of them relate to my work at PCLOB and another relates to some pro bono work I've done for the Constitution Project in the past on video surveillance in public places. The three aspects of the Fourth Amendment I wanted to discuss are, basically, narrowing aspects of the protections it provides: (1) the reasonable expectation of privacy standard, (2) the third-party doctrine and (3) the foreign intelligence exception. The first two have already been touched on previously today.

But I think, as people know, the Fourth Amendment requires a warrant in most cases. The protections of the Fourth Amendment prior to the famous *Katz* decision[2] focused on the home, which was the subject of the first panel. And then after *Katz*, it focused more on people than places which, in some ways, expands on the second panel in terms of people out and about, and not just in their home, getting protection under the Fourth Amendment.

And the standard that was enunciated is that there be a reasonable expectation of privacy in terms of when the Fourth Amendment would apply. The *Katz* case looked at wiretapping one phone booth and listening in on one person's conversations. The standard was developed at a time before the government had the powers we've heard about today that are sometimes used for pervasive surveillance. The government uses video cameras, license plate readers, sometimes GPS. And these tools allow for more than a snapshot, or for those students in the room, Snapchat, of people's lives and how they operate. And these inputs from a variety of devices as mentioned before can be linked together and merged using facial recognition, as Yana [Welinder] mentioned, and other devices to create a profile of someone, a near complete picture of what they do every day and all day.

The question is: is there a reasonable expectation of privacy in collecting all this information about people that creates a very detailed profile about people's lives, what they do, who they meet with, what they talk about? Under the *Katz* expectation of privacy, if you have a video surveillance camera on the wall and a sign underneath it that says, "CCTV Monitoring Here" or "This area is being surveilled," one could argue that negates any expectation of privacy and so, therefore, the Fourth Amendment would not apply to that type of collection activity.

One could also argue that when you drive on the road, you know that you're in public and don't have an expectation of privacy. And so when a license plate reader picks up your car and knows where you've gone all throughout the city, you're acting in public and therefore, also didn't expect to be private.

I guess another thing I should mention is policemen. We think of it as being appropriate for police to tail people—[we think of this] as permissible. But what if we assigned a policeman to, say, a dissident, and they tail him day after day after day, night after night? At some point you reach the point—even if you're operating in public—where it tips the balance and you're gathering so much information about someone over such a long period of time that it should be considered a search under the Fourth Amendment.

We also now have publically available information, Facebook, Twitter, all kinds of social media that give not only what people do, but oftentimes their location. And so we can, again, map where they've been throughout the day. You post your picture on Facebook—that indicates where the picture is taken. And again [if] people don't use privacy settings, [the government] can gather that information together and create a very detailed profile of how its citizens are operating.

Now, some have argued that there isn't an expectation of privacy that the government will create these detailed profiles of you throughout your day, but I'm not sure that the courts are going to recognize that as a limiting factor on government surveillance activities. So I don't think that the expectation of privacy standard is really appropriate as we move forward into a new generation where we can live our lives virtually and in the cloud. This is one area where the Fourth Amendment, I think, could benefit from some changes and interpretation to adopt a more substantive standard of protection. Not looking at the individual's view of whether the government is invading their privacy, but looking at the nature of the government's activity collectively and decide, essentially, has that crossed a line. [A standard] where notice of surveillance is not enough, if you're being surveilled in the Panopticon [as referenced earlier by Jeffrey Vagle] or wherever it happens to be. At some point, the government should be limited in its powers to surveil citizens.

The second area I wanted to talk about is the third-party doctrine which is, to some extent, an element of the reasonable expectation of privacy standard. [This doctrine states that] if you give your information to a company, you can't reasonably expect that that information is supposed to be kept private. Margot Kaminski made a stunning comment earlier today, which is that, at least to some extent, the way the law is developing now, citizens have more protection against companies' surveillance activities, under consumer protection law, than they may have under the Fourth Amendment when the government surveils their activities. And if that's true, I think that's a somewhat troubling development in terms of the power balance between citizens and the government.

But I want to talk a little bit about how our Board came to bump up against the third-party doctrine. This happened with one of the first programs that we looked at: the Section 215 telephony metadata program. And for those who may not be aware of it, it's a program in which the NSA goes to phone companies and gathers information, not about the contents of your phone calls, but the metadata, which is the number that your phone number dialed, whether the call connected, how long the call lasted, and some basic information like that. And they gather all that information into a massive database. The purpose of that is, say, you find a terrorist in a cave in Afghanistan who called someone in the United States, that is certainly potentially interesting. If someone from Al-Qaeda is calling someone in Cincinnati, you might want to know if there's a terrorist plot underway and maybe someone has been planted in Cincinnati or there's some cooperative person in the United States that's helping out Al-Qaeda.

So what the government can do under this program is not only see that call coming in, but then find out who the person in Cincinnati called on the theory that maybe they're in on a terrorist plot and the government can find who the co-conspirators were. And then [the government can] go out another level to see who those people, every one of those people, called and everyone who those people called. So it's a growing number of steps that are taken in terms of understanding—of reaching out to see if there's a terrorist plot underway. We looked at the program from three perspectives. One, is it legal? Two, is it constitutional? And the third is, on policy grounds: does it strike the right balance between privacy and civil liberties and national security?

On the legal side we concluded that the program did not fall properly under the statute for a number of reasons. One is that the statute says . . . that if the government wants to collect this type of information it has to be relevant to an investigation.[3] And the question is: How could the collection of every American's phone records be relevant to any investigation and have *relevance* have any meaning? And so in our view, that statute and the program did not match up.

In addition just as a somewhat technical matter, the Electronic Communications Privacy Act[4] restricts phone companies' ability to provide metadata to the government, and it provides specific programs under which that data can be provided; Section 215 is not one of those programs. And so the statute doesn't match there as well.

Just a third example is the statute says that the FBI shall collect this information. And as we know, the NSA collects the information; not a totally trivial difference. The FBI is a domestic law enforcement agency and we're looking at potentially domestic crimes. The NSA, obviously, has a more international focus. So for a number of reasons the board concluded the program didn't match up with its statute.

On the policy side—and Jennifer Lynch talked about this earlier, about some of the privacy implications of having a map of your phone calls and who you're interacting with—just the mere fact that the government is collecting information about your phone calls has the real potential to chill freedom of association, freedom of speech, and freedom of religion. Just think of someone who's a whistleblower who wants to call a reporter at a newspaper knowing that the government knows about that call. Or some of the more typical examples: you call an oncologist and the next call is to a funeral home, I think you have a pretty good sense, unfortunately, of what's going on. And there are lots more examples: of religious groups meeting together, political groups meeting together, et cetera.

So the mere fact that the government is collecting this information raises some significant civil liberties issues and privacy issues. But our job is not to look at just the privacy and civil liberties side of the equation, it's also to look at the national security side. And so as many of you may know, right after the Snowden leaks, the government advanced a number of success stories under which 215 was asserted to be successful. So we were able to go to the government—and there were about a dozen of those ultimately—and get the files on each of those cases, some of which included classified information, and see what role the 215 played in the asserted success in each of those cases.

We looked at a number of metrics: catching co-conspirators, evidence of other crimes, and also thwarting terrorists' plots and identifying co-conspirators. And we concluded, based on all of those metrics, that the program was not effective. It had certainly not thwarted any terrorist plots, but it also had been of limited efficacy in those other areas. And we also found that what limited efficacy it had, could have been achieved through other legal resources, like national security letters or grand jury subpoenas. The most typical case that was mentioned was the Zazi case where someone from Colorado came to bomb the New York City subway. That was asserted to be a 215 success story. But 215 didn't come into play until Mr. Zazi stopped, realized they were onto him, left New York, went back to Colorado, was arrested in Colorado and they picked up, through 215, one of his co-conspirators. [The 215 program] had nothing to do with thwarting the plot and bombing the subway in New York.

Just on a policy ground the board said, that based on various significant privacy and civil liberties concerns, [the program was] not effective on the national security side, and recommended that the program be discontinued in its current form. And instead that the government [should] go on a case-by-case basis to phone companies when they have a particular need for phone information and get the records from the phone companies instead of having the bulk collection. We essentially did not accept the argument that you can't find the needle in a haystack unless you have the haystack. There are other ways of finding needles that are more privacy and civil liberties protective than having the government hold all this transactional information.

So then the third part of our analysis was constitutional. And the question is: Did this collection of information on Americans run again afoul on the Fourth Amendment? It certainly seems very troubling that the government—without a warrant—is gathering massive amounts of information with no suspicion about any individual. But what we quickly found is there is this *Smith v. Maryland* case.[5]

And I want to just briefly tell you some of the facts of the *Smith v. Maryland* case on which the NSA's collection of millions of phone records is based. [In *Smith,*] a woman in Baltimore was robbed and the robber then proceeded to call her and harass her on the phone. As a matter of fact, one day he even called her and said if you just look outside I'll be outside your door in my car. And so she looked out and there was this Monte Carlo driving by. She reported it to the police that this robber was driving around and harassing her. The police put out a lookout for this particular car with this particular person's description. And on March 16th of that year, someone identified that car and that person.

The police went to the phone company and put a pen trap on his phone, which, basically, is a primitive device that would allow [them to collect] what numbers he was calling out to. Not nearly as sophisticated as what the NSA does in terms of its telephony metadata program of seeing if the phone call was connected and how long it lasted; [the pen register] simply [collected] what calls were made. That was on March 16th. On March 17th, they found him calling her number. Bingo! They got what they wanted one day later. And on the basis of that, they got a search warrant, searched his home, found he had put a fold on the page of his phone directory that had her number on it, and arrested him and prosecuted him.

He was convicted. And he went to the Supreme Court and argued that the search warrant was based on information that was collected [in violation] of the Fourth Amendment and the search was unconstitutional. His case went to the Supreme Court and the Supreme Court said no, you give your phone records to the phone company when you make a phone call, and you know that. And so, therefore, when the police put the pen trap on your phone and got the information it wasn't really private—[it was] public in the sense of giving it to the phone company and not keeping it private. And so, therefore, the pen trap search of your phone records was constitutional and didn't violate the Fourth Amendment.

Just as a side note, we invited in the lawyer who argued the case for Maryland who won. He said he tried to make it as narrow of a case as possible. And he said he's horrified that his little decision in this Baltimore . . . robbery case has now become the foundation for an NSA collection program; but sure enough, it has been. And the question is: Should it be?

I should say what we concluded was that the government was reasonable in relying on *Smith v. Maryland* as the basis for this program because at least up until now, *Smith v. Maryland* is good law and the third-party doctrine, which allows the government to collect this information, is still viable.

But the question is, as we go forward, as cases are working their way up through the system, one judge has held the program unconstitutional, some have held it constitutional: Should the Fourth Amendment restrict this kind of government collection?

There are some important distinctions between the 215 program and the *Smith v. Maryland* case. One is, obviously, everyone's records are being collected. In *Smith*, [collection] was for a few days, but the 215 program goes on for months and years. In *Smith*, there was suspicion about this particular person. Hopefully, not all of us are suspect in an investigation of the government, and yet [under 215] all of that information is being collected. And so it's really quite an extension of *Smith* . . . admittedly it probably has to work its way to the Supreme Court to have changes made to the third-party doctrine.

The same principle has been found in other cases in other contexts in the Supreme Court. There's the *Miller* case,[6] where records also fell under the third-party doctrine and weren't protected under the Fourth Amendment. In response, Congress passed the Right to Financial Privacy Act that protected financial records.[7] But the same principles apply to credit card records, online shopping, library records—all held by third parties.

As was mentioned earlier, there's some language in the *Jones* case in the Supreme Court that suggests that maybe five of the justices are willing to revisit these issues.[8] Justice Alito, concurring in that case, contrasted the short-term monitoring that might have occurred in prior cases, to the longer term collection of information with the GPS tracking device, [arguing] that's something that might tip the balance.[9] Justice Sotomayor suggested that there might be a need to reevaluate the third-party doctrine given the reasonableness of how much information was being collected.[10]

So I guess my view is that the third-party doctrine should either be abandoned or sufficiently narrowed, so that it doesn't allow massive bulk collection of information by the government on citizens every day on constitutionally protected activities. I think it's appropriate the Fourth Amendment has evolved from one's home, to expectations of privacy, to people's virtual existence now, and it should recognize that we live our lives in the cloud and online. Merely the fact that a third-party company is handling our information should not take it out of the protections of the Fourth Amendment with regard to the government's collection activities.

And the third potential narrowing of the Fourth Amendment I wanted to mention is the foreign intelligence exception. According to the Supreme Court, warrantless searches are per se unreasonable, except in well-delineated exceptions. And the Court left open, in a case many, many decades ago, whether there might be an exception for national security or the activities of foreign powers. The lower courts that have considered the question of whether there's a foreign intelligence exception to the Fourth Amendment have generally found that there is one. Although, it's yet to make it up to the Supreme Court. Even the Foreign Intelligence Surveillance Court has indicated that the surveillance directed at a foreign power, or agent of a foreign power, would be exempt from the Fourth Amendment. But it's worth noting that U.S. citizens or U.S. persons can be agents of a foreign power, and so that exception would allow surveillance of U.S. persons without a warrant. So I think it's something important to consider.

We came up against this in the 702 program, which was the other program that Snowden leaked back in 2013. It's a targeted program; it's not a bulk connection program. Under 702, the government targets accounts that belong to people who are not Americans, who are overseas and where there's a foreign intelligence purpose. But unlike the 215 program, it's actually collecting the contents of emails and the contents of phone calls. The government has to go to court to approve this overall program, but does not have to go to court and get approval for each individual email account that's been targeted.

And so the first question is: Why does this impact the Fourth Amendment at all? And the answer is: Even though you're collecting communications of non-U.S. persons overseas, occasionally those people talk to or email with Americans. And so the government is collecting a database of contents of communications and phone calls of Americans even though their targets may have been non-U.S. persons.

And so the question is: How does the Fourth Amendment apply in this context? For the purposes of our 702 report, we assumed without deciding that there was a foreign intelligence exception. And what that meant is that there was not a warrant requirement in this case. Now, I think that that's something that certainly the courts could, and may well, revisit as there are also challenges underway to the 702 program. But, even without a warrant, that's not the end of the story under the Fourth Amendment. Even a warrantless search has to be reasonable under the Fourth Amendment. And one of the things we looked at in this program was whether the protections on the way the program operates in targeting and oversight, and so forth, were reasonable. Our conclusion as a board is that this program went, essentially, right up to the line of reasonableness, but the Board was not prepared to say the program was unreasonable under the Fourth Amendment.

However, one of my fellow board members, a former federal appellate judge, Patricia Wald, and I dissented from the Board's report and argued that, at least in one context, there should be court approval for searches. [There is a] big database now of communications, collected on foreign targets that the U.S. government can search for U.S. persons. Basically, it can gather my communications with folks overseas over a period of time and with different people, and compile those, looking at me and my communications.

Judge Wald's view and my view was that that this type of collection on U.S. persons at least requires court approval, whether it's in the national security context by NSA, or in the law enforcement context by FBI. This information wasn't gathered with a warrant and even if that's acceptable, this is a use of the information, now shifting the focus to Americans, that at least in our view ought to trigger the protections of a federal judge approving the collection.

So going forward, the foreign intelligence exception is another area where we could really benefit from some court guidance on whether, first of all, an exception exists at all, because we have not gotten any expression from the Supreme Court [in that area]. And if it exists, what are the contours of that exception?

Our Board has now shifted our focus from the 215 and 702 programs, which were the initially leaked programs, to Executive Order 12333[11] which is not a program; it's an authority. It's something that President Reagan issued to govern the entire intelligence community and, essentially, talk about what each of the elements of the intelligence community could do, how you could target Americans under that program if they didn't fall under 215 and 702, and a variety of other aspects of how the intelligence community operates. And so we have begun working on that last July [2014]. It's a challenging effort to look at how this massive authority applies, but we've been digging in and getting briefings from the intelligence community.

[There are] three aspects of Executive Order 12333 [that raise constitutional issues]. The first is separation of powers. [Executive Order] 12333 is really based primarily on presidential power from Article II, the commander-in-chief power. The question is: To what extent, if Congress wanted to, could Congress legislate in this space in which the current president currently operates purely based on presidential power? Just a few months ago, Congress did legislate in this space with the Intelligence Reau-thorization Act.[12] Section 309 [effectively] said that, under 12333, the government couldn't keep most records more than five years in its collection activities. So Con-gress, without a lot of debate on the constitutional side, went ahead and legislated in the space. [As part of our inquiry,] we're going to hear some discussion from academics on both sides of whether these are pure presidential powers or whether these are areas where the Congress can legislate.

We're also going to look at the First and Fourth Amendments and see where the president is operating on pure presidential power how much, if at all, do the First and Fourth Amendments restrict the president's power to conduct surveillance activities.

We'll also look at some of the operational aspects of 12333, including what oversight mechanisms are in place, because there is no judicial oversight of 12333 activities. Unlike 215, where a court now, after some reforms, has to approve every search of records and make sure the government has a reasonable articulable suspicion before the government does the search. And unlike 702, as I mentioned, at least a court approves the program, 12333 has no judicial oversight. And the question is: What types of oversight exist under 12333 that might compensate for the absence of judicial oversight? Congress has, of course, conducted oversight and is continuing to conduct oversight of these programs as well, but we're looking at, how effective that [12333] oversight function is.

So in conclusion, I think it's time now, with both the advances of technology and the government's abilities to collect information, that there be some reconsideration of the expectation of privacy standard, of the third-party doctrine, and some better fleshing out of the foreign intelligence exception.

Thank you very much.

Notes

1. National Commission on Terrorist Attacks upon the United States, the 9/11 Commission Report (2004).

2. *Katz v. United States,* 389 U.S. 347 (1967).
3. *See* 50 U.S.C. § 1861(b)(2) (2006).
4. 18 U.S.C. § 2510 (2006).
5. *Smith v. Maryland*, 442 U.S. 735 (1979).
6. *United States v. Miller*, 425 U.S. 435 (1976).
7. 2 U.S.C. § 3401 (2006).
8. *United States v. Jones*, 132 S. Ct. 945 (2012).
9. *Id.* at 964 (Alito, J. concurring).
10. *Id.* at 967(Sotomayor, J., concurring).
11. Exec. Order No. 12,333, 3 C.F.R. 200 (1981), *reprinted as amended in* 50 U.S.C. 401 (2006).
12. Intelligence Authorization Act for Fiscal Year 2015, Pub. L. No. 113-293.

5
A Year in Review

© Jason Szenes/epa/Corbis

Former U.S. Secretary of State, U.S. Senator, and First Lady Hillary Rodham Clinton joins Beatrice Biira, Community Engagement Coordinator at Heifer International, left, and British journalist and CEO of the Women in the World Summit, Tina Brown, right, and members of the Manhattan Girls Chorus after addressing the Sixth Annual Women in the World Summit at the David H. Koch Theater at Lincoln Center in New York, New York, April 23, 2015.

Creating the Future of Health Care Today

By Steven J. Stack

In his inaugural address to the American Medical Association, President Steven J. Stack addresses the role of emergency physicians in healthcare, present-day practices in the medical industry, and various obstacles that physicians currently face, including outdated technology, bureaucratic systems that work against patient interest, and insurance companies that threaten lives by questioning the necessity of treatments. With poignant anecdotes about treating patients and saving lives, Stack reminds his audience of the rewarding and meaningful work they do every day. Steven J. Stack, MD, an emergency physician residing in Lexington, Kentucky, became the 170th president of the American Medical Association in June 2015.

Thank you. I am both honored and humbled to stand before you tonight as AMA president. Of course, I would not be here were it not for the love and encouragement of my family; the support of my colleagues, both in medical practice and in organized medicine; the inspiring examples of previous AMA presidents; or the ongoing labors of our leadership on behalf of the profession. To each of you—to all of you—I am eternally grateful.

It is a special privilege to become the first emergency physician to serve as AMA president. Like many in this room, my specialty has profoundly shaped who I am as a physician, and as a person.

One thing I love about emergency medicine is its capacity to teach. Every day I'm in the emergency department I learn something about life. For one thing, I learn what not to do in life. For example, never put a firecracker in an upside down beer can, light the fuse, and put your foot on top to see what happens.

And if you're going to hammer a nail into a board, don't swing the hammer toward your face. Believe it or not, you may miss the board entirely and etch a hammer-shaped arc in your two front teeth. It's been said truth is stranger than fiction. Let me assure you, truth in the ED is a lot stranger than fiction.

Of course, it's the deeper, more profound lessons that truly leave their mark. The emergency department is the great equalizer in the health care system – a place where rich and poor, insured and uninsured, those at death's door, and those with minor aches and pains, lay side by side. You quickly realize that illness does not discriminate – that the C-suite executive is no more immune to accidents or emergencies than the homeless man living under a bridge.

Delivered June 9, 2015, at the American Medical Association Annual Meeting, Chicago, Illinois, by Steven J. Stack.

You also become increasingly aware of society's failings and the people who fall through the cracks in the system. . . The elderly woman who visits the ED week after week because she is lonely. The man so addicted to opioids he makes the rounds of all the area emergency departments, scoping out the new physicians and duping them into writing a prescription.The young mother who works two jobs but can't afford health care, so now she seeks care in the ED with a large mass in her pelvis.

Being an emergency physician also teaches you how important it is to be able to adapt. Sometimes there aren't enough beds available. Sometimes there aren't enough nurses or specialists on hand to attend to a patient. So you quickly move from plan A to B. And from B to C. When lives are at stake, there's no time to lament the challenges before you. You make the most of what you've got and move forward. And, more often than not, it works out.

These lessons have furnished me with a sense of perspective regarding the challenges we face in organized medicine. If one lesson stands above the rest, however, it's how tenuous and precious life is – and what a gift it is to be a physician.

I recall a particular patient who drove this point home for me. It was about 4 a.m. Christmas morning, 2010. I was working the night shift. A young man arrived in the emergency department with symptoms about as vague as it gets. For the sake of anonymity, I'll call him Joe.

Joe had been sitting at his computer doing some work, when he got a funny feeling in his back – a strange pain that just wouldn't go away. So he went to the hospital to get it checked out. Obviously, many conditions – mostly minor – can trigger a funny feeling in the back. But something about the way he described his symptoms led me to suspect a 1 in 100,000 diagnosis: a thoracic aortic dissection.

Joe was in his thirties, by all indications healthy, and his pain could best be described as mild. Nevertheless, something didn't sit right with me. So I ordered a CT scan, and sure enough, my fear was confirmed.

I went to Joe and explained that we needed to immediately transfer him to a bigger hospital for emergency surgery. Some of his family had shown up by this point, and I had to make sure they understood the gravity of the situation. If Joe's aorta ruptured, he would die in transit. They needed to take this opportunity to exchange last words.

At the same time, I didn't want to deprive them of hope. This was one of those situations where both the patient and his family needed to have the utmost confidence in his physicians. So I did my best to walk that fine line between being compassionate and being strong.

As we were getting him ready to leave, Joe asked his nurse to write down a phone number. He said to the nurse, "Please, don't let me die. But if I do, promise me you'll call my girlfriend and tell her I'm sorry we argued."

As I said, it was Christmas morning. After my shift ended, my wife drove us to Cincinnati to spend the holiday with her family. All day, I kept logging on to check the university health records. As long as laboratory data kept showing up, I knew he was still alive.

Now, fast forward to Christmas 2011. I didn't work the holiday that year, but suddenly the phone rings and it's my colleague. He says, "Some guy just stopped by and said you took care of him last year. He wanted to thank you for saving his life."

For many, that life-changing moment—that defining moment when what's important suddenly draws into focus and the mundane falls back into relief—occurs in a physician's care. The birth of a child. The loss of a loved one. An unexpected diagnosis. The physician's life is defined not by one, but by hundreds of these moments. Our profession is literally built around them. And to play a part in these moments is a priceless gift. These are the moments we went to medical school for. These are the moments for which we forego nights with our families. These are the moments that sustain us.

Unfortunately, too often these life-changing moments are overshadowed by other, more mundane matters—the day-to-day trials and tribulations we face as we navigate the health care system. During my travels across the country I've been struck by the sense that so many physicians feel under siege. It's easy to understand why.

These days just about everyone has an opinion about how we should do our jobs. The government compels us, under threat of penalty, to purchase electronic health records. So we go out and buy them. But instead of increasing efficiency they slow us down, eating up valuable time that would be far better spent at the bedside.

The health system executive institutes policies that don't make clinical sense—abandoning patient interests in favor of spreadsheets and financial models. And physicians are left scrambling to fill in the gaps.

The insurance company steps in with its medical opinion, questioning whether a particular procedure was necessary—denying payment for tests that in cases like my patient Joe's—can mean the difference between life and death.

And the lawyer circles like a hawk above us, witnessing the failures of the system, looking for any opportunity to assign blame to the person most easily accountable under law—the physician.

All these demands leave us exhausted—accountable to everyone, yet without the autonomy needed to deliver on everyone's expectations. And the highest expectations, of course, come from ourselves. We know the level of care our patients need and deserve. And we are unwilling to compromise on that care, regardless of the obstacles and burdens the system throws in our path.

I experience these trials and tribulations regularly in the ED. I've labored through the 70-page transition-of-care documents. I've been forced, in this day of nanotechnology and genetic sequencing, to head over to the fax machine because our hospital computer can't talk to the one across town.

I've marveled at the sparkling legibility of the reams of paper produced. Perfectly legible. . . yet utterly incomprehensible. I've marveled at the fact that an industry responsible for one fifth of this nation's economy can be less technologically adept than a fantasy football website or an online video game.

These kinds of daily frustrations are disheartening. And there are days when I feel overwhelmed. Powerless to shape my own future, let alone those of my patients. But that is only part of the story.

A couple of months ago, I attended the 200th meeting of the World Medical Association in Norway. During my stay, I had the opportunity to tour some of Oslo's highlights, including a dramatic bridge by the artist Gustav Vigeland. What makes the bridge so striking are the 58 life-size sculptures perched along its two rails.

As you approach one of the rails, the first thing you encounter is a woman fighting a dragon. Further down, there's a man and woman arguing. A bit further along a child clenches his fists in anger. The images continue in this way, captivating in their own right.

But then when you look across the bridge to the other rail you're surprised to see the polar opposites portrayed. The other side of the story. There's a sculpture of a child, but this time he's skipping in reverie. The couple that was so fiercely arguing is now kissing. And the woman who bravely fought the dragon. . . is now clutching it in warm embrace.

All along the bridge this duality is movingly displayed. The joys of love. The anguish of love. The pleasures of childhood. The frustrations of childhood. It's all part of the human condition. Part of the rich pageantry of life.

When I reflect on being a physician today, I see many challenges. But for each story of frustration, there is a story of vision, perseverance, and success. There is a story of hope. Think of some of the AMA's recent victories. . .

For well over a decade, America's physicians toiled to fix the broken Medicare payment system. Year after year we marched to Capitol Hill with solutions. And year after year we were turned away. But we refused to give up.

In the face of adversity, we gathered our strength. As the obstacles mounted, we redoubled our efforts. With every passing year, our voice grew stronger. With every year, our voice grew louder. Until finally, we could not be ignored.

Two months ago, because of a quest that started right here in the House of Medicine, Congress passed the Medicare Access and CHIP Reauthorization Act. And because of this law, today 49 million seniors and 10 million members of the military and their families are assured access to care in their time of need. And the 1 million physicians who serve them, have the stability we need to provide the best possible care.

This is just one example—just the most recent example—of the kind of impact America's physicians can have when we stand together. And there are more.

Today, because of a quest that started in the House of Medicine, the number of uninsured Americans has dropped to the lowest level in seven years. Today, because of a quest that started in the House of Medicine, 10 million more Americans are taking control of their health—engaging with the system in times of wellness, as well as in illness. Today, because of a quest that started in the House of Medicine, physician-led accountable care organizations have become the top performers in Medicare. They're not only improving patient care. . . they're saving tens of millions of dollars for the system.

Since the AMA was founded in 1847, physicians have faced one obstacle after another. Medical quackery. Substandard medical education. Ethical dilemmas. The perils of smoking. HIV/AIDS. Whatever the obstacles, the AMA has faced them head on. And together, we have overcome them.

As some of you know, I studied the Classics during my undergraduate years. This background has furnished me with a wealth of useful knowledge. For example, when most people hear the name Cicero they think of history's most famous orator. I think of hummus. That's because the Latin word for Cicero essentially translates to chickpea.

In addition to giving me a clear advantage in Trivial Pursuit, studying the Classics affords valuable insight into human behavior and politics – lessons as valid today as they were two millennia ago.

For me, one figure that always stood out is Alexander the Great. Crowned king of Macedonia at age 20, by 30 he had amassed one of the largest empires of antiquity. It stretched 3,000 miles across parts of modern-day Europe, Asia and Africa. With unparalleled ambition and endurance, Alexander conquered nations, founded cities in his name, and built a personal legacy that endures to this day. But just a few years after Alexander died, his massive empire had fragmented and fallen apart. Rome, by contrast, thrived for centuries. The lesson from the pages of history could not be more clear: an empire built by one man will not stand. An empire built by many endures.

I have always felt that the power of the AMA lies in the sheer diversity of our membership. Instead of representing one particular specialty, or one particular state, we represent all physicians, in all states. We represent medical students, residents, young physicians, international medical graduates. We represent minority physicians, senior physicians, LGBT physicians. Our membership is as diverse as the patients we serve. Each one of us brings something different to the equation. And together, our collective voice is as rich and nuanced as it is strong.

Today our quest is broader, bolder, and more visionary than ever before. Rather than reacting to the changes and challenges transforming health care, the AMA is stepping out to lead the way forward. Rather than waiting for tomorrow, we're creating the future of health care today. Our vision is ambitious:

- To profoundly improve health outcomes for the 86 million people in this country with pre-diabetes and the 70 million with hypertension.
- To forge a generation of physicians prepared to meet the needs of our twenty-first century health care system.
- To restore the joy in medicine and enable physicians to spend their time where it matters most – helping patients.

These are lofty goals, and achieving them will not be easy. Nothing worthwhile ever is. But as physicians, we have never shied away from challenges. Rather, by working together, we have always found a way to overcome them – one patient at a time, one family at a time, one community at a time.

I recall a truck driver I treated early in my career in Memphis. Let's call him Matt. Matt arrived to the ED in a taxi. I point that out because some folks don't hesitate to call an ambulance for a runny nose. But Matt was the opposite. He made his living crossing the continent in an 18-wheeler, and he'd been having chest pain for hours before he finally decided to pull over.

He walked into a truck stop and asked the cashier, "Can you call me a cab? And by the way, can you recommend a hospital?"

Matt found us, and we immediately did an EKG. It showed he was clearly having a heart attack – he'd probably been having it for hours. My team and I administered numerous medications and were able to stabilize him to such a degree that he could be admitted to the hospital.

The next night when I arrived for my shift in the ED, a "Code Blue" was called in the operating room. One of the nurses turned to me and said, "I think the fellow we took care of last night just went up there." So I went up to the OR and sure enough, there was Matt on the table—a cardiac surgeon leaning over him. I asked the surgeon what had happened, and he filled me in on the extraordinary chain of events.

After leaving the ED, Matt had spent an uneventful night in the hospital. In the morning he saw a cardiologist for a catheterization. The cardiologist discovered blockage so severe that stents would not be enough, so he scheduled Matt for an urgent open heart bypass. At the appointed time, Matt arrived in the operating room. But the moment the anesthesiologist put him under, he went into cardiac arrest. A code blue was called, and for all intents and purposes, Matt was dead.

That's when the cardiac surgeon made a series of split-second decisions. With lightning speed he attempted to put Matt on the bypass pump so the surgery could proceed. But when he tried to insert the catheters into Matt's femoral artery and vein, they were so calcified that the catheters would not pass. Without blinking, the surgeon moved to plan B. He cracked open Matt's chest, inserted the bypass catheters directly into Matt's aorta and vena cava, and commenced open heart surgery. All of this, within the four or so minutes necessary to prevent brain damage.

A few days later, I stopped by Matt's room to see how he was doing. And in a surreal moment, this man who had nearly died before my eyes in the ED – and literally died before my eyes in the OR—stood up, walked across the room, and gave me a bear hug.

When it comes to something as important as saving a life, numerous factors come into play. Speed. Mental dexterity. Decades of training. Hope. Above all, it takes a team. At the end of the day, which one of us was responsible for saving Matt's life? Was it the quick-thinking cardiac surgeon? Was it the cardiologist who detected the blockage? Was it those of us in ED who stabilized his heart attack? What about the nurses who cared for him, or the assistants in the OR?

Like everyone in this room, I was drawn to organized medicine because I realized that the only way to take on big problems is through collaboration with others. Each one of us has a role to play. Each one of us contributes something the other cannot.

The same can be said of health care in this country. When it comes to something as important as shaping a better, healthier future, it will take every single one of us. Physicians. Payers. Policymakers. Patients. Every one of us has a part to play. We cannot do it alone.

As that famous orator Cicero once said, "We were born to unite with our fellow men, and to join in community with the human race."

Colleagues, it is my honor to join with you in the year ahead. It is my honor to fight alongside you, on behalf of this country's physicians and patients. Today the AMA tenaciously pursues a healthier future. And we will get there because of our past.

We will get there because of the rich foundation that supports us. We will get there because of the vision and fortitude that are the hallmarks of this profession. We will get there because America's physicians have always stood—and still stand today—united as one.

Thank you.

Raising Wages as the Standard for 2016 Presidential Candidates

Richard L. Trumka

At the outset of the 2016 U.S. presidential campaign, President of the American Federation of Labor and Congress of Industrial Organizations (AFL-CIO) Richard L. Trumka delivers a speech noting that after two generations of American politicians pursuing policies that have stagnated wages and worsened inequality, working Americans remain skeptical of both the Republican and Democratic parties. Observing that "since 1978, CEOs have increased their own pay by almost 1,000 percent [while] the wages of 90% of us have gone down," Trumka voices the need for a presidential candidate who will commit to improving a host of issues that affect the lower and middle classes—by raising wages, increasing benefits, and investing in infrastructure and education—in order to serve the interests of the majority of working Americans. Richard Trumka is president of the 12.5 million-member AFL-CIO, the largest organization of labor unions in the country. Born into a family of coal miners in Pennsylvania, Trumka worked as a miner himself while attending Penn State and then Villanova University Law School before joining the labor movement.

Thank you, Liz [Shuler],for your words of introduction. Before I get into the main substance of my remarks, I want to acknowledge Workers Memorial Day. Today, we remember the 150 men and women who die every day from a workplace injury or occupational disease.

Please join me in a moment of silence in their honor.

[Moment of silence.]

Thank you. The arrival of spring in Washington has brought baseball—as well as the other D.C. obsession and America's second-favorite pastime: presidential politics.

The election is more than 18 months away, but already ideas are percolating and candidates are stepping forward to announce for the presidency.

Working people are stepping forward, too. We are not waiting for an invitation. We have created an agenda for shared prosperity called Raising Wages. It will be our inspiration and our measuring stick throughout the presidential campaign. Raising

---

Delivered April 28, 2015, at the AFL-CIO headquarters, Washington D.C., by Richard L. Trumka, © AFL-CIO, used with permission.

Wages is grounded in a fundamental idea—that we can become a high-wage society, a society in which the people who do the work share in the wealth we create.

That idea faces a political landscape characterized by two powerful forces: one, there is an enormous need in America. Our nation is struggling, and has been struggling for almost two generations. Two, there is an equal amount of skepticism in America. For decades, we have given politicians the benefit of the doubt. Today, there is much more doubt than there is benefit.

As the presidential campaigns begin, workers have a very clear question: Will candidates be and think and act big enough to seize this historic opportunity?

Will they look past what Washington says can't be done and do what America needs? Will they overcome our skepticism? Will they present a vision that's authentic, bold and unequivocal? Will our candidates meet the moment?

It is early and, although many candidates are already in the race, the field remains open. And the labor movement's doors are open to any candidate who is serious about transforming our economy with high and rising wages. We want to talk to candidates who will deliver and who we can trust to always be on the side of all working people.

Over nearly two generations, national leaders have either taken steps that worsened inequality or fiddled around the edges, trying to raise wages in an economy fundamentally built to lower wages. President Obama has spent much of his presidency getting our nation out of a deep economic crisis. Now we have an economy where GDP is up, and the stock market is up, but wages remain flat—and this has happened again and again since the 1970s. Once again, America is emerging from an economic crisis—but those of us who count on paychecks are not. And that's not an accident. Workers are being held down on purpose.

For almost two generations, our economic policies—the very structure of our economy—have been designed to push incomes down for the vast majority of working people. This was planned. It's not the accidental result of the wandering and clumsy hand of capitalism.

Since the 1980s, the growing political power of the wealthiest among us has rewritten our labor laws, our trade laws, our tax laws, our monetary policies, our fiscal policies, our financial regulations, all to push wages down and to increase corporate profits, to put speculation over private investment and tax cuts over public investment.

The results: Runaway inequality. Unemployment. Falling wages. Rising economic insecurity. Collapsing infrastructure. Deteriorating national competitiveness. All driven by gigantic imbalances in economic and political power.

One simple comparison captures the whole story: since 1978, CEOs have increased their own pay by almost 1,000 percent. In the same 37 years, the wages of 90% of us have gone down. That is a violation of the American Promise. It's not just the poor who are falling behind; it's the middle class, too.

And now, this story threatens to grow in scale, with Fast Track and the Trans-Pacific Partnership.

But all across the country, workers are leading a fierce and broad social movement to defeat Fast Track. We are rebelling against corporate-written free trade agreements—and we are succeeding. The TPP [Trans-Pacific Partnership] is the latest example of a long-term approach to trade that, starting with NAFTA [North American Free Trade Agreement], was designed to drive wages down, create special rights for corporations and export jobs.

The labor movement opposes Fast Track. We expect those who seek to lead our nation forward to oppose Fast Track. There is no middle ground, and the time for deliberations is drawing to a close.

In the 2016 campaign, there will be no place to hide for those who aspire to lead America. The problems of income inequality and stagnant wages are so clear, so abundant, that only direct, sweeping action to change the rules will put our nation on a fresh path of progress.

We are hungry for a path to a prosperous twenty-first century. And America's workers know that the first step on that path is Raising Wages.

Yes, Raising Wages includes lifting national wages—but it's far broader than that. We want earned sick leave and paid family leave. We want full employment, fair overtime rules and fair scheduling so people don't have to guess whether they'll get enough hours to pay the rent. We want student debt relief. We want to tax Wall Street to pay for massive investments in infrastructure and education, so Wall Street serves Main Street, not the other way around. And we want to be able to bargain collectively with our employers for good wages and benefits without fear of retaliation.

We want to raise wages. And that's exactly what we're doing, despite policies designed to hold us down. Working people, and the collective voice, are rising. Look at the people who work at Walmart, McDonald's and Target, and TJMaxx and Marshalls. In those fights alone, a combined 2 million people have won raises in just the past few months. It's not enough, but it's a start. We are fighting in new ways with new ideas—and starting to win.

We are swarming ballot boxes, city halls and state houses. Initiatives to raise the minimum wage won last November in every state they were on the ballot. Red State, Blue State, it didn't matter, from Alaska to Illinois. Cities across the country have been adopting universal earned sick leave. San Francisco passed a retail workers bill of rights. Seattle raised the minimum wage to $15 an hour.

And working people are bargaining with employers like never before. In 2015, more union members will bargain for new contracts than in any other year in American history. Five million union members are negotiating this year for contracts with employers in every conceivable industry. Together, through collective bargaining, we are asking for a raise.

Five million workers sitting down with employers to bargain in a straightforward way, to make the case to raise wages. That's what the collective voice is about. That's what American democracy is about.

Our whole country deserves that same conversation.

Working people, together, are rising. The question is, will our candidates listen? Will they seize this opportunity? I wonder, and so do the vast majority of working Americans. The truth is we're skeptical.

Are we wrong to be skeptical? I don't think so. A surging army of workers, activists and families are tired of taking "maybe" for an answer. We're tired of scared politicians who won't stand up for what's right. Listen to this: About one-third—30%—of working-class voters after the last election said they couldn't see any significant difference between the two parties.

Both parties, they said, side with the wealthy over working people. Both parties are too close to big corporations. Neither party cares deeply enough about creating jobs. Neither party cares enough about raising wages or protecting Social Security or Medicare.

Of the working-class voters we surveyed, 80% of Democrats and Republicans, 80%, say both parties do far too much for Wall Street and not nearly enough to help average folks.

That's what America thinks.

Are we wrong? I don't think so. Anyone who thinks it's OK for women to get 78 cents on the dollar is willingly betraying the American Promise. Anyone letting corporate America write our economic rules while expressing surprise at the outcome is willingly betraying the American Promise.

That's why we're skeptical. And our skepticism will only be overcome by an honest conversation about how we can all benefit from what we produce and expand the American Promise. We want to make our case and get an authentic, meaningful response. That's what we want from employers, and that's what we want from our presidential candidates.

That's why we at the AFL-CIO are creating Raising Wages Summits in each of the first four presidential primary states. At these summits, beginning next month in Iowa, working people will make the case for a Raising Wages agenda. Together, we will declare the standard by which presidential aspirations will be judged.

And that brings me back to the opportunity in front of us, both for our country and for the men and women who might want to lead it.

To candidates who have just discovered that there is an income inequality problem in America, we say "Welcome." We encourage them to dig deeper, to understand and respond to the history, the intent and the impact of this problem.

And we say to them, we appreciate your words of acknowledgment. But now what? After almost two generations of intentional assault on our incomes, our families and our dignity, working people are not going to be satisfied with words of acknowledgment. We want action. We want big ideas, and we want structural change. We want Raising Wages.

That also means no candidate can be all things to all people and still meet this standard. Standing with working people once in a while won't work. Candidates can't hedge bets any longer.

Workers have swallowed the politics of hedged bets for almost two generations. We've waited for the scraps that remain after the pollsters shape the politics.

Those days are over. America doesn't need relentlessly cautious half-measures. Any candidate who wants to appeal to workers has to put forth a bold and comprehensive Raising Wages agenda. They must be committed to investing in a prosperous future for America. They must have an authentic voice and a commitment, from the candidate down through his or her economic team, to see this agenda through to completion.

We have an agenda for shared prosperity, and we want the same from candidates. They must address essential questions like these: How will you make sure the incomes of working people regain lost ground and grow? How will you show us that corporations will no longer write America's economic rules? How will you establish public investment in America's common goals as a priority over narrow special interests? How will you make sure we all rise together with justice in our communities, dignity for immigrants and fairness for all, regardless of gender or sexuality, race, ethnicity or wealth?

We call on all of America's working men and women—Democrat and Republican, white collar, blue collar and no collar—to join us in supporting the candidate who can and will deliver on the American Promise. That is the standard. We will not settle for less.

Thank you.

Finding Common Ground

By Bernie Sanders

In a speech at Liberty University, the school founded by evangelical Southern Baptist pastor, televangelist, and conservative political commentator Jerry Falwell, Senator Bernie Sanders, an avowed liberal, appeals for those of diverging political beliefs to find common ground. While acknowledging that he and his audience do not share many of the same views, for instance on homosexuality and abortion, he raises other issues where they might have common interests, for instance regarding the wealth discrepancy in the United States, where "the top one-tenth of 1 percent ... owns almost as much wealth as the bottom 90 percent." With allusions to biblical morals as embodied by the "golden rule" and the need to care for the poor and the wretched, Sanders discusses the injustice and immorality of having people die from poverty and lack of health care in the world's wealthiest country. By invoking the bible and a common ethical system that he says all of the world's great religions agree upon, Sanders makes the case for more moral economic policies that will serve the majority of people in the United States and around the world. Bernie Sanders is a self-described democratic socialist and the junior U.S. Senator from Vermont. He worked in the non-profit world before being elected mayor of Burlington, Vermont in 1981. In 1990 he won a seat in the House of Representatives, where he served until 2007, when he was elected to the Senate. As of the publication of this book, Sanders is running for the office of President of the United States.

Thank you, President Falwell and David. Thank you very much for inviting my wife, Jane, and me to be with you this morning. We appreciate the invitation very much.

And let me start off by acknowledging what I think all of you already know. And that is the views that many here at Liberty University have and I, on a number of important issues, are very, very different. I believe in a woman's rights. . . .

And the right of a woman to control her own body.

I believe in gay rights and gay marriage.

Those are my views, and it is no secret. But I came here today, because I believe from the bottom of my heart that it is vitally important for those of us who hold different views to be able to engage in a civil discourse.

Too often in our country—and I think both sides bear responsibility for us—there is too much shouting at each other. There is too much making fun of each other.

Now, in my view, and I say this as somebody whose voice is hoarse, because I

Delivered September 14, 2015, at Liberty University, Lynchburg, Virginia, by Bernie Sanders.

have given dozens of speeches in the last few months, it is easy to go out and talk to people who agree with you. I was in Greensboro, North Carolina, just last night. All right. We had 9,000 people out. Mostly they agreed with me. Tonight, we're going to be in Manassas, and have thousands out and they agree with me. That's not hard to do. That's what politicians by and large do.

We go out and we talk to people who agree with us.

But it is harder, but not less important, for us to try and communicate with those who do not agree with us on every issue.

And it is important to see where if possible, and I do believe it is possible, we can find common ground.

Now, Liberty University is a religious school, obviously.

And all of you are proud of that.

You are a school which, as all of us in our own way, tries to understand the meaning of morality. What does is mean to live a moral life? And you try to understand, in this very complicated modern world that we live in, what the words of the Bible mean in today's society.

You are a school which tries to teach its students how to behave with decency and with honesty and how you can best relate to your fellow human beings, and I applaud you for trying to achieve those goals.

Let me take a moment, or a few moments, to tell you what motivates me in the work that I do as a public servant, as a senator from the state of Vermont. And let me tell you that it goes without saying, I am far, far from being a perfect human being, but I am motivated by a vision, which exists in all of the great religions, in Christianity, in Judaism, in Islam and Buddhism, and other religions.

And that vision is so beautifully and clearly stated in Matthew 7:12, and it states,"So in everything, do to others what you would have them to do to you, for this sums up the war and the prophets."That is the golden rule. Do unto others what you would have them do to you. That is the golden rule, and it is not very complicated.

Let me be frank, as I said a moment ago. I understand that the issues of abortion and gay marriage are issues that you feel very strongly about. We disagree on those issues. I get that,but let me respectfully suggest that there are other issues out there that are of enormous consequence to our country, and in fact to the entire world, that maybe, just maybe, we do not disagree on and maybe, just maybe, we can try to work together to resolve them.

Amos 5:24, "But let justice roll on like a river, righteousness like a never-failing stream."Justice treating others the way we want to be treated, treating all people, no matter their race, their color, their stature in life, with respect and with dignity.

Now here is my point. Some of you may agree with me, and some of you may not, but in my view, it would be hard for anyone in this room today to make the case that the United States of America, our great country, a country which all of us love,it would be hard to make the case that we are a just society, or anything resembling a just society today.

In the United States of America today, there is massiveinjustice in terms of income and wealth inequality.Injustice is rampant. We live, and I hope all of you know this, in thewealthiest country in the history of the world.

But most Americans don't know that. Because almost all of that wealth and income is going to thetop 1 percent.

You know, that is the truth. We are living in a time—and I warn all of you if you would, put this in the context of the Bible, not me, in the context of the Bible —we are living in a time where a handful of people have wealth beyond comprehension. And I'm talking about tens of billions of dollars, enough to support their families for thousands of years.With huge yachts, and jet planes and tens of billions. More money than they would ever know what to do with.

But at that very same moment, there are millions of people in our country, let alone the rest of the world, who are struggling to feed their families. They are struggling to put a roof over their heads, and some of them are sleeping out on the streets. They are struggling to find money in order to go to a doctor when they are sick.

Now, when we talk about morality, and when we talk about justice, we have to, in my view, understand that there is no justice when so few have so much and so many have so little.

There is no justice, and I want you to hear this clearly, when the top one-tenth of 1 percent—not 1 percent, the top one-tenth of 1 percent—today in America owns almost as much wealth as the bottom 90 percent. And in your hearts, you will have to determine the morality of that, and the justice of that.

In my view, there is no justice, when here, in Virginia and Vermont and all over this country, millions of people are working long hours forabysmally low wages of $7.25 an hour, of $8 an hour, of $9 an hour, working hard, but unable to bring in enough money to adequately feed their kids.

And yet, at that same time,58 percent of all new income generated is going to the top 1 percent. You have got to think about the morality of that, the justice of that, and whether or not that is what we want to see in our country.

In my view, there is no justice when, in recent years, we have seen a proliferation of millionaires and billionaires, while at the same time the United States of America has the highest rate of childhood poverty of any major country on Earth. How can we? I want you to go into your hearts, how can we talk about morality, about justice, when we turn our backs on the children of our country?

Now you have got to think about it. You have to think about it and you have to feel it in your guts. Are you content? Do you think it's moral when 20 percent of the children in this country, the wealthiest country in the history of the world, are living in poverty? Do you think it is acceptable that 40 percent of African American children are living in poverty?

In my view, there is no justice, and morality suffers when in our wealthy country, millions of children go to bed hungry. That is not morality and that is not in my view. . . what America should be about.

In my view, there is no justice when the 15 wealthiest people in this country in the last two years—two years—saw their wealth increase by $170 billion. Two years. The wealthiest 15 people in this country saw their wealth increase by $170 billion.

My friends, that is more wealth acquired in a two-year period than is owned by the bottom 130 million Americans. And while the very, very rich become much richer, millions of families have no savings at all. Nothing in the bank. And they worry every single day that if their car breaks down, they cannot get to work, and if they cannot get to work, they lose their jobs.

And if they lose their jobs,they do not feed their family. In the last two years, 15 people saw a $170 billion increase in their wealth; 45 million Americans live in poverty. That in my view is not justice. That is a rigged economy, designed by the wealthiest people in this country to benefit the wealthiest people in this country at the expense of everybody else.

In my view, there is no justice when thousands of Americans die every single year because they do not have any health insurance and do not go to a doctor when they should.I have talked personally to doctors throughout Vermont and physicians around the country. And without exception, they tell me there are times when patients walk into their office very, very sick and they say, why didn't you come in here when you're sick? And the answer is, I do not have any health insurance or I have a high deductible or I thought the problem would get better. And sometimes it doesn't, and sometimes they die because they lack health insurance.

That is not justice. That is not morality. People should not be dying in the United States of America when they are sick.

What that is is an indication that we are the only major country on earth that does not guarantee health care to all people as a right, and I think we should change that.

And I think—I think that when we talk about morality, what we are talking about is all of God's children. The poor, the wretched, they have a right to go to a doctor when they are sick.

You know, there is a lot of talk in this country from politicians about family values. You have all heard that. Well, let me tell you about a family value.

In my view, there is no justice when low-income and working-class mothers are forced to separate from their babies one or two weeks after birth and go back to work because they need the money that their jobs provide. Now I know everybody here—we all are, maybe in different ways, but all of us believe in family values.

Jane and I have four kids. We have seven beautiful grandchildren. We believe in family values. But it is not a family value when all of you know that the most important moments and time of a human being's life is the first weeks and months after that baby is born. That is the moment when a mother bonds with the baby; gets to love and know her baby—dad is there as well. That is what a family is about. And those of you—at least those of you who are parents—more parents back here than there I suspect. You know what an unforgettable moment that is. What an important moment that is. And I want you to think, whether you believe it is a family value, that the United States of America is the only—only—major country on earth that does not provide paid family and medical leave.

Now in English, what that means is that all over the world when a woman has her baby she is guaranteed the right because society understands how important that moment is. She is guaranteed the right to stay home and get income in order to nurture her baby. And that is why I believe when we talk about family values that the United States government must provide at least 12 weeks of paid family and medical leave.

In my view there is no justice in our country when youth unemployment exists at tragically high levels. I requested a study last month from a group of economists. And what they told me is that 51 percent of African American high school graduates between the ages of 17 and 20 are unemployed or underemployed—51 percent.

We have in this country sufficient amounts of money to put more people in jail than any other country on earth.The United States has more people in jail than China, a communist authoritarian country.

But apparently we do not have enough money to provide jobs and education to our young people. I believe that's wrong. I am not a theologian, I am not an expert on the Bible, nor am I a Catholic. I am just a United States senator from the small state of Vermont. But I agree with Pope Francis, who will soon be coming to visit us in the United States.

I agree with Pope Francis when he says, and I quote, "The current financial crisis originated in a profound human crisis, the denial of the primacy of the human person," and this is what he writes: "We have created new idols. The worship of the ancient golden calf has returned in a new and ruthless guise in the idolatry of money and the dictatorship of an impersonal economy lacking a truly human purpose," end of quote.

And the pope also writes, quote, "There is a need for financial reform along ethical lines that would produce in its turn an economic reform to benefit everyone. Money has to serve, not to rule," end of quote.

Now those are pretty profound words, which I hope we will all think about. In the pope's view, and I agree with him, we are living in a nation and in a world, and the Bible speaks to this issue, in a nation and in a world which worships not love of brothers and sisters, not love of the poor and the sick, but worships the acquisition of money and great wealth. I do not believe that is the country we should be living in.

Money and wealth should serve the people. The people should not have to serve money and wealth. (APPLAUSE)

Throughout human history, there has been endless discussion. It is part of who we are as human beings, people who think and ask questions, endless discussion and debate about the meaning of justice and about the meaning of morality. And I know that here at Liberty University, those are the kinds of discussions you have every day, and those are the kinds of discussions you should be having and the kinds of discussions we should be having all over America.

I would hope, and I conclude with this thought, I would hope very much that as part of that discussion and part of that learning process, some of you will conclude that if we are honest in striving to be a moral and just society, it is imperative that we have the courage to stand with the poor, to stand with working people and when necessary, take on very powerful and wealthy people whose greed, in my view, is doing this country enormous harm.

Thank you all very much.

Intelligence Community Pride

By Stephanie O'Sullivan

Principal Deputy Director of National Intelligence Stephanie O'Sullivan delivers a speech on behalf of Director of National Intelligence James Clapper at the LGBTA Summit of 2015. Beginning by noting Clapper's past regret at having to enforce policies like "Don't Ask, Don't Tell" that discriminated against the LGBT community in the armed forces, O'Sullivan expresses relief that such policies are no longer in effect and applauds the current climate that is increasingly aware of the lived experiences of gay, lesbian, bisexual, and transgender individuals. O'Sullivan especially commends new laws and policies that protect the equal rights of this community and the more open and accepting beliefs in the medical industry and society in general. Stephanie O'Sullivan was sworn in as the Principal Deputy Director of National Intelligence (PDDNI) in 2011. Previously, she served as the Associate Deputy Director of the Central Intelligence Agency (CIA) and as the CIA's Directorate of Science and Technology (DS&T).

Thank you for the introduction and for welcoming me here today in place of Director Clapper. He had a personal issue that pulled him away, and there is simply no way he could be here today. I know it's the standard line to say, "I know he wishes he could be here." In this case, that's a vast understatement. He was very much looking forward to making this speech—which now, I get to make.

He's talked a lot about how much last year's LGBTA [Lesbian, Gay, Bisexual, Transgender, and Allies] Summit meant to him, and he asked me to relay some things. Over the past 14 months, he's spent a good bit of time ruminating on that speech, and he told me that what he said last year—he's felt that way for years, decades. But he's never before spoken out in public like that about his experiences.

He said it took him a while to process just how much the injustice he'd seen during his career bothered him, particularly his personal experience 50 years ago when he was a very young lieutenant, when he had to process the dishonorable discharges of two fine airmen who had been "outed" as homosexuals.

They were model airmen: superb Russian linguists and meticulous about their military responsibilities. And they loved serving their country. He says that five decades later, it still stings him to think of being asked to out-process them. It was a waste of superb talent, as well as a profound injustice.

Decades later, when Director Clapper was wing commander for all Air Force troops at NSA [National Security Agency], he saw Admiral Bobby Inman take a stand and go in a different direction. The standing logic at the time was that

Delivered May 6, 2015, to the Intelligence Community Lesbian, Gay, Bisexual, Transgender and Allies Summit, National Reconnaissance Office Headquarters, Chantilly, Virginia.

anyone who was gay was open to blackmail and therefore should not hold a security clearance.

Of course, that is and was very flawed logic. The main reason gay clearance holders were open to blackmail is because, if anyone found out their orientation, they'd lose their clearance. You'd lose your clearance, because of the threat of losing your clearance.

It's funny, in a tragic sense, because the consequences are terrible.

So, when DNI [Director of National Intelligence] Clapper was Colonel Clapper, Wing Commander at NSA, and a gifted crypto-mathematician there was outed and lost his clearance, NSA Director Bobby Inman restored his clearance, asking only that this officer acknowledge his sexual orientation to his coworkers, so that there was no longer any threat of blackmail.

Of course, that's a big "only." That forced the officer to follow someone else's timeline with his very personal process of coming out. But it was a courageous and at the time unprecedented decision.

A decade later, (Jim Clapper has a lot of "decades" in this business) [laughter], he was profoundly grateful for the example Inman set, because as the Chief of Air Force Intelligence, then-General Clapper was given a similar opportunity to correct an injustice, by restoring the clearance of a civilian employee who'd been outed.

He says he doesn't think that act makes up for out-processing the two airmen at the start of his career, but he says with that second chance, he had the power to do something about it. So he did. And this is a quote from Director Clapper, "Damn, it felt good."

And he says, more importantly, it was the right thing to do. And it helped the Air Force retain talent they desperately needed. He says, in the weeks and months after that decision, he wore it as a badge of honor when his fellow General and Flag Officers gave him a hard time about it.

At the 2014 LGBTA Summit here, he talked with you about those experiences and a few others. He says it felt good to him to get those things off his chest and out in the open. So the first thing he asked me to pass on is his appreciation for that invitation to speak last March. I believe that speech was cathartic for him. He used the term *cleansing*.

I think he understands the influence he has as DNI, but he underestimates the impact he can have personally, because he's been a bit taken aback by how much that discussion meant to you. This February, when he was on travel in Paris, an NSA integree caught him between meetings and, with a good deal of emotion, said she'd been at the March summit, 11 months earlier. She said hearing him talk about his experiences made a huge impact on her, and the way she felt about the Intelligence Community, and her career choice to join this community.

That's fantastic, and it shows, not only what an impact he can have, but the impact you have by holding this summit, and by establishing an LGBTA community in the IC.

I want to give you the words the DNI had planned to say about that interaction in Paris and to her: "I'm amazed and humbled that I—a 74-year-old, straight, white man— can say anything that has that kind of impact on you, because I can only imagine the obstacles you've had to overcome, not for your personal gain, but so that you can serve our country. You inspire me, I believe, far more than I could inspire you." And since you all know him, you know he means that sincerely.

That passion reminds me of another senior leader I think we can find inspiration in. In the fall of 2012, OPM [Office of Personnel Management] Director John Berry came to visit our office and spoke at an ODNI [Office of the Director of National Intelligence] town hall. His enthusiasm for the federal workforce was evident in his remarks. When he said the government is a great place to work, he wasn't just feeding us a line.

He said he'd taken a visit to Google's campus and told an auditorium full of their employees that, for a small pay cut [laughter], and fewer stock options [laughter] they could do truly meaningful work as part of the federal workforce. As you can imagine, that's a bit of a tough sell to make on Google's home turf, but he meant it.

At our town hall, John talked about working to streamline federal hiring practices and boost hiring of veterans, about making recruitment of students and recent graduates easier and about improving the diversity of the federal workforce. What John didn't mention in his speech was his own personal story. But with our very first question, someone from my office thanked him for being "out" as the most-senior openly-gay official in the history of the federal government.

We asked John what obstacles he'd had to overcome to achieve his position. John laughed and talked about going through his very first security clearance interview, just 90 days after President Clinton signed the executive order to allow people to hold a clearance while serving openly. John said his security interviewers were more nervous than he was. They had no idea what questions they could or couldn't ask him. And being John, he ended up having to comfort them and tell them it would be okay.

We then asked John what advice he would give to gay, lesbian, bisexual, and transgender employees in the IC as they progress through their careers. He advised everyone, and this advice stands for everyone in this room, no matter what orientation, background, or experiences you've had, "Be open with who you are, because life is simply too short not to be yourself." Our auditorium erupted with applause that went on for almost a minute. I was proud of us for that.

I started my career as an engineer, contracted to work for the Office of Naval Intelligence. I worked as an ONI [Office of Naval Intelligence] civilian, and then joined the CIA through the directorate of science and technology. I've got far fewer decades than DNI Clapper, okay, two fewer, but I've been around a while. And I've known many gay, and some bisexual, men and women; both civilians and uniformed military.

I cannot imagine the stress they were forced to endure to serve their country. It's simply incomprehensible to me, trying to keep and live with such a secret. It was wrong to have compelled people to live that way under "Don't Ask, Don't Tell" and under our regulations to hold clearances. I'm glad those things are in our past. And

I'm happy that those draconian rules also no longer hang over the heads of transgender employees.

By the way, I just found out, getting ready for today—that there's a label for me. Apparently, I am "Cis-gender."

That means my body, the gender I was assigned at birth, and my personal identity all match. It was really only a few years ago that I, and many of us, first thought about how it would feel if those didn't match.

The past couple of years have been huge for the transgender community. Case law precedents that protect transgender employees from being fired have been stacking up. And a 2012 ruling on Title 12 by the Equal Employment Opportunity Commission extends protections to transgender workers in all 50 states.

Then, in May of 2013, the diagnosis manual for psychology stopped listing being transgender as a "mental disorder." That was a big step forward, for the medical establishment to decide that, if your body and your assignment don't match your identity, there are much more constructive ways to help you than with a diagnosis of mental illness. It's good for the medical establishment to catch up to something most people have known for a long time.

Of course, that won't be the end of the struggle. We know that, because homosexuality was pulled from the list of "disorders" in 1973, and yet there are still outliers that try to "cure" homosexuality. So that, just a month ago, President Obama took a stand and called for an end to "conversion therapy." I like having a boss who publicly does things I'm proud of.

In January, for the first time ever, the president used the word *transgender* in his State of the Union speech. He was talking about how we as Americans respect human dignity, and he said, "That's why we defend free speech and advocate for political prisoners, and condemn the persecution of women or religious minorities or people who are lesbian, gay, bisexual, or transgender." The president's remarks show how, just in the past few years, we as a society have become much more attuned to how being transgender is simply a part of the human experience.

And very recently, Bruce Jenner has brought this into the public consciousness. I think we could have a reasonable debate about whether the media circus is a good thing or not, but nationally, I think we're ready for the discussion. I think the national transgender community has laid a lot of the groundwork to define terms and help us understand. And, media circus or not, personally I think airing the difficulties that transgender people experience is a good thing.

I'm happy, for instance, we can have a public discussion about "passing," specifically the idea that transgender people don't need, and shouldn't feel the need for other people to immediately identify them with the gender that they identify with. Transgender people can, in fact, dress and present according to who they are, and nothing that other people believe should drive what they do. Some people may not be ready to hear that message, but I don't consider that to be my opinion. That's just truth.

Just five or 10 years ago, it was acceptable for pop culture to use confusion over perceived sex and gender for low-brow comedy. But the transgender community has made a huge, positive impact in the past few years, and when Bruce Jenner came out with his transition, the few Paleolithic comedians who tried to make a joke of it very quickly found out how unacceptable that is today.

That's a lot of progress, very quickly made. However, just because mainstream America is learning what actions and reactions are unacceptable, that doesn't mean everyone knows how to be supportive. That's why I'm particularly proud of the work your transgender working group has done since it stood up after the first IC LGBTA Summit in 2012.

You filled a much needed gap with your publication of your, "Best Practices Guide for Transgender Employees, Their Colleagues, and Managers," and I think more importantly, you've formed what I'd have to describe as a "cross-agency rapid-response team" [laughter] to help, across the community, anyone considering gender transition, and to help that person's managers and coworkers. Beyond a sense of duty, that shows a true love for our Intelligence Community and for the people who work here.

So, thank you. So I've addressed the lesbian, gay, bisexual, and transgender members of this alliance. I want to take just a couple minutes to talk to the allies, the people who put the "A" in "LGBTA."

First, I'd like to officially add my name to your ranks. Thank you. That's humbling.

I'd like to add my name by repeating something the DNI said last year: "There's no way I can ever really know what members of the LGBT community go through and have gone through, but I can absolutely proclaim myself to be an ally." I'm proud to be one, and I'm proud of everyone else who's here today as an ally, because we, as allies, need to find a way to translate personal support into public advocacy.

The director and I both spend a lot of time talking about the "business case" for diversity in the Intelligence Community. Put simply, if we get together a bunch of people who all look and think alike to brainstorm about some problems we have, we'll all come up with similar ideas about what to do. If you look back at prominent intelligence failures, particularly as laid out by the Iraq WMD [Weapons of Mass Destruction] Commission, you'll see that each time, diverse thinking by people with diverse life experiences might have prevented the mistakes we made.

But here's an important distinction: hiring a diverse workforce is not enough. We won't reap the benefits of that diversity unless we also foster a culture of inclusion. People who belong to a minority group in our IC, whether that's because of their national origin, native language, race, color, disability, ethnicity, gender, age, religion, sexual orientation, or gender identity, need to feel welcome in our community, and they need to know they don't need to hide what makes them unique. It's from our differences that we draw our strengths. That's the "business and mission case" for diversity.

To me, there's an equally important reason to convert personal support into public advocacy. It's the right thing to do, to treat everyone, especially IC professionals, with dignity and respect. That may mean, if you pass someone cracking an inappropriate joke in the hallway, you stop and say, "That's not how we act here." Or that may mean actually speaking out in public.

As a rule, the director and I try not to take ourselves or the positions we occupy too seriously, but we realize that we can and should use our positions as, and this is how Director Clapper puts it, a "bully pulpit" when the occasion calls for it.

I do have to remind him he's not actually old enough to have been Teddy Roosevelt's principal intelligence advisor.

This occasion calls for using that bully pulpit. After the 2014 LGBTA Summit, we published his remarks on ODNI's public website, and we got outside publications to print them as well. I intend to continue talking about IC pride after today's summit, and Director Clapper has assured me that he'll be doing the same for the 87 weeks he has left to serve this community; not that he's counting.

By the way, I love the name of this group: IC Pride. I checked online for a definition of gay pride or LGBT pride, and I found this: "It's is the positive stance against discrimination and violence toward lesbian, gay, bisexual, and transgender (LGBT) people, to promote their self-affirmation, dignity, equality rights, increase their visibility as a social group, build community, and celebrate sexual diversity and gender variance."

The phrase in there that jumped out at me was, "build community." That's been our goal at ODNI, building a community of diverse intelligence agencies. Each Intelligence Community agency and element has its own unique intelligence tradecraft that it brings to the table. And we work best, as a community, when we celebrate how each agency is different, and we take advantage of the strengths inherent in their different cultures and ways of doing business. That's true at a macro level with agencies and at a micro level with individual intelligence officers.

So, going forward, I plan to be even more public with my support, because it's good for our community to be inclusive, and because it's right for our IC to welcome everyone who's a member. We should all take pride in doing so.

The work you do here, work that cuts across agency lines and brings people together as a community, is an important part of intelligence integration. That goes for the transgender working group, the ally engagement group, the recruitment and retention group, the communications and technology group, and the group that put this summit together. Thank you all for the work you do every day, and particularly for the work you're doing with IC Pride and at today's summit.

I want to leave you with a few words from the president. Two weeks ago, my office celebrated our tenth anniversary, and our celebration was capped off by a visit from President Obama. He spoke to our workforce and asked us to go out to all the agencies and pass along his message. He said first to tell you—simply—"You can take great pride in your service."

He talked about integrity. He said, "The work you provide is vital for me being able to make good decisions. And the fact that the work you prepare is giving it to me straight, that it doesn't look at the world through rose-colored glasses, that it doesn't exaggerate threats, but doesn't underplay the significant challenges that we face around the world—that's vitally important to me."

Then he talked about the great successes we've had over the past few years. . . and the great challenges, and he wrapped up with this message. He said, "I know what you do. We're more secure because of your service. We're more secure because of your patriotism and your professionalism. And I'm grateful for that."

So that's the president's message he wanted me to pass along, and because of the challenges we've faced over the past few years, that message comes from a president who has a better understanding of how the intelligence enterprise works than any of his predecessors.

I know he'd agree with me, that in our twenty-first century world, your work here with IC Pride is critical to our Intelligence Community and to the defense of our nation. So I want to leave you with the president's words: "You can all take great pride in your service." Thank you.

Keynote Address at the Women in the World Summit

By Hillary Clinton

In a speech at the sixth annual Women in the World Summit in New York City, Hillary Clinton addresses the various obstacles that face women in the United States and around the world, as well as the progress they have made over the years. Clinton begins with a personal story of her mother who grew up poor but persevered largely spurred on by moments of kindness from others. Discussing the impressive strides that women have made globally just in the last twenty years, Clinton cites domestic violence laws and other developments toward "closing gaps for women and girls." She proceeds to acknowledge that despite great advances much more work must be done. Addressing a wide range of women's issues from sexual violence to health care and equal pay, Clinton observes that the United States ranks 65th out of 142 nations on equal pay. "Imagine that," she says. "We should be number one." Noting "the full participation of women and girls in every aspect of their societies is the great unfinished business of the 21st century," Clinton urges her audience to work toward this important goal. Former First Lady, U.S. Senator for New York, and Secretary of State, Hillary Clinton, as of the publication of this book, is, for the second time, running for the office of President of the United States.

Oh, thank you. Wow.

Hasn't this been an extraordinary conference? I mean, all of the amazing people!

I want to thank Beatrice [Biira]. I have known Beatrice for a number of years. I know the story of her and her family, and how one goat helped get her on her way.

But then I have watched her make it through college, and graduate school, and just demonstrate all those qualities of grit and grace that really are there within so many people if they're just given a chance. And particularly women and girls, who just need that extra bit of encouragement. Who need to be surrounded by people who believe in them, that lift them up and help them find their paths as well.

If you're interested in Beatrice's story, there's a book—a children's book—about Beatrice and her goat. I highly recommend it. It's in my collection to read to my granddaughter.

Well, today, it's wonderful for me to be back here at Women in the World. I wanted to be here regardless of what else I was doing.

Delivered April 23, 2015 at the 2015, Women in the World Summit, New York, New York, by Hillary Clinton.

And, as usual, Tina [Brown] has done a masterful job planning three days to inspire not just awareness but action.

And every one of you proves that no matter who you are, or where you come from, you too can be a champion for change.

It doesn't matter whether you're a student or an artist, a journalist, and ambassador, maybe even a future president. We all have our stories.

We all have those moments where it just falls into place. When we realize we can't ignore the world around us. When we have something to say, something to do, and we can name the people who have inspired us to be able to take those risks. To care about what's going on in the world around us.

For me, the earliest inspiration, and really, still today my guiding light, was my mother. She had a childhood that none of us would want. Abandoned. Mistreated. First by her parents, then by her grandparents. Starting to work on her own by fourteen as a housemaid and a babysitter.

I didn't know this when I was growing up. I just knew she was my mom. And she believed in me, and she encouraged me, and set high standards for me.

And then as I got a little older, and I learned about her story, I was stunned.

I mean, there I was in our house. Secured, cared for, and I said to her, "How could you. . . how could you have survived? How could you have built a family of your own? Taking such good care of your children?"

And she told me about those moments of kindness that kept her going. The teacher who realized she had no food, in the first-grade classroom where they all ate at their desks. And without embarrassing her, without condescending or patronizing her, said one day, "You know, Dorothy? I just brought too much food to eat. Would you like to share what I have?"

And my mother said it wasn't until she was an adult, thinking through all those stages along her life when things could have gone so terribly wrong, that she realized there were people who reached out to her.

And when I was old enough to understand the challenges that my own mother faced, that lit a spark.

No one deserves to grow up like that. Everyone deserves the chance to live up to his or her God-given potential.

Those core values inculcated by my family and reinforced by my church and the people that I met in my experiences in public school and so much else.

And that's been the common thread, and it's really connected to what this conference is about. Because you're here understanding that there is a movement, a necessary movement that requires you to be involved in advancing the rights and opportunities of women and girls, here at home and around the world.

This work is far from finished, and every one of us, every single one of us, can make our own contribution.

Some of you, I know were with me in Beijing back in 1995 at the United Nations fourth World Conference on Women. Representatives from 189 countries came together to declare with one voice that human rights are women's rights and women's rights are human rights, once and for all. And finally, the world began to listen.

And in the years that followed, we have seen change. We passed laws prohibiting violence against women. Women elected to lead communities and countries. We made significant strides in closing gaps in health and education for women and girls around the world. And last month, the Clinton Foundation and the Gates Foundation unveiled a sweeping new report that gathers twenty years of data from around the world to document how far we have come and how far we still have to go.

All the evidence tells us that despite the enormous obstacles that remain, there has never been a better time in history to be born female. Think about that.

A girl born twenty years ago in Tanzania could not hope to one day own or inherit property. Today she can.

If she was born in Nepal, there was a tragically high chance that her mother, and even she, would die in childbirth. Today, thankfully, that is far less likely.

A girl born twenty years ago in Rwanda grew up in the shadow of genocide and rape. Today, she can be proud that women led the way out of that dark time, and now there are more women serving in her country's Parliament than anywhere else in the world.

But the data leads to a second conclusion, that despite all this progress, we're just not there yet.

Yes, we've nearly closed the global gender gap in primary school, but secondary school remains out of reach for so many girls around the world.

Yes, we've increased the number of countries prohibiting domestic violence, but still, more than half the nations in the world have no such laws on the books, and an estimated one in three women still experience violence.

Yes, we've cut the maternal mortality rate in half, but far too many women are still denied critical access to reproductive health care and safe childbirth.

All the laws we have don't count for much if they're not enforced. Rights have to exist in practice, not just on paper. Laws have to be backed up with resources and political will, and deep-seated cultural codes, religious beliefs, and structural biases have to be changed.

As I have said, and as I believe, the advancement of the full participation of women and girls in every aspect of their societies is the great unfinished business of the twenty-first century.

And not just for women, but for everyone. And not just in faraway countries, but right here in the United States.

We know that when women are strong, families are strong. When families are strong, countries are strong. So this is about more than just unleashing the full potential of women.

In our country, women moved into the workforce in large numbers over the past forty years. That helped to drive unprecedented economic growth.

In fact, the average American family earns $14,000 more today, and our gross domestic product is about $2 trillion larger, because all those women went to work and brought home a paycheck.

But if we close the gap that remains in the workforce between men and women, our economy in the United States would grow by nearly ten percent by 2030. Think about what that would mean in terms of rising wages and more opportunities.

But unfortunately, there are still far too many policies and too many pressures that make it tougher for parents, men and women alike, to work at a job, to go to school, while also raising a family.

The lack of quality affordable childcare, unequal pay, work schedules that are not only far from predictable or flexible, but also simply unfair, fall disproportionately heavily on women.

It is outrageous that America is the only country in the developed world that doesn't guarantee paid leave to mothers of newborns.

When I was at the hospital with Chelsea, while she was there to give birth to my most amazing, fabulous, unbelievable granddaughter, I was talking to some of the nurses. And one of the nurses said to me, "Thank you for fighting for paid family leave." She said, "I see so many women who have their babies who are just distraught."

At a time that should be so exciting and joyful, they have to immediately go back to work. They don't know how they're gonna manage. They don't have any kind of childcare, let alone quality affordable childcare.

It's hard to believe that in 2015, so many women still pay a price for being mothers.

It is also hard to believe that so many women are still paid less than men for the same work, with even wider gaps for women of color.

And if you doubt what I say, look to the World Economic Forum, hardly a hotbed of feminist thought.

Their rankings show that the United States is 65th out of 142 nations and other territories on equal pay.

Imagine that.

We should be number one.

And this isn't just about women. So many of our families today depend on two incomes to make ends meet, and 40 percent of all women are now the sole or primary breadwinners. That's a fact of life in the twenty-first century.

So when any parent is shortchanged, the entire family is shortchanged, often by thousands of dollars a year. Real money in your pockets that could mean a better home to rent or even buy. Or a little more food on the table, or something in a college savings account or your retirement fund. So you'd have a little less worry, and more means to be able to meet your needs.

Now when I talk to men about this, which I frequently do, I remind them, "If it was your wife, or your sister, or your daughter, or your mother getting taken advantage of at work, you would suffer, your kids would suffer, your family would suffer, and you'd want to do something about it."

Well, that's the point.

When women are held back, our country is held back. When women get ahead, everyone gets ahead.

And it's important to realize that it's not just in the economic arena that women are held back.

When women of any age, whether on college campuses, or on military bases, or even in their homes, face sexual assault, then no woman, no woman is secure.

Every woman deserves to have the safety and the security they need.

That means we have to guarantee that our institutions respond to the continuing scourge of sexual assault.

America moves forward when all women are guaranteed the right to make their own health care choices, not when those choices are taken away by an employer like Hobby Lobby.

And it's not just enough for some women to get ahead.

We need to make sure that all women, no matter where you live or who you are, and particularly, African-American and Hispanic women, who've worked their entire careers, can retire with dignity.

I was at a roundtable discussion at a small factory in Keene, New Hampshire, the other day, and one of the people sitting at the table with me was an older woman. And she said she had worked at the factory for a number of years and she had retired.

And I thought, "Well, that's nice. They asked a retiree to come back to be part of the discussion."

But she quickly said, "I had some big house repairs, and based on what I was getting in Social Security, I couldn't afford it. I had to come back to work."

When we deny women access to retirement that is secure. When we continue, as we do, to discriminate against women in the Social Security system. We are leaving too many women on their own. And those women do the very best they can under really difficult circumstances.

We move forward when gay and transgender women are embraced as our colleagues and our friends, not fired from good jobs because of who they love or who they are.

We move forward when women who came to this country in search of a better life can earn a path to citizenship.

Right now, they are being forced to work outside the formal economy, often being subjected to discrimination and even worse.

You know, our mothers and sisters and daughters are on the frontlines of all these battles, but these are not just women's fights. These have to be America's fights and the world's fights.

We have to take them on, we have to win them together, and we have to have leaders who recognize that the time has come.

Yet there are those who offer themselves as leaders who take a very different view.

Who offer themselves as leaders who see nothing wrong with denying women equal pay.

Who offer themselves as leaders who would defund the country's leading provider of family planning, and want to let health insurance companies, once again, charge women just because of our gender.

There are those who offer themselves as leaders who would deport mothers working to give their children a better life, rather than risk the ire of talk radio.

There are those who offer themselves as leaders who even play politics with the nomination of our nation's chief law enforcement officer and victims of human trafficking.

Finally, finally, Loretta Lynch will be able to assume the position she has trained her lifetime to hold.

These are not the way to move America forward.

It isn't leadership.

It's not going to create a single job, raise anyone's wages, or strengthen our families.

I have been so struck by meeting women who have, like my mother, dealt with tough odds, far tougher than anything I've had to face.

Last week, I met a woman in Iowa named Bethany. A single mom of three. She recognized that today, education is more than an opportunity; it's a necessity. So she enrolled in the local community college, thanks to Pell Grants and work study.

Now she's juggling a job, school, and raising her kids. But she is determined to see it through.

Of course she's worried about piling up debt. But she hopes to earn that two-year degree, and then go on to a four-year degree. And she is looking forward to her daughter starting at the same community college next fall.

She's not content to just get by any longer. She wants to get ahead and she wants to stay ahead.

She doesn't expect anything to come easy, but she did ask me, "What more can we do so it isn't quite so hard?"

The answer is, We can do a lot. If we do it together.

That's what this conference is all about. It's why we're here today. Because we believe that we can build a future where if you do your part, you can, in fact, get ahead.

And we know that the future would be in our reach.

And we can't get there unless women are empowered, not only on behalf of themselves, but others.

We have seen women all over the world become agents of change, drivers of progress, makers of peace.

I've seen penniless women in India and Bangladesh banding together to secure micro-financed loans and start their own businesses.

I've sat with Catholic and Protestant women in northern Ireland who finally have the courage to reach across ancient divides.

I've met the women in Liberia who forced an end to a bloody civil war and then took their place in government to forge a better future.

Here in the United States, just this week, we saw fast-food workers marching in the streets, asking for nothing more than a living wage and a chance at the American dream. (Applause)

So what I ask all of you is to recognize that by coming here and being part of this extraordinary gathering, you now must be an agent of change as well.

Because it's up to all of us—women, men, business leaders, policy makers, people of faith, community leaders—to be part of the progress we want to see.

My mother was born before women had the right to vote, and she never graduated from college.

But she was determined to make the most of her own life, and to give me and my brothers opportunities far beyond anything she had known.

Now, when I look at my own granddaughter, I feel that same determination.

It's not just what I want for her, because her family will do whatever we must to make sure she has every chance to go as far as her hard work and talent will take her.

It's not about her that I worry. It's about what we need to do to make sure that every child, every single child, has the same chance at equality and opportunity.

That's the dream we share. That's the fight we must wage.

We are so close, closer than we've ever been.

I'm grateful that there is now a new burst of energy around the rights and opportunities of women and girls.

There is still much to be done in our own country, much more to be done around the world.

But I am confident and optimistic that if we get to work, we will get it done together.

Thank you all very much.

6
A Global Perspective

Julián Castro, the U.S. Secretary of the Department of Housing and Urban Development, speaks during the National Council of La Raza annual conference in Kansas City, Missouri, July 13, 2015.

Ending the Embargo

Raúl Castro

In his first speech before the United Nations, President Raúl Castro of Cuba calls for an end to the fifty-three-year-old economic embargo of his country since diplomatic relations were restored between the two countries as of July 2015. In addition, Castro also calls on the United States to close the American military base in Guantánamo Bay and return that land to Cuba and to end anti-government radio and television broadcasts as well as other programs he called "subversive and destabilizing." Aligning his country with other leftist governments in Latin America including Venezuela and Ecuador, Castro also pledges to aid Haiti and to support the goals of Puerto Rico for self-determination, calling for the cooperation of all countries in the hemisphere to join together to support international humanitarian causes in spite of any political differences. Raúl Castro succeeded Fidel Castro as president of Cuba in 2008 and prior to that served as the head of Cuba's armed forces and defense minister.

His Excellency Juan Carlos Varela, President of the Republic of Panama;
Presidents and Prime Ministers;
Distinguished guests;

I appreciate the solidarity of all Latin American and Caribbean countries that made possible Cuba's participation in this hemispheric forum on equal footing, and I thank the President of the Republic of Panama for the kind invitation extended to us. I bring a fraternal embrace to the Panamanian people and to the peoples of all nations represented here.

The establishment of the Community of Latin American and Caribbean States (CELAC) on December 2–3, 2011, in Caracas, opened the way to a new era in the history of Our America, which made clear its well-earned right to live in peace and develop as their peoples freely decide, and chart the course to a future of peace, development and integration based on cooperation, solidarity and the common will to preserve their independence, sovereignty and identity.

The ideals of Simón Bolívar on the creation of a "Grand American Homeland" were a source of inspiration to epic campaigns for independence.

In 1800, there was the idea of adding Cuba to the North American Union to mark the southern boundary of the extensive empire. The nineteenth century witnessed the emergence of such doctrines as the Manifest Destiny, with the purpose of dominating the Americas and the world, and the notion of the "ripe fruit,"

Delivered April 11, 2015, at United Nations headquarters in New York, New York, by Raúl Castro.

meaning Cuba's inevitable gravitation to the American Union, which looked down on the rise and evolution of a genuine rationale conducive to emancipation.

Later on, through wars, conquests and interventions that expansionist and dominating force stripped Our America of part of its territory and expanded as far as the Rio Grande.

After long and failing struggles, José Martí organized the "necessary war," and created the Cuban Revolutionary Party to lead that war and to eventually found a Republic "with all and for the good of all" with the purpose of achieving "the full dignity of man."

With an accurate and early definition of the features of his times, Martí committed to the duty "of timely preventing the United States from spreading through the Antilles as Cuba gains its independence, and from overpowering with that additional strength our lands of America."

To him, Our America was that of the Creole and the original peoples, the black and the mulatto, the mixed-race and working America that must join the cause of the oppressed and the destitute. Presently, beyond geography, this ideal is coming to fruition.

One hundred and seventeen years ago, on April 11, 1898, the president of the United States of America requested congressional consent for military intervention in the independence war already won with rivers of Cuban blood, and that legislative body issued a deceitful joint resolution recognizing the independence of the Island "de facto and de jure." Thus, they entered as allies and seized the country as an occupying force.

Subsequently, an appendix was forcibly added to Cuba's Constitution, the Platt Amendment that deprived it of sovereignty, authorized the powerful neighbor to interfere in the internal affairs, and gave rise to Guantánamo Naval Base, which still holds part of our territory without legal right. It was in that period that the Northern capital invaded the country, and there were two military interventions and support for cruel dictatorships.

At the time, the prevailing approach to Latin America was the "gunboat policy" followed by the "Good Neighbor" policy. Successive interventions ousted democratic governments and in twenty countries installed terrible dictatorships, twelve of these simultaneously and mostly in South America, where hundreds of thousands were killed. President Salvador Allende left us the legacy of his undying example.

It was precisely 13 years ago that a coup d'etat staged against beloved President Hugo Chavez Frías was defeated by his people. Later on, an oil coup would follow.

On January 1st, 1959, sixty years after the U.S. troops entered Havana, the Cuban Revolution triumphed and the Rebel Army commanded by Fidel Castro Ruz arrived in the capital.

On April 6, 1960, barely one year after victory, Assistant Secretary of State Lester Mallory drafted a wicked memorandum, declassified tens of years later, indicating that "The majority of Cubans support Castro. . . An effective political opposition does not exist. . . ; the only foreseeable means of alienating internal support [to the government] is through disenchantment and disaffection based on economic dissatisfaction and hardship. . . to weaken the economic life of Cuba. . . denying it money and supplies to decrease monetary and real wages, to bring about hunger, desperation, and overthrow of government."

We have endured severe hardships. Actually, 77% of the Cuban people [were] born under the harshness of the blockade, but our patriotic convictions prevailed. Aggression increased resistance and accelerated the revolutionary process. Now, here we are with our heads up high and our dignity unblemished.

When we had already proclaimed socialism and the people had fought in the Bay of Pigs to defend it, President Kennedy was murdered, at the exact time when Fidel Castro, leader of the Cuban Revolution, was receiving his message seeking to engage Cuba in a dialogue.

After the Alliance for Progress, and having paid our external debt several times over while unable to prevent its constant growth, our countries were subjected to a wild and globalizing neoliberalism, an expression of imperialism at the time that left the region dealing with a lost decade.

Then, the proposal of a "mature hemispheric partnership" resulted in the imposition of the Free Trade Association of the Americas (FTAA)—linked to the emergence of these Summits—that would have brought about the destruction of the economy, sovereignty and common destiny of our nations, if it had not been derailed at Mar del Plata in 2005 under the leadership of Presidents Kirchner, Chavez and Lula. The previous year, Chavez and Fidel had brought to life the Bolivarian Alternative known today as the Bolivarian Alliance for the Peoples of Our America.

Excellencies;

We have expressed to President Barack Obama our disposition to engage in a respectful dialogue and work for a civilized coexistence between our states while respecting our profound differences.

I welcome as a positive step his recent announcement that he will soon decide on Cuba's designation in a list of countries [that] sponsor of terrorism, a list in which it should have never been included.

Up to this day, the economic, commercial and financial blockade is implemented against the Island with full intensity causing damages and scarcities that affect our people and becoming the main obstacle to the development of our economy. The fact is that it stands in violation of international law, and its extraterritorial scope disrupts the interests of every State.

We have publicly expressed to President Obama, who was also born under the blockade policy and inherited it from 10 former presidents when he took office, our appreciation for his brave decision to engage the U.S. Congress in a debate to put an end to such policy.

This and other issues should be resolved in the process toward the future normalization of bilateral relations.

As to us, we shall continue working to update the Cuban economic model with the purpose of improving our socialism and moving ahead toward development and the consolidation of the achievements of a Revolution that has set to itself the goal of "conquering all justice."

Esteemed colleagues;

Venezuela is not, and it cannot be, a threat to the national security of a superpower like the United States. We consider it a positive development that the U.S. president has admitted it.

I should reaffirm our full, determined and loyal support to the sister Bolivarian Republic of Venezuela, to the legitimate government and civilian-military alliance headed by President Nicolas Maduro, and to the Bolivarian and chavista people of that country struggling to pursue their own path while confronting destabilizing attempts and unilateral sanctions that should be lifted; we demand the repeal of the Executive Order, an action that our Community would welcome as a contribution to dialogue and understanding in the hemisphere.

We shall continue encouraging the efforts of the Republic of Argentina to recover the Falklands, the South Georgia and the South Sandwich Islands, and supporting its legitimate struggle in defense of financial sovereignty.

We shall maintain our support for the actions of the Republic of Ecuador against the transnational companies causing ecological damages to its territory and trying to impose blatantly unfair conditions.

I wish to acknowledge the contribution of Brazil, and of President Dilma Rouseff, to the strengthening of regional integration and the development of social policies that have brought progress and benefits to extensive popular sectors, the same that the thrust against various leftist governments of the region is trying to reverse.

We shall maintain our unwavering support for the Latin American and Caribbean people of Puerto Rico in its determination to achieve self-determination and independence, as the United Nations Decolonization Committee has ruled tens of times.

We shall also keep making our contribution to the peace process in Colombia.

We should all multiply our assistance to Haiti, not only through humanitarian aid but also with resources that help in its development, and, in the same token, support a fair and deferential treatment of the Caribbean countries in their economic relations as well as reparations for damages brought on them by slavery and colonialism.

We are living under threat of huge nuclear arsenals that should be removed, and are running out of time to counteract climate change. Threats to peace keep growing and conflicts spreading out.

As President Fidel Castro has said "The main causes rest with poverty and underdevelopment, and with the unequal distribution of wealth and knowledge prevailing in the world. It cannot be forgotten that current poverty and underdevelopment are the result of conquest, colonization, slavery and plundering by colonial powers in most of the planet, the emergence of imperialism and the bloody wars for a new division of the world. Humanity should be aware of what they have been and should be no more. Today, our species has accumulated sufficient knowledge, ethical values and scientific resources to move forward to a historical era of true justice and humanism. Nothing of what exists today in economic and political terms serves the interests of Humanity. It cannot be sustained. It must be changed," he concluded.

Cuba shall continue advocating the ideas for which our people have taken on enormous sacrifices and risks, fighting alongside the poor, the unemployed and the sick without healthcare; the children forced to live on their own, to work or be submitted to prostitution; those going hungry or discriminated; the oppressed and the exploited who make up the overwhelming majority of the world population.

Financial speculation, the privileges of Bretton Wood, and the unilateral removal of the gold standard have grown increasingly suffocating. We need a transparent and equitable financial system.

It is unacceptable that less than ten big corporations, mostly American, determine what is read, watched or listened to worldwide. The Internet should be ruled by an international, democratic and participatory governance, particularly concerning its content. The militarization of cyberspace, and the secret and illegal useof computer systems to attack other States are equally unacceptable. We shall not be dazzled or colonized again.

Mister President;

It is my opinion that hemispheric relations need to undergo deep changes, particularly in the areas of politics, economics and culture, so that, on the basis of international law and the exercise of self-determination and sovereign equality, they can focus on the development of mutually beneficial partnerships and cooperation in the interest of all our nations and the objectives proclaimed.

The adoption in January 2014, during the Second Summit of CELAC in Havana, of the Proclamation of Latin America and the Caribbean as a Peace Zone made a transcendental contribution to that end, marked by Latin American and Caribbean unity in diversity.

This is evident in the progress we are making toward genuinely Latin American and Caribbean integration processes through CELAC, UNASUR, CARICOM, MERCOSUR, ALBA-TCP, SICA and the ACS, which underline our growing awareness of the necessity to work in unison in order to ensure our development.

Through that proclamation we have committed ourselves "to have differences between nations resolved peacefully, through dialogue and negotiation, and other ways consistent with International Law."

Living in peace, and engaging in mutual cooperation to tackle challenges and resolve problems that, after all, are affecting and will affect us all, is today a pressing need.

As the Proclamation of Latin America and the Caribbean as a Peace Zone sets forth, "the inalienable right of every State to choose its political, economic, social and cultural system, as an essential condition to secure peaceful coexistence between nations" should be respected.

Under that proclamation we committed to observe our "obligation to not interfere, directly or indirectly, in the internal affairs of any other State, and to observe the principles of national sovereignty, equality of rights and free determination of the peoples," and to respect "the principles and standards of International Law. . . and the principles and purposes of the United Nations Charter."

That historical document urges "all member states of the International Community to fully respect this Declaration in its relations with the CELAC member States."

We now have the opportunity, all of us here, as the proclamation also states, of learning "to exercise tolerance and coexist in peace as good neighbors."

There are substantial differences, yes, but also commonalities which enable us to cooperate making it possible to live in this world fraught with threats to peace and to the survival of the human species.

What is it that prevents cooperation at a hemispheric scale in facing climate change?

Why is it that the countries of the two Americas cannot fight together against terrorism, drug-trafficking and organized crime without politically biased positions?

Why can we not seek together the necessary resources to provide the hemisphere with schools, hospitals, employment, and to advance in the eradication of poverty?

Would it not be possible to reduce inequity in the distribution of wealth and infant mortality rates, to eliminate hunger and preventable diseases, and to eradicate illiteracy?

Last year, we established hemispheric cooperation to confront and prevent Ebola, and the countries of the two Americas made a concerted effort. This should stimulate our efforts toward greater achievements.

Cuba, a small country deprived of natural resources, that has performed in an extremely hostile atmosphere, has managed to attain the full participation of its citizens in the nation's political and social life; with universal and free healthcare and education services, a social security system ensuring that no one is left helpless, significant progress in the creation of equal opportunities and in the struggle against all sorts of discrimination, the full exercise of the rights of children and women, access to sports and culture, and, the right to life and to public safety.

Despite scarcities and challenges, we abide by the principle of sharing what we have. Currently, 65,000 Cuban collaborators are working in 89 countries, basically in the areas of healthcare and education, while 68,000 professionals and technicians from 157 countries have graduated in our Island, 30,000 of them in the area of healthcare.

If Cuba has managed to do this with very little resources, think of how much more the hemisphere could do with the political will to pool its efforts to help the neediest countries.

Thanks to Fidel and the heroic Cuban people, we have come to this Summit to honor Marti's commitment, after conquering freedom with our own hands proud of

Our America, to serve it and to honor it "with the determination and the capacity to contribute to see it loved for its merits and respected for its sacrifices."

Thank you.

On the Iran Nuclear Deal

By Barack Obama

Defending his Iran nuclear deal at American University, President Barack Obama makes a speech that pushes for what he calls a diplomatic solution, which limits Iran's nuclear ability in exchange for lifting international oil and financial sanctions against the country. While critics on the right claim that the deal does not go far enough in limiting Iran's ability to create nuclear energy, Obama contends that those who oppose the deal are too eager to resort to war. He insists that the deal "cuts off all of Iran's pathways to a bomb [and] contains the most comprehensive inspection and verification regime ever negotiated to monitor a nuclear program." Invoking the legacy of President John F. Kennedy, who spoke on the same campus in 1963 to advocate for a nuclear test ban treaty with the Soviet Union, Obama reiterates a stance that helped him gain political power—his strong opposition to the war in Iraq as a first-term senator. President Obama is the forty-fourth president of the United States, having been elected to office in 2008 and reelected in 2012.

Thank you. (Applause.) Thank you so much. Everybody, please have a seat. Thank you very much. I apologize for the slight delay. Even presidents have problems with toner. (Laughter.)

It is a great honor to be back at American University, which has prepared generations of young people for service in public life. I want to thank President Kerwin and the American University family for hosting us here today.

Fifty-two years ago, President Kennedy, at the height of the Cold War, addressed this same university on the subject of peace. The Berlin Wall had just been built. The Soviet Union had tested the most powerful weapons ever developed. China was on the verge of acquiring a nuclear bomb. Less than 20 years after the end of World War II, the prospect of nuclear war was all too real. With all of the threats that we face today, it's hard to appreciate how much more dangerous the world was at that time.

In light of these mounting threats, a number of strategists here in the United States argued that we had to take military action against the Soviets, to hasten what they saw as inevitable confrontation. But the young president offered a different vision. Strength, in his view, included powerful armed forces and a willingness to stand up for our values around the world. But he rejected the prevailing attitude among some foreign policy circles that equated security with a perpetual war footing. Instead, he promised strong, principled American leadership on behalf of what

Delivered August 5, 2015, at American University, Washington, D.C., by Barack Obama.

he called a "practical" and "attainable peace"—a peace "based not on a sudden revolution in human nature but on a gradual evolution in human institutions—on a series of concrete actions and effective agreements."

Such wisdom would help guide our ship of state through some of the most perilous moments in human history. With Kennedy at the helm, the Cuban Missile Crisis was resolved peacefully. Under Democratic and Republican presidents, new agreements were forged—a Non-Proliferation Treaty that prohibited nations from acquiring nuclear weapons, while allowing them to access peaceful nuclear energy; the SALT and START Treaties which bound the United States and Soviet Union to cooperation on arms control. Not every conflict was averted, but the world avoided nuclear catastrophe, and we created the time and the space to win the Cold War without firing a shot at the Soviets.

The agreement now reached between the international community and the Islamic Republic of Iran builds on this tradition of strong, principled diplomacy. After two years of negotiations, we have achieved a detailed arrangement that permanently prohibits Iran from obtaining a nuclear weapon. It cuts off all of Iran's pathways to a bomb. It contains the most comprehensive inspection and verification regime ever negotiated to monitor a nuclear program. As was true in previous treaties, it does not resolve all problems; it certainly doesn't resolve all our problems with Iran. It does not ensure a warming between our two countries. But it achieves one of our most critical security objectives. As such, it is a very good deal.

Today, I want to speak to you about this deal, and the most consequential foreign policy debate that our country has had since the invasion of Iraq, as Congress decides whether to support this historic diplomatic breakthrough, or instead blocks it over the objection of the vast majority of the world. Between now and the congressional vote in September, you're going to hear a lot of arguments against this deal, backed by tens of millions of dollars in advertising. And if the rhetoric in these ads, and the accompanying commentary, sounds familiar, it should—for many of the same people who argued for the war in Iraq are now making the case against the Iran nuclear deal.

Now, when I ran for president eight years ago as a candidate who had opposed the decision to go to war in Iraq, I said that America didn't just have to end that war—we had to end the mindset that got us there in the first place. It was a mindset characterized by a preference for military action over diplomacy, a mindset that put a premium on unilateral U.S. action over the painstaking work of building international consensus, a mindset that exaggerated threats beyond what the intelligence supported. Leaders did not level with the American people about the costs of war, insisting that we could easily impose our will on a part of the world with a profoundly different culture and history. And, of course, those calling for war labeled themselves strong and decisive, while dismissing those who disagreed as weak—even appeasers of a malevolent adversary.

More than a decade later, we still live with the consequences of the decision to invade Iraq. Our troops achieved every mission they were given. But thousands of lives were lost, tens of thousands wounded. That doesn't count the lives lost among

Iraqis. Nearly a trillion dollars was spent. Today, Iraq remains gripped by sectarian conflict, and the emergence of al Qaeda in Iraq has now evolved into ISIL. And ironically, the single greatest beneficiary in the region of that war was the Islamic Republic of Iran, which saw its strategic position strengthened by the removal of its long-standing enemy, Saddam Hussein.

I raise this recent history because now more than ever we need clear thinking in our foreign policy. And I raise this history because it bears directly on how we respond to the Iranian nuclear program.

That program has been around for decades, dating back to the Shah's efforts—with U.S. support—in the 1960s and 1970s to develop nuclear power. The theocracy that overthrew the Shah accelerated the program after the Iran-Iraq War in the 1980s, a war in which Saddam Hussein used chemical weapons to brutal effect, and Iran's nuclear program advanced steadily through the 1990s, despite unilateral U.S. sanctions. When the Bush administration took office, Iran had no centrifuges—the machines necessary to produce material for a bomb—that were spinning to enrich uranium. But despite repeated warnings from the United States government, by the time I took office, Iran had installed several thousand centrifuges, and showed no inclination to slow—much less halt—its program.

Among U.S. policymakers, there's never been disagreement on the danger posed by an Iranian nuclear bomb. Democrats and Republicans alike have recognized that it would spark an arms race in the world's most unstable region, and turn every crisis into a potential nuclear showdown. It would embolden terrorist groups, like Hezbollah, and pose an unacceptable risk to Israel, which Iranian leaders have repeatedly threatened to destroy. More broadly, it could unravel the global commitment to nonproliferation that the world has done so much to defend.

The question, then, is not whether to prevent Iran from obtaining a nuclear weapon, but how. Even before taking office, I made clear that Iran would not be allowed to acquire a nuclear weapon on my watch, and it's been my policy throughout my presidency to keep all options—including possible military options—on the table to achieve that objective. But I have also made clear my preference for a peaceful, diplomatic resolution of the issue—not just because of the costs of war but also because a negotiated agreement offered a more effective, verifiable and durable resolution.

And so, in 2009, we let the Iranians know that a diplomatic path was available. Iran failed to take that path, and our intelligence community exposed the existence of a covert nuclear facility at Fordow.

Now, some have argued that Iran's intransigence showed the futility of negotiations. In fact, it was our very willingness to negotiate that helped America rally the world to our cause, and secured international participation in an unprecedented framework of commercial and financial sanctions. Keep in mind: unilateral U.S. sanctions against Iran had been in place for decades but had failed to pressure Iran to the negotiating table. What made our new approach more effective was our ability to draw upon new U.N. Security Council resolutions, combining strong enforcement with voluntary agreements from nations like China and India, Japan and

South Korea to reduce their purchases of Iranian oil, as well as the imposition by our European allies of a total oil embargo.

Winning this global buy-in was not easy—I know. I was there. In some cases, our partners lost billions of dollars in trade because of their decision to cooperate. But we were able to convince them that absent a diplomatic resolution, the result could be war, with major disruptions to the global economy and even greater instability in the Middle East. In other words, it was diplomacy—hard, painstaking diplomacy—not saber-rattling, not tough talk that ratcheted up the pressure on Iran.

With the world now unified beside us, Iran's economy contracted severely, and remains about 20 percent smaller today than it would have otherwise been. No doubt this hardship played a role in Iran's 2013 elections, when the Iranian people elected a new government that promised to improve the economy through engagement with the world. A window had cracked open. Iran came back to the nuclear talks. And after a series of negotiations, Iran agreed with the international community to an interim deal—a deal that rolled back Iran's stockpile of near 20 percent enriched uranium, and froze the progress of its program so that the P5+1—the United States, China, Russia, the United Kingdom, Germany, France, and the European Union—could negotiate a comprehensive deal without the fear that Iran might be stalling for time.

Now, let me pause here just to remind everybody that when the interim deal was announced, critics—the same critics we're hearing from now—called it "a historic mistake." They insisted Iran would ignore its obligations. They warned that sanctions would unravel. They warned that Iran would receive a windfall to support terrorism.

The critics were wrong. The progress of Iran's nuclear program was halted for the first time in a decade. Its stockpile of dangerous materials was reduced. The deployment of its advanced centrifuges was stopped. Inspections did increase. There was no flood of money into Iran, and the architecture of the international sanctions remained in place. In fact, the interim deal worked so well that the same people who criticized it so fiercely now cite it as an excuse not to support the broader accord. Think about that. What was once proclaimed as a historic mistake is now held up as a success and a reason to not sign the comprehensive deal. So keep that in mind when you assess the credibility of the arguments being made against diplomacy today.

Despite the criticism, we moved ahead to negotiate a more lasting, comprehensive deal. Our diplomats, led by Secretary of State John Kerry, kept our coalition united. Our nuclear experts—including one of the best in the world, Secretary of Energy Ernie Moniz—worked tirelessly on the technical details. In July, we reached a comprehensive plan of action that meets our objectives. Under its terms, Iran is never allowed to build a nuclear weapon. And while Iran, like any party to the Nuclear Non-Proliferation Treaty, is allowed to access peaceful nuclear energy, the agreement strictly defines the manner in which its nuclear program can proceed, ensuring that all pathways to a bomb are cut off.

Here's how. Under this deal, Iran cannot acquire the plutonium needed for a bomb. The core of its heavy-water reactor at Arak will be pulled out, filled with concrete, and replaced with one that will not produce plutonium for a weapon. The spent fuel from that reactor will be shipped out of the country, and Iran will not build any new heavy-water reactors for at least 15 years.

Iran will also not be able to acquire the enriched uranium that could be used for a bomb. As soon as this deal is implemented, Iran will remove two-thirds of its centrifuges. For the next decade, Iran will not enrich uranium with its more advanced centrifuges. Iran will not enrich uranium at the previously undisclosed Fordow facility, which is buried deep underground, for at least 15 years. Iran will get rid of 98 percent of its stockpile of enriched uranium, which is currently enough for up to 10 nuclear bombs, for the next 15 years. Even after those 15 years have passed, Iran will never have the right to use a peaceful program as cover to pursue a weapon.

And, in fact, this deal shuts off the type of covert path Iran pursued in the past. There will be 24/7 monitoring of Iran's key nuclear facilities. For decades, inspectors will have access to Iran's entire nuclear supply chain—from the uranium mines and mills where they get raw materials, to the centrifuge production facilities where they make machines to enrich it. And understand why this is so important: For Iran to cheat, it has to build a lot more than just one building or a covert facility like Fordow. It would need a secret source for every single aspect of its program. No nation in history has been able to pull off such subterfuge when subjected to such rigorous inspections. And under the terms of the deal, inspectors will have the permanent ability to inspect any suspicious sites in Iran.

And finally, Iran has powerful incentives to keep its commitments. Before getting sanctions relief, Iran has to take significant, concrete steps like removing centrifuges and getting rid of its stockpile. If Iran violates the agreement over the next decade, all of the sanctions can snap back into place. We won't need the support of other members of the U.N. Security Council; America can trigger snapback on our own. On the other hand, if Iran abides by the deal and its economy begins to reintegrate with the world, the incentive to avoid snapback will only grow.

So this deal is not just the best choice among alternatives—this is the strongest nonproliferation agreement ever negotiated. And because this is such a strong deal, every nation in the world that has commented publicly, with the exception of the Israeli government, has expressed support. The United Nations Security Council has unanimously supported it. The majority of arms control and nonproliferation experts support it. Over 100 former ambassadors—who served under Republican and Democratic presidents—support it. I've had to make a lot of tough calls as president, but whether or not this deal is good for American security is not one of those calls. It's not even close.

Unfortunately, we're living through a time in American politics where every foreign policy decision is viewed through a partisan prism, evaluated by headline-grabbing sound bites. And so before the ink was even dry on this deal—before Congress even read it—a majority of Republicans declared their virulent opposition. Lobbyists and pundits were suddenly transformed into arm-chair nuclear scientists, disputing the assessments of experts like Secretary Moniz, challenging his findings, offering multiple—and sometimes contradictory—arguments about why Congress should reject this deal. But if you repeat these arguments long enough, they can get some traction. So let me address just a few of the arguments that have been made so far in opposition to this deal.

First, there are those who say the inspections are not strong enough because inspectors can't go anywhere in Iran at any time with no notice.

Well, here's the truth: Inspectors will be allowed daily access to Iran's key nuclear sites. If there is a reason for inspecting a suspicious, undeclared site anywhere in Iran, inspectors will get that access, even if Iran objects. This access can be with as little as 24 hours' notice. And while the process for resolving a dispute about access can take up to 24 days, once we've identified a site that raises suspicion, we will be watching it continuously until inspectors get in. And by the way, nuclear material isn't something you hide in the closet. It can leave a trace for years. The bottom line is, if Iran cheats, we can catch them—and we will.

Second, there are those who argue that the deal isn't strong enough because some of the limitations on Iran's civilian nuclear program expire in 15 years. Let me repeat: The prohibition on Iran having a nuclear weapon is permanent. The ban on weapons-related research is permanent. Inspections are permanent. It is true that some of the limitations regarding Iran's peaceful program last only 15 years. But that's how arms control agreements work. The first SALT Treaty with the Soviet Union lasted five years. The first START Treaty lasted 15 years. And in our current situation, if 15 or 20 years from now, Iran tries to build a bomb, this deal ensures that the United States will have better tools to detect it, a stronger basis under international law to respond, and the same options available to stop a weapons program as we have today, including—if necessary—military options.

On the other hand, without this deal, the scenarios that critics warn about happening in 15 years could happen six months from now. By killing this deal, Congress would not merely pave Iran's pathway to a bomb, it would accelerate it.

Third, a number of critics say the deal isn't worth it because Iran will get billions of dollars in sanctions relief. Now, let's be clear: The international sanctions were put in place precisely to get Iran to agree to constraints on its program. That's the point of sanctions. Any negotiated agreement with Iran would involve sanctions relief. So an argument against sanctions relief is effectively an argument against any diplomatic resolution of this issue.

It is true that if Iran lives up to its commitments, it will gain access to roughly $56 billion of its own money—revenue frozen overseas by other countries. But the notion that this will be a game-changer, with all this money funneled into Iran's pernicious activities, misses the reality of Iran's current situation. Partly because of our sanctions, the Iranian government has over half a trillion dollars in urgent requirements—from funding pensions and salaries, to paying for crumbling infrastructure. Iran's leaders have raised the expectations of their people that sanctions relief will improve their lives. Even a repressive regime like Iran's cannot completely ignore those expectations. And that's why our best analysts expect the bulk of this revenue to go into spending that improves the economy and benefits the lives of the Iranian people.

Now, this is not to say that sanctions relief will provide no benefit to Iran's military. Let's stipulate that some of that money will flow to activities that we object to. We have no illusions about the Iranian government, or the significance of the Revolutionary Guard and the Quds Force. Iran supports terrorist organizations like Hezbollah. It supports proxy groups that threaten our interests and the interests of our allies—including proxy groups who killed our troops in Iraq. They try to destabilize our Gulf partners. But Iran has been engaged in these activities for decades. They engaged in them before sanctions and while sanctions were in place. In fact, Iran even engaged in these activities in the middle of the Iran-Iraq War—a war that cost them nearly a million lives and hundreds of billions of dollars.

The truth is that Iran has always found a way to fund these efforts, and whatever benefit Iran may claim from sanctions relief pales in comparison to the danger it could pose with a nuclear weapon.

Moreover, there's no scenario where sanctions relief turns Iran into the region's dominant power. Iran's defense budget is eight times smaller than the combined budget of our Gulf allies. Their conventional capabilities will never compare with Israel's, and our commitment to Israel's qualitative military edge helps guarantee that. Over the last several years, Iran has had to spend billions of dollars to support its only ally in the Arab World—Bashar al-Assad—even as he's lost control of huge chunks of his country. And Hezbollah has suffered significant blows on the same battlefield. And Iran, like the rest of the region, is being forced to respond to the threat of ISIL in Iraq.

So contrary to the alarmists who claim that Iran is on the brink of taking over the Middle East, or even the world, Iran will remain a regional power with its own set of challenges. The ruling regime is dangerous and it is repressive. We will continue to have sanctions in place on Iran's support for terrorism and violation of human rights. We will continue to insist upon the release of Americans detained unjustly. We will have a lot of differences with the Iranian regime.

But if we're serious about confronting Iran's destabilizing activities, it is hard to imagine a worse approach than blocking this deal. Instead, we need to check the behavior that we're concerned about directly: By helping our allies in the region strengthen their own capabilities to counter a cyber-attack or a ballistic missile, by improving the interdiction of weapons shipments that go to groups like Hezbollah, by training our allies' special forces so that they can more effectively respond to situations like Yemen. All these capabilities will make a difference. We will be in a stronger position to implement them with this deal. And, by the way, such a strategy also helps us effectively confront the immediate and lethal threat posed by ISIL.

Now, the final criticism—this sort of a catch-all that you may hear—is the notion that there's a better deal to be had. "We should get a better deal"—that's repeated over and over again. "It's a bad deal, need a better deal"—(laughter)—one that relies on vague promises of toughness, and, more recently, the argument that we can apply a broader and indefinite set of sanctions to squeeze the Iranian regime harder.

Those making this argument are either ignorant of Iranian society, or they're just not being straight with the American people. Sanctions alone are not going to force Iran to completely dismantle all vestiges of its nuclear infrastructure—even those aspects that are consistent with peaceful programs. That oftentimes is what the critics are calling "a better deal." Neither the Iranian government, nor the Iranian opposition, nor the Iranian people would agree to what they would view as a total surrender of their sovereignty.

Moreover, our closest allies in Europe, or in Asia—much less China or Russia—certainly are not going to agree to enforce existing sanctions for another 5, 10, 15 years according to the dictates of the U.S. Congress. Because their willingness to support sanctions in the first place was based on Iran ending its pursuit of nuclear weapons. It was not based on the belief that Iran cannot have peaceful nuclear power. And it certainly wasn't based on a desire for regime change in Iran.

As a result, those who say we can just walk away from this deal and maintain sanctions are selling a fantasy. Instead of strengthening our position as some have suggested, Congress's rejection would almost certainly result in multilateral sanctions unraveling. If, as has also been suggested, we tried to maintain unilateral sanctions, beefen them up, we would be standing alone. We cannot dictate the foreign, economic and energy policies of every major power in the world.

In order to even try to do that, we would have to sanction, for example, some of the world's largest banks. We'd have to cut off countries like China from the American financial system. And since they happen to be major purchasers of or our debt, such actions could trigger severe disruptions in our own economy and, by the way, raise questions internationally about the dollar's role as the world's reserve currency.

That's part of the reason why many of the previous unilateral sanctions were waived. What's more likely to happen, should Congress reject this deal, is that Iran would end up with some form of sanctions relief without having to accept any of the constraints or inspections required by this deal. So in that sense, the critics are right: Walk away from this agreement and you will get a better deal—for Iran. (Applause.)

Now, because more sanctions won't produce the results that the critics want, we have to be honest. Congressional rejection of this deal leaves any U.S. administration that is absolutely committed to preventing Iran from getting a nuclear weapon with one option—another war in the Middle East.

I say this not to be provocative. I am stating a fact. Without this deal, Iran will be in a position—however tough our rhetoric may be -- to steadily advance its capabilities. Its breakout time, which is already fairly small, could shrink to near zero. Does anyone really doubt that the same voices now raised against this deal will be demanding that whoever is president bomb those nuclear facilities?

And as someone who does firmly believe that Iran must not get a nuclear weapon, and who has wrestled with this issue since the beginning of my presidency, I can tell you that alternatives to military action will have been exhausted once we reject a hard-won diplomatic solution that the world almost unanimously supports.

So let's not mince words. The choice we face is ultimately between diplomacy or some form of war—maybe not tomorrow, maybe not three months from now, but soon. And here's the irony. As I said before, military action would be far less effective than this deal in preventing Iran from obtaining a nuclear weapon. That's not just my supposition. Every estimate, including those from Israeli analysts, suggest military action would only set back Iran's program by a few years at best, which is a fraction of the limitations imposed by this deal. It would likely guarantee that inspectors are kicked out of Iran. It is probable that it would drive Iran's program deeper underground. It would certainly destroy the international unity that we've spent so many years building.

Now, there are some opponents—I have to give them credit; there are opponents of this deal who accept the choice of war. In fact, they argue that surgical strikes against Iran's facilities will be quick and painless. But if we've learned anything from the last decade, it's that wars in general and wars in the Middle East in particular are anything but simple. (Applause.) The only certainty in war is human suffering, uncertain costs, unintended consequences. We can also be sure that the Americans who bear the heaviest burden are the less than 1 percent of us, the outstanding men and women who serve in uniform, and not those of us who send them to war.

As Commander-in-Chief, I have not shied from using force when necessary. I have ordered tens of thousands of young Americans into combat. I have sat by their bedside sometimes when they come home. I've ordered military action in seven countries. There are times when force is necessary, and if Iran does not abide by this deal, it's possible that we don't have an alternative.

But how can we in good conscience justify war before we've tested a diplomatic agreement that achieves our objectives, that has been agreed to by Iran, that is supported by the rest of the world, and that preserves our options if the deal falls short? How could we justify that to our troops? How could we justify that to the world or to future generations?

In the end, that should be a lesson that we've learned from over a decade of war. On the front end, ask tough questions. Subject our own assumptions to evidence and analysis. Resist the conventional wisdom and the drumbeat of war. Worry less about being labeled weak; worry more about getting it right.

I recognize that resorting to force may be tempting in the face of the rhetoric and behavior that emanates from parts of Iran. It is offensive. It is incendiary. We do take it seriously. But superpowers should not act impulsively in response to taunts, or even provocations that can be addressed short of war. Just because Iranian hardliners chant "Death to America" does not mean that that's what all Iranians believe. (Applause.)

In fact, it's those hardliners who are most comfortable with the status quo. It's those hardliners chanting "Death to America" who have been most opposed to the deal. They're making common cause with the Republican caucus. (Laughter and applause.)

The majority of the Iranian people have powerful incentives to urge their government to move in a different, less provocative direction—incentives that are strengthened by this deal. We should offer them that chance. We should give them that opportunity. It's not guaranteed to succeed. But if they take it, that would be good for Iran; it would be good for the United States. It would be good for a region that has known too much conflict. It would be good for the world.

And if Iran does not move in that direction, if Iran violates this deal, we will have ample ability to respond. The agreements pursued by Kennedy and Reagan with the Soviet Union, those agreements, those treaties involved America accepting significant constraints on our arsenal. As such, they were riskier. This agreement involves no such constraints. The defense budget of the United States is more than $600 billion. To repeat, Iran's is about $15 billion. Our military remains the ultimate backstop to any security agreement that we make. I have stated that Iran will never be allowed to obtain a nuclear weapon. I have done what is necessary to make sure our military options are real. And I have no doubt that any president who follows me will take the same position.

So let me sum up here. When we carefully examine the arguments against this deal, none of them stand up to scrutiny. That may be why the rhetoric on the other side is so strident. I suppose some of it can be ascribed to knee-jerk partisanship that has become all too familiar; rhetoric that renders every decision that's made a disaster, a surrender—"you're aiding terrorists; you're endangering freedom."

On the other hand, I do think it's important to acknowledge another, more understandable motivation behind the opposition to this deal, or at least skepticism to this deal, and that is a sincere affinity for our friend and ally, Israel—an affinity that, as someone who has been a stalwart friend to Israel throughout my career, I deeply share.

When the Israeli government is opposed to something, people in the United States take notice. And they should. No one can blame Israelis for having a deep skepticism about any dealings with a government like Iran's—which includes leaders who have denied the Holocaust; embrace an ideology of anti-Semitism; facilitate the flow of rockets that are arrayed on Israel's borders, are pointed at Tel Aviv. In such a dangerous neighborhood, Israel has to be vigilant, and it rightly insists that it cannot depend on any other country—even its great friend the United States—for its own security. So we have to take seriously concerns in Israel.

But the fact is, partly due to American military and intelligence assistance, which my administration has provided at unprecedented levels, Israel can defend itself against any conventional danger—whether from Iran directly or from its proxies. On the other hand, a nuclear-armed Iran changes that equation.

And that's why this deal ultimately must be judged by what it achieves on the central goal of preventing Iran from obtaining a nuclear weapon. This deal does exactly that. I say this as someone who has done more than any other president to strengthen Israel's security. And I have made clear to the Israeli government that we are prepared to discuss how we can deepen that cooperation even further. Already we've held talks with Israel on concluding another 10-year plan for U.S. security assistance to Israel. We can enhance support for areas like missile defense, information sharing, interdiction—all to help meet Israel's pressing security needs, and to provide a hedge against any additional activities that Iran may engage in as a consequence of sanctions relief.

But I have also listened to the Israeli security establishment, which warned of the danger posed by a nuclear-armed Iran for decades. In fact, they helped develop many of the ideas that ultimately led to this deal.

So to friends of Israel, and to the Israeli people, I say this: A nuclear-armed Iran is far more dangerous to Israel, to America, and to the world than an Iran that benefits from sanctions relief.

I recognize that Prime Minister Netanyahu disagrees—disagrees strongly. I do not doubt his sincerity. But I believe he is wrong. I believe the facts support this deal. I believe they are in America's interest and Israel's interest. And as president of the United States, it would be an abrogation of my constitutional duty to act against my best judgment simply because it causes temporary friction with a dear friend and ally. I do not believe that would be the right thing to do for the United States. I do not believe it would be the right thing to do for Israel. (Applause.)

Over the last couple weeks, I have repeatedly challenged anyone opposed to this deal to put forward a better, plausible alternative. I have yet to hear one. What I've heard instead are the same types of arguments that we heard in the run-up to the Iraq War: Iran cannot be dealt with diplomatically; we can take military strikes without significant consequences; we shouldn't worry about what the rest of the world thinks, because once we act, everyone will fall in line; tougher talk, more military threats will force Iran into submission; we can get a better deal.

I know it's easy to play on people's fears, to magnify threats, to compare any attempt at diplomacy to Munich. But none of these arguments hold up. They didn't back in 2002 and 2003; they shouldn't now. (Applause.) The same mindset, in many cases offered by the same people who seem to have no compunction with being repeatedly wrong, led to a war that did more to strengthen Iran, more to isolate the United States than anything we have done in the decades before or since. It's a mindset out of step with the traditions of American foreign policy, where we exhaust diplomacy before war, and debate matters of war and peace in the cold light of truth.

"Peace is not the absence of conflict," President Reagan once said. It is "the ability to cope with conflict by peaceful means." President Kennedy warned Americans, "not to see conflict as inevitable, accommodation as impossible, and communication as nothing more than the exchange of threats." It is time to apply such wisdom. The deal before us doesn't bet on Iran changing; it doesn't require trust; it verifies and requires Iran to forsake a nuclear weapon, just as we struck agreements with the Soviet Union at a time when they were threatening our allies, arming proxies against us, proclaiming their commitment to destroy our way of life, and had nuclear weapons pointed at all of our major cities—a genuine existential threat.

We live in a complicated world—a world in which the forces unleashed by human innovation are creating opportunities for our children that were unimaginable for most of human history. It is also a world of persistent threats, a world in which mass violence and cruelty is all too common, and human innovation risks the destruction of all that we hold dear. In this world, the United States of America remains the most powerful nation on Earth, and I believe that we will remain such for decades to come. But we are one nation among many.

And what separates us from the empires of old, what has made us exceptional, is not the mere fact of our military might. Since World War II, the deadliest war in human history, we have used our power to try to bind nations together in a system of international law. We have led an evolution of those human institutions President Kennedy spoke about—to prevent the spread of deadly weapons, to uphold peace and security, and promote human progress.

We now have the opportunity to build on that progress. We built a coalition and held it together through sanctions and negotiations, and now we have before us a solution that prevents Iran from obtaining a nuclear weapon, without resorting to war. As Americans, we should be proud of this achievement. And as members of Congress reflect on their pending decision, I urge them to set aside political concerns, shut out the noise, consider the stakes involved with the vote that you will cast.

If Congress kills this deal, we will lose more than just constraints on Iran's nuclear program, or the sanctions we have painstakingly built. We will have lost something more precious: America's credibility as a leader of diplomacy; America's credibility as the anchor of the international system.

John F. Kennedy cautioned here, more than 50 years ago, at this university, that "the pursuit of peace is not as dramatic as the pursuit of war." But it's so very important. It is surely the pursuit of peace that is most needed in this world so full of strife.

My fellow Americans, contact your representatives in Congress. Remind them of who we are. Remind them of what is best in us and what we stand for, so that we can leave behind a world that is more secure and more peaceful for our children.

Thank you very much. (Applause.)

A Nation of Immigrants

By Julián Castro

Julián Castro, Secretary for the U.S. Department of Housing and Urban Development, delivers a speech at the Annual Conference of the National Council of La Raza held in Kansas City, Missouri. Addressing issues from the social conditions of Latino community, to job training and employment, to bias and discrimination against Latinos, Castro says that "Latinos comprise the youngest and fastest growing segment of our nation's population" and that "now, more than ever, America's destiny is intertwined with the Latino destiny." Julián Castro has been the United States Secretary of Housing and Urban Development (HUD) since July 28, 2014. Prior to that he served three terms as the mayor of San Antonio, Texas, from 2009 to 2014.

Hello, NCLR [National Council of La Raza]! Thank you very much for that warm welcome, and good afternoon. My thanks to Arantxa Loizaga for her very kind introduction. It's always nice to see a former San Antonian doing great things.

I'd also like to thank NCLR's President and CEO, the one and only, Janet Murguia. She's been a champion for the Latino community, and I'm proud to call her a friend. My thanks to your Chair Daniel Ortega, and NCLR's Board of Directors and staff for their incredible leadership.

Finally, let me thank all of you for the work you're doing across the United States to make a difference. I'm grateful for your efforts and honored to be with you this afternoon.

Nine days ago, on July 4th, families, friends and neighbors across the nation gathered together to celebrate the birth of American independence. With flags in our hands and pride in our hearts, we remembered the band of patriots who, with conviction and courage, decided to risk everything for the cause of freedom.

We honored the single, but powerful idea that guides our democracy and our way of life: that all people are created equal and endowed with certain unalienable rights, including life, liberty and the pursuit of happiness. And we reflected on the rich history that's unfolded since 1776—a journey that's proven our great nation to be a place of unlimited possibilities and a beacon of hope around the world.

Back in the nineteenth century it was said that "America is another name for opportunity" and through the course of history, people from all backgrounds have proven these words to be true in their own lives, in their own way, in their own time.

This is where Ellen Ochoa was able to reach the stars, making the journey from humble beginnings in La Mesa, California, to become the first Latina in outer

---

Delivered July 13, 2015, at the National Council of La Raza 2015 Annual Conference, Kansas City, Missouri, by Julián Castro.

space. This is where, nearly 80 years ago, the Unanue family was able to buy the "Goya" name for one dollar and build that brand into a business empire. This is where one of our nation's greatest legal minds, Sonia Sotomayor, was able to go from public housing in The Bronx all the way to the Supreme Court.

But it's important to remember that opportunity has never been guaranteed. Each generation has had to strive, to work, and to fight to make it real. Now it's our generation's challenge to build on this legacy by answering a fundamental question: how do we ensure that the United States remains the undisputed land of opportunity in the twenty-first century?

The answer is by shaping a future where every child has the chance to thrive, where every person has the chance to succeed, and where every idea can flourish—and Latinos will play a vital role in meeting this challenge.

The Latino community stands at the intersection of two dynamics that will determine prosperity in the twenty-first century global economy. The first is that brainpower is the new currency of success.

And, for the first time, America finds itself in an unprecedented competition for jobs and investment with rising nations around the world that are producing millions of young, talented graduates with the intelligence, drive and ability to innovate and to develop new technologies that will define progress in this century.

The second is that Latinos comprise the youngest and fastest growing segment of our nation's population. The 2010 Census revealed that 23 percent of children under 17 are Latino.

Now, more than ever, America's destiny is intertwined with the Latino destiny. If educated well, Latinos can be a game-changing asset in keeping America tremendously competitive in this twenty-first century and beyond.

And that's something all Americans can get behind—like all Americans, Latinos love this nation, and want it to prosper and remain strong. Unfortunately there are some who continue to attack this community for who we are and where we're from.

Last month, as he announced his campaign for president, Republican Donald Trump stated that immigrants coming from Mexico were criminals and rapists. Mr. Trump's remarks would be laughable, if they weren't so insulting to the very notion of America.

Ours is a nation of immigrants, a nation that's made stronger in this twenty-first century by the energy and entrepreneurial spirit that they bring into the larger American family. Consider the story of 17-year-old Fernando Rojas from Fullerton, California.

The son of Mexican immigrants—his father a machine operator and his mother a seamstress—Fernando graduated from high school earlier this year as a national speech and debate champion, and a co-valedictorian with a 4.8 GPA. And incredibly, he was accepted to all eight Ivy League schools—every single one of them.

Fernando credits his parents for teaching him to work hard and never give up. That strength, that determination, that success—that's the immigrant story, that's our American story.

That's why Americans from all backgrounds are standing up to, and speaking out against Trump's rhetoric. As mothers and fathers; sons and daughters; sisters and brothers; CEOs, small business owners and hard-working employees; Soldiers, cops, firefighters and teachers who serve our nation every single day—Latinos are making America stronger.

So Donald Trump and his conservative allies ought to hear this: Americans will not stand for your rhetoric or your hatred—not today, not tomorrow, not ever.

We are one America, and we must choose a different course for our nation—not one where personal success comes at the expense of others—but a future where opportunity and prosperity expand.

Just look at the last two weeks. First, the Supreme Court upheld the Affordable Care Act, and now millions of Americans will be able to keep their healthcare. Then the Court ruled for marriage equality. It told us what we already knew in our hearts: that all Americans have the right to live and love freely.

Last week we watched that symbol of division, of hate—the Confederate flag—finally come down from the State Capital in South Carolina. And we also learned that more Americans are working again. The unemployment rate is down to 5.3 percent, and we've seen a record 64 straight months of private-sector job growth and 12.8 million new jobs.

So how do we build on that success? The answer is to invest in opportunity. It means making pre-K universal so that every child can get a strong start in life. It means making college more affordable so that all folks who're willing to work hard can get the skills they need to compete.

It means investing in job training and apprenticeships to give folks of modest means a pathway to the middle class. It means raising the minimum wage. It means finally, once and for all, passing comprehensive immigration reform, and not settling for the second-class status that Republicans would impose on some immigrant families.

And it means putting good and decent housing within reach of all hardworking Americans. At HUD [Housing and Urban Development], we call ourselves the Department of Opportunity because where you live impacts how you live—the education your children receive, the grocery stores you have access to, the financial security you can build for the future.

We work hard to help people achieve their dreams. Our Federal Housing Administration insures half of all home loans to Latinos, and we've taken strong steps to make homeownership more affordable and accessible for responsible families, helping spark the growth we're seeing in our housing market.

Through our Community Development Block Grants and our HOME initiative, we're investing in neighborhoods to lift up communities across the nation, which is why we're fighting against the congressional Republican proposal to cut HOME by 93 percent, so we can keep affordable housing development, construction jobs and economic investment going across the nation.

And last Wednesday, we produced a new fair housing rule to help give every family an equal chance to access quality housing near good schools, transportation and jobs—no matter who they are, what they look like, how they worship or where they're from.

Our entire nation is richer when everyone has the chance to prosper, and we look forward to collaborating with you to build a future where there are no limits for any American.

Janet, you and I know this won't be easy. Progress is never a given. We've got to work for it. But we can accomplish incredible things if we keep working together to advance opportunity for all.

And I know that NCLR will keep on doing what you do: advocating, educating, negotiating, collaborating, legislating, activating, facilitating, mediating, reinvigorating, coordinating, validating, motivating, jubilating, sometimes agitating and always elevating our nation to greater progress.

Oh, and making sure that the Latino community elects the next president of the United States in 2016. You know that when we invest in people, we invest in our nation's future. That when opportunity reaches all, everyone benefits. That when the Latino community succeeds, our entire nation succeeds.

I still believe that the American Dream isn't a sprint or a marathon, but a relay. Fernando Rojas's parents came from Mexico to America. They didn't go to college or even finish high school. But they worked hard and 51 days from now, their son will give them a kiss and an abrazo, wave goodbye and start college at Yale.

That, my fellow Americans, is the magic of our nation, and the future of our Latino community.

Thank you very much.

Index